Famous Faces, Famous Places & Famous Food

Famous *Faces*
Famous *Places*
Famous *Food*

Victoria Brooks

Greatest Escapes
PUBLISHING

08 07 06 05 04   1 2 3 4 5 6

First published in 2004 by
Greatest Escapes Publishing
Suite 310, 318 Homer Street
Vancouver, British Columbia
Canada V6B 2V2
www.GreatestEscapes.com
www.LiteraryTrips.com

National Library of Canada Cataloguing in Publication Data
Brooks, Victoria
    Famous faces, famous places, famous food / Victoria Brooks.

Includes index.
ISBN 0-9686137-3-X

    1. Authors—Travel—Anecdotes. 2. Cookery, International. I. Title.

PN164.B76 2004   910.4   C2004-906940-0

Edited by Michael Carroll
Text design and typesetting by Jen Hamilton
Cover design by Adam Swica

Printed and bound in Canada by Friesens

For Tyson Brooks, who was instrumental in the making of this book,
and who, more important, is instrumental to my life

Contents

Acknowledgments

*M*y eternal thanks to Tyson, my son, my friend, and my collaborator. During the past year, the time it took for this book to become a reality finally, Tyson helped me through the onerous and traumatizing emotional breakup of a 19-year marriage. Sharing the burden of my personal trouble, Tyson successfully executed the difficult task of contacting the restaurants and hotels in far-flung foreign places for recipes and collated them. The long distances and language barriers made this a job for a detective with fortitude. Late-night calls and conversations in tongues neither of us knew finally brought all the famous recipes to this biographically charged cookbook. Tyson also wrote the interesting notes that go with the recipes, explaining exotic ingredients, and compiled the hotel contact information and famous hotel and restaurant descriptions.

I can't forget to thank the amazing Sir Arthur C. Clarke and sportsman novelist Dick Francis for their time and for their letters, which lend a personal touch to this book. Musicians Willie and Lobo also showed kindness and the importance of food in providing their own personal recipes.

Thanks to Jenny Wood and Cathy Snipper of Goldeneye in Jamaica for their exceptional job of researching what foods Ian Fleming preferred while he resided on that siren island. Also in Jamaica I thank the talented hotelier Jane Issa both for her friendship and her generous assistance with the delicious recipes for the Jamaica chapters. I must thank the creative duo, Greer-Ann and Bertram Saulter, who lovingly created Chris Blackwell's hideaway resort The Caves and who run the chi-chi Hungry Lion Restaurant that lends a truly Jamaican sophistication to the ramshackle charm of West End Road.

Tyson and I also thank Earl Smith of the Cayman Island Tourist Board for researching and contacting the appropriate links for recipes on the Cayman Islands; Joseph Sampermans and

Patrick Behrens of Raffles Grand Hôtel D'Angkor for their help with the recipes taken from that lovely colonial hotel in faraway Cambodia; and Diana Mason, neighbor and cook extra-ordinaire, for her pragmatic assistance with the recipe editing. Diana and her husband, Tom, have supported me in many ways through this difficult and busy year.

Almost last, but never least, I thank my parents, David and Katherine Friesen, for their continual belief in me; my sister and her husband, Ruth and Brian Hastings; and my nieces who love and are proud of me, Lisa Hastings and Treena Hastings. Thanks, too, to Adam Swica for his cover work, and to Jen Hamilton for layout and interior design. And finally, a simple thanks to my editor, Michael Carroll, who knows all that this means.

Introduction

I want to tell you what this collection of literary travel pieces and recipes means to me. I've begun to think that the nature of a biographical story and the added flavor of eating emulate the beginning of a love affair. When I met someone special, as happened to me after the emotional meltdown of a 19-year relationship, I was fascinated by the details of his life, in short, his history or biography. Then, as our paths joined further, we began to celebrate our knowing each other by eating, even cooking together, something my ex-husband did alone for me (his choice) for many years. My ex-husband's keeping me from the kitchen lent a mystique to the art of cooking that has finally been quashed by my new role as sole entertainer, and by this collection of recipes that illuminates details of the lives of famous creative people.

The reflection upon the famous personalities I've researched and written about, and the act of following in their trails, have in each case led me to an adventure and a discovery of myself as well as given me knowledge about the countries I've traveled to. Each chapter I've written is wrapped up in a human being, and in each case the particular landscape affected that person's personality and history and, naturally, eventually mine. Through writing these stories I have the incredible fortune to share my own experiences and personality with the reader. The format of delving into the lives of writers such as Ernest Hemingway and Graham Greene, and the exotic locales that burned fevers into them, is, to me, a fascinating and romantic task. I hope the stories entertain and provide dinner conversation, if nothing else.

I've included four stories previously published in my *Literary Trips* series. The Paul Bowles piece is included because he was the spark that lit the flame for my purposeful wanderings. The incredible author and composer, now deceased, came to me in a dream, and through my subconscious planted the seed that soon became my passion: discovering history, people, and their cultures through the famous literary figures that have written about them and spent time there. The inclusion of Sir Arthur C. Clarke, I think, is self-explanatory once one reads the piece. He is more than the author of *2001: A Space Odyssey*, made famous as a film by his dear friend, the late director Stanley Kubrick. Not many people know that Clarke is the brains behind satellite communication, though. As he wryly pointed out to me, he would have been a very wealthy man if he had patented his discovery. On another note, Sri Lanka, Clarke's adopted country, has extricated itself from years of terrorism, something that might give us hope in the Western world. The Hemingway piece also published in the *Literary Trips* series is here simply because it won an award—the TMAC Excellence in Caribbean Travel Writing Award—that I am proud of, and Greene's Vietnam is included because the new Greene's Cuba chapter adds a different dimension to the Greeneland myth and offers yet another perspective on Cuba.

The idea of pairing biographical travel stories with recipes from the celebrated places where the artistic greats wined and dined is meant to transport to exotic destinations those who can't escape the boredom of everyday life that many of us fall prey to. At the same time I've attempted to provide implements, the recipes, to fashion a little bit of the magic right at home. The photographs, too, are meant to sweep the reader off to the scenes depicted, and in each instance I've tried to choose a shot of the new face that represents the soul of each locale.

I hope, too, that when the reader tries out these recipes, he or she regales guests with details of the famous personages' lives and landscapes encountered in these pages. I should point out, too, that Tyson, my son, has provided a helpful Ingredients Glossary at the end of the book that will illuminate anything that's unfamiliar in these recipes.

Personally I can't think of having a better time—a little gossip, a little storytelling spiked with dishes and drinks from establishments that have entertained some of the wildest talents of all time. So, with those last words, let the feast that is these special people's lives begin!

From 1951 to 1955 Graham Greene "wintered" in Vietnam where he covered the French wars for the *Sunday Times* and the French newspaper *Le Figaro*.

Courtesy
Hotel Sevilla/Havana

Graham Greene
Our Man in Vietnam

*S*aigon is a house without walls from the moment the sun ascends on the magnificent river that snakes past Dong Khoi Street right through to the unfolding of the tattered night—a muffled time when the mandarins' moon and the new capitalists' neon-green Heineken beer sign melt into a single reflection on the citrine water. To wander at will in such a place is to be privy to history, to the smashing of dreams and to the bright blaze of hope.

I first discovered Ho Chi Minh City, still commonly called Saigon, in 1987, 10 years before President Bill Clinton lifted the U.S. trade embargo. I was collecting background color for my novel *Red Dream*, a romantic melodrama set in Vietnam in the 1950s, the first half of which is Graham Greene's Vietnam period. Before this initial excursion, my characters and landscape were drawn from the fascinating picture of Southeast Asia I had gained from books. Chief among them were *Vietnam: A History* by Stanley Karnow, Marguerite Duras's novella *The Lover*, a guidebook translated from French, and especially Greene's *The Quiet American* in which, quite by accident, he prophesied the outcome of America's Vietnam War before it had really begun.

Greene's influence on my normally romantic cast of mind was so strong that I chose his evocative description for my novel's epigraph: "To take an Annamite to bed with you is like taking a bird: they twitter and sing on your pillow."

Since then, on five different occasions, I have found myself in what is still Greene's Indochina. Standing on the magnificent sweep of marble stairs on Dong Khoi Street in front of the pink-columned L'Hôtel Majestic—Greene's favorite and mine—I conjure up the vision of a Vietnamese schoolgirl sitting upright and tall on a wide-handled bicycle. She is Greene's Annamite pedaling elegantly down a dusty road or staring straight ahead with serene trust as she negotiates her way along the highway's hurl of ageless motorcycles, rumbling Russian buses, leather-seated trishaws, 1950s Citroëns, and nifty U.S. jeeps abandoned at the end of what the Vietnamese term "the American War." Vietnam's feminine image cycles through this waste of history, clad in see-through silk and always in white. Her trousers flute at the bottom like upside-down tulips, and her high-necked *aoi dai* is slit to the waist at each slim hip. From Annamite she transforms into Phuong in *The Quiet American* and into my protagonist, the exquisite Doctoress Jade Minh. Finally she is Suzette, Jade Minh's unfortunate half-caste daughter from her illicit affair with a young Frenchman.

Vietnam has had as many invaders as shots in a fully loaded Luger, a sad fact that augments its exoticism and attracts adventurers like Greene. European interference in Vietnam began in the early 17th century when the French assisted the exiled Mandarin Nguyen Anh in a civil uprising. French missionaries dabbled in politics while converting the Vietnamese to Catholicism. Politics and religion are compelling themes in Greene's fiction (the enigmatic novelist eventually became a Catholic convert).

Near the end of the French colonial era the Americans feared that if Vietnam fell to the Communists, a domino effect would be triggered and all of Southeast Asia would soon be under Communist rule. Nationalist leader Ho Chi Minh remarked, "The last time the Chinese came they stayed a thousand years! The French are foreigners…. Colonialism is dying out…the white man is finished in Asia. But if the Chinese stay now, they will never leave. As for me, I prefer to sniff French shit for five years, rather than Chinese shit for the rest of my life."

After the French came the Japanese, the British, and then the Americans.

The Quiet American, begun by Greene as one of his "entertainments," a term he invented to distinguish his lighter works from his serious novels, is based on the author's own experiences in Indochina at the end of the Franco–Viet Minh War. The novel follows Pyle, a high-minded American and CIA agent who naively meddles in Vietnamese politics and initiates a bomb attack in Saigon's Place Garnier, now Lam Son Square. "I never knew a man who had better motives for all the trouble he caused," remarks Greene's protagonist Fowler, who finds it impossible to stand aside and remain an observer. The very human Fowler is not dissimilar to the peripatetic and adulterous Greene, a jaded British war correspondent estranged from his wife.

Greene's novel is ultimately about involvement, both personal and political—an attribute that Vietnam, especially Saigon, inspires in those who dare to linger within her invisible gates. A quote from the novel explains it best: "Sooner or later…one has to take sides. If one is to remain human."

Jane Fonda's stint in Vietnam in August 1972 as Hanoi Jane, propaganda artiste for Ho Chi Minh's side, is further modern evidence of the country's lure. In her live Radio Hanoi broadcast to American servicemen, she counseled then-U.S. President Richard Nixon "to read Vietnamese history, particularly their poetry, and particularly the poetry written by Ho Chi Minh."

℘

Graham Greene forged an international reputation with his 1932 novel *Stamboul Train,* and the next year, *Orient Express.* His critically acclaimed and bestselling contemporary thrillers eventually included *The Third Man,* written first as a film treatment in 1949. As a sideline, he established himself as one of London's cleverest film and book reviewers. The hype that revolved around Greene was so intense that his face was splashed on the cover of *Time* in October 1951. The caption "Adultery can lead to sainthood" referred to his latest novel *The End of the Affair* and to his tryst with a married woman. Greene fled this intrusion into his double life, seeking refuge in the beleaguered French colony of Indochina.

The adventurous author first visited Vietnam in 1950 at the invitation of old friend Trevor Wilson, the British consul in Hanoi. In his 1980 autobiography *Ways of Escape,* Greene confessed: "So it was that in the fifties I found myself tempting the end to come…. I hadn't the courage for suicide, but it became a habit with me to visit troubled places." (His first perilous adventure, possibly one he never meant to survive, was a 300-mile trek across malaria-ridden West Africa. The result was *Journey Without Maps,* his 1936 travelogue about Liberia, a squalid republic founded for released slaves.)

From 1951 to 1955, Greene "wintered" in Vietnam where he covered the French wars for the *Sunday Times* and the French newspaper *Le Figaro.* To supplement his writing income, he became a part-time operative, moonlighting for Britain's Secret Intelligence Service (SIS). He reported to another independent operative, Alexander Korda, famous filmmaker of the 1930s, who is remembered for his imperial epic *Sanders of the River.*

Greene's first sortie into espionage was in the heat of World War II, six years after *Journey Without Maps* was published. Stationed in Sierra Leone by the British Foreign Office, he

By the mid-1960s America was no longer "quiet" in Vietnam and there were hundreds of thousands of U.S. soldiers embroiled in a savage war that finally ended in 1975.

reported enemy activity in the neighboring French colonies. Greene once quipped, "A writer should be careful where he goes for pleasure in peacetime, for in wartime he is only too likely to return there to work."

This second set of experiences in West Africa produced the novel *The Heart of the Matter*. His protagonist, Major Scobie, was modeled on a colleague, a weary middle-aged colonial police commissioner. Greene had calling cards made up in that fictitious name for his frequent excursions to brothels. There, he had cigarette burns inflicted on his own pale flesh to satisfy his need for self-punishment. When Greene's backwater posting ended, he was transferred to wartime London, where he was given a position in Section V of the SIS, headed by Kim Philby, the British double agent whose dramatic 1963 defection to Russia would astonish the world.

A handful of operatives under Philby's tutelage worked from a secret location, a comfortable house outside London. Greene's role was to supervise counterintelligence operations for a neutral Portugal. More to the point, the author kept a card-index file on known German spies. Like Greene's postwar Vienna in *The Third Man*, Portugal was a hotbed of enemy agents.

Havana, too, was a magnet for spies. Greene's darkly comedic 1958 "entertainment" *Our Man in Havana* was inspired by "Garbo," the legendary double agent who pretended to recruit a spy ring in London for German intelligence and his own financial gain. Greene's own futile attempts to gather intelligence for the SIS on aspects of life in Communist China under the guise of a cultural tour was fruitful fodder for his bumbling *Our Man in Havana* hero, a British vacuum-cleaner salesman.

Greene's real-life experience as the SIS's man in Beijing was a farcical bungle. He couldn't ditch the cultural delegation as planned and quarreled publicly with his fellow travelers. Privately the boyish Greene pinned the blame on *mou-tai*, a wine with an explosive alcohol content. To authenticate the backdrop of *Our Man in Havana*, Greene traveled to Cuba the year before Fidel Castro boldly wrenched the island's reins of power from dictator Fulgencio Batista. Greene demonstrated an allegiance to the underdog Castro's cause by layering warm clothing under his own and smuggling them to the rebels' mountain hideout.

A colleague in Greene's cloak-and-dagger world described the writer as an espionage "dilettante," but the same associate admitted in retrospect that "his visits to Indochina proved of assistance to the local station." That understatement included Greene's potentially deadly game of passing on information from personal interviews with both major players in the Vietnamese drama: the North's Ho Chi Minh and the South's President Ngo Dinh Diem.

I am going to church in the rain. My *cyclo* driver Shan was a colonel in President Diem's South Vietnamese army. Shan once squared his slight shoulders side by side with his brawny and powerful American heroes. Together they pitted their fighting prowess against Shan's Communist cousins, the seemingly fearless Vietcong. Now Shan pedals people for a living. The ARVN officers who didn't escape after their failed bid for a democratic government were deemed disloyal to Ho's regime, and not worthy of employment.

An obsolete automobile bears down from Le Loi Boulevard, its chrome bumper threatening like the teeth of a shark as our *cyclo* crosses diagonally through the six lanes of Nguyen Hue Street. The charging, misshapen relic that I recognize as a Lada is joined by a throbbing three-stroke Honda motorcycle, a bicycle with a cargo of trussed and squawking chickens wedged in the rusting wire basket, and a hiccuping, honking bus of Russian origin crammed with a big-eyed sea of small faces staring out of glassless windows.

Shan stabs his bare arm into the seething maelstrom, not as a hand signal but to shield me. I notice a brand on the delicate skin of his wrist. The precise scar is a mandatory stigmata, along with his identity card. When I ask his opinion of Americans and the deceased Diem, Shan shows me a puckered hole in his chest and says, "Only the VC are bad."

After the fall of Saigon, Shan and thousands like him were jailed as traitors and shipped to "reeducation camps" where he and other "detainees" memorized Communist dogma and

Children in the street close by the Continental Hotel often supplement their parents' income by selling Chiclets and postcards.

wielded pickaxes and shovels. His arms have the color and consistency of overcooked beef, thanks to years spent in the glaring heat of Vietnam's countryside. And the blue veins that writhe in his sinewy forearms move like Saigon's traffic—nervous and fast.

The antiquated and open *cyclo-pousse*, with its worn and shiny leather seat, weaves and bobs within the traffic's flow. The rain that at first fell stingily now comes in generous splashes, and Shan pulls to the curb to raise the folded leather roof. It is as if I am a baby and he a solicitous father who has made a wrong turn. The *cyclo's* protective top seems to me as cracked and delicate as a 1,000-year-old Chinese egg. While Shan fiddles, I notice a boy of about 12 asleep on a bench. He is curved in a pose that knows no borders: one arm flung forgetfully behind his small head. It is noon at its most feverish, and a rat saunters brazenly by, its coat dark from dirt and sleek from rain. The rodent lunges nose-first for the open canal roiling with the downpour, then dives into the escalating green, a soup filthy with sewage and debris. The snoozing boy is oblivious to the rat and the rain and a Seiko billboard that looms like a wild delusion above his head. The advertisement depicts a handsome young Asian in an expensive suit casually consulting his watch.

Shan remounts, pushes down one wide, splayed, rubber-thonged foot on the right pedal, and we are off with barely a lurch. The traffic gyrates like a drunken dance troupe in a cantankerous mood. I hold my breath as an old woman ambles head-on across the double-laned road, her spindly yellow legs and bony knees akimbo. She eats fried bread as she cries. I am so close I can see that her bread is soggy, and I watch as crumbs and tears mingle on her gaunt cheeks, then disappear. We are in Cholon, Saigon's Chinese district.

Shan lowers the *cyclo* and I descend. Mud squishes through the soft leather straps of my sandals as I make the damp dash to the entrance of Nha Tho Phanxico Xavie. The double doors hang wide and the sweet soprano strains of "Ava Maria" flutter like doves taking flight. I stand concealed behind the wooden collection box in the sacrosanct hall, the tall podium of my blind polished to a thick, greasy glaze. My camera is miraculously dry in its protected place beneath my linen jacket, though I am soaked with perspiration from the high heat and drenched from the steaming monsoon rain.

As I click my camera, light from its flash blinks rudely in the dim edifice. Fortuitously the innocent mouths of youths begin a Latin litany, and I am mesmerized. Swallowed by the dark church, I blur into the primeval drone of a Gregorian chant and am cast into the past of my own novel: *It is mid-morning, November 2, 1963. The church's double doors yawn, and under a thick sky* cyclos *play dodge-'em in Cholon's slummy streets.*

In 1955, almost a decade before Diem's violent demise in a 1963 coup by his own generals, Greene personally interviewed the president. He recalled in his *Collected Essays*: "I thought with more sympathy now of the southern President Diem…. One pictured him there in the Norodom Palace, sitting with his blank, brown gaze, incorruptible, obstinate, ill-advised, going to his weekly confession, bolstered by his belief that God is always on the Catholic side, waiting for a miracle. The name I would write under his portrait is the Patriot Ruined by the West."

Converted to Catholicism at age 26 and tempted by communism in the 1950s, Greene admitted a childish hero worship for Ho Chi Minh, likening him to an Asian Mr. Chips, 1930s novelist James Hilton's much-admired schoolmaster. Ho's political rivals tagged the revolutionary of many pseudonyms "the man as pure as Lucifer." Ho thought of himself as the "bringer of light."

Before Greene interviewed Ho in the leader's modest house in Hanoi for the *Sunday Times* of London, he stopped to suck on paradise, as he did on desultory afternoons at the notorious and now-defunct opium *fumerie* on what was once Saigon's Rue d'Ormay.

Fat Toan struts nearby, his partially exposed belly arriving before the rest of him. The lucrative corner of Dong Khoi and Mac Thi Buoi is his. He saunters back and forth across the 300 yards of sidewalk between the Majestic and the Continental Hotel, stridently calling out *"Cyclo, cyclo!"* to well-heeled tourists. Fat Toan's turf is prime American-dollar territory, and the brute steams in his own sweat and boils with bravado. He is the *cyclo* driver's pimp, a small-time hoodlum. They must pay or take their *cyclos* to Cholon and Tran Phu Street, another of Greene's stomping grounds.

Greene knew Cholon intimately, from the Arc-en-Ciel on Tan Da Street, a perennial favorite for Chinese food and in Greene's day infamous for its taxi girls, to Chinese mafia leader Bay Vien's cavernous establishments, the Grande Monde Casino and the House of 500 Women. In the 1950s, opium dens and brothels cuddled cheek to sensual cheek, but now the women that slink down Cholon's sordid side streets are as unhealthy-looking as the motley, moth-eaten civet cats seemingly frozen above medicine shops. Shan stops so I can photograph the disreputable Arc-en-Ciel Restaurant, and I take the stairs in a cockroach-infested building up to another of Greene's favorite opium *fumeries*, now a dollar-a-dance venue. Like Greene, I have purchased an opium pipe for memory's sake. Mine is smooth ivory with a rosewood bowl and a silver needle attached by a slim chain.

I lean, elbows out, over the ornate balcony of my splendid fourth-floor suite in the French colonial L'Hôtel Majestic, having forsaken a late-afternoon snooze. The white ceiling fan stirs

The Cao Dai Temple, where clerics worship the All-Seeing Eye, was described by Graham Greene as the "Walt Disney *Fantasia* of the East."

the languid air, and when I splash my face to refresh, I run my fingers over the colonial trademark of Lyon etched in the sink's ceramic bowl. On a previous stay I was rousted from my lovely lair so French President Jacques Chirac could occupy the suite, but that is yet another Saigon story.

On the street below my curvaceous windows, *cyclo* drivers congregate, and children hawk grainy sepia postcards and foursomes of Chiclets wrapped in clear plastic. Lazily I gaze at a pod of freighters, their sienna hulls slung low in the river's calm southern crawl.

From 1941 to 1975, Ho's Communist guerrillas controlled the swamp on the other side of Saigon, guns trained tight and twitchy. Dressed in trademark black pajamas, the Viet Minh hoisted Russian AK-47s and stolen MK-18s, unwieldy weapons supplied by America for the French, later pried from GI Joe's idealistic grip. With his usual suicidal complacency, Greene would have watched the sparks from the Viet Minh's tracer bullets ride ruby across the tinted sky. He would have sipped cassis, the hue of dried blood, from Baccarat crystal on the Majestic's wrought-iron balcony, the protruding retinas of his cool gaze held steady like a camera on a tripod. Greene was addicted to risk, by "that feeling of exhilaration which a measure of danger brings to the visitor with the return ticket."

Saigon's opposite shore has always been enemy territory, but now the guns are light-alloy M-16s firing 650 to 680 rounds per minute. The sawed-off handles are more suitable for the grips of smaller-boned Vietnamese and are clutched with greed, not nationalism. Just as the drug dealers have replaced the dreaded Viet Minh and Vietcong, Benzedrine and the needle high of heroin and crack cocaine are substituted for opium's smoke-ringed kiss. British writer Thomas De Quincey, whose autobiographical *Confessions of an English Opium-Eater* is a 19th-century classic, thought the drug was a celestial panacea for all human woes. Greene discovered opium's ethereal white night in the brothels and *fumeries* of Vietnam, where he puffed up to four pipes a day, reclining sanguinely on a divan while a patient Vietnamese prostitute or a pipe maker kneaded "his little ball of brown gum over the flame until it bubbles and alters shape like a dream…"

Yesterday afternoon in front of Ciao Café, the glassed-in ice-cream shop on Nguyen Hue, I jounced over the crammed and bullet-pocked streets in a spanking new imported Jeep with a hawk mascot, wings clipped and one leg chained to a tree limb securely anchored by the spare tire. The hawk was regal, nonplussed by the searing heat and bumptious traffic. I took photographs while riding shotgun beside a total stranger, an American of Vietnamese descent and dubious employment, dressed in jungle khakis. My host had rescued the hawk while hunting in the nether regions along the nearby Cambodian border, but the sad and beautiful creature could just as easily have been purchased from the live-animal market where dogs, cats, snakes, turtles, and monkeys are sold to specialty restaurants. He confirmed what I had suspected: that the opium dens where Greene puffed and drifted from depression no longer existed. Echoing the warning of a foreign-exchange banker I had met earlier, he advised me to be careful whom I talked to.

The sky is evening's pewter. I walk the former Rue Catinat with a seller of postcards. My charming companion is a street urchin, a precocious gamin whose shiny dark hair is cut short, pixie-style, and whose eyes sparkle like black marbles. Tintin, the French children's character, is stenciled on the apron of her clean dress. The little girl is 10 going on 20, yet in size can be compared to a North American five-year-old. Her English is perfect, Americanized. Like Greene's character, her name is Phuong, and she has managed to procure a copy of the British author's *Quiet American* for me.

In the crook of Dong Khoi (once known as Radio Catinat because of the war gossip that flourished in the cafés) and Le Loi, and beneath the dazzling golden Art Deco globe that hangs in the portico of the four-story Continental Hotel, we eat croissants and sip thimblefuls of *sua*, the sweet black filtered coffee loved by Vietnamese of all ages. Young women flit by on

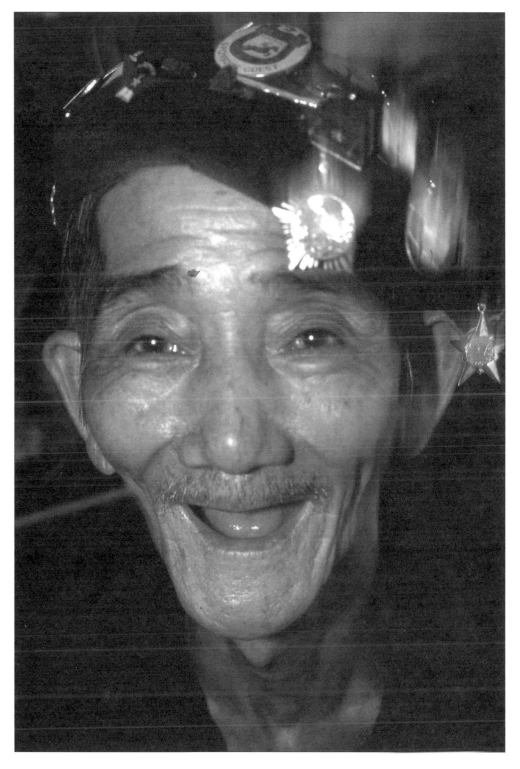

In Ho Chi Minh City, the former Saigon, one encounters many elderly sidewalk artists who still speak French and make a living as well as they can.

motorcycles, their *aoi dais* flashing like bright swallows' tails and their luminous long hair fluttering behind like silken black streamers. Vietnamese youths stroll in T-shirts and jeans, holding hands in simple affection. Old crones, faces like yellowed maps, squat on freshly swept pavement mouthing greetings, their few teeth black, their gums and lips scarlet with the age-old stain of betel.

Phuong leads the way to the square near the 1880s Neo-Romanesque red-bricked, twin-spired Notre-Dame that Greene describes in his novel as "the hideous pink Cathedral," and there she introduces me to a middle-aged couple. Her friends are hearing-impaired and can't speak. Phuong looks out for them. In daylight the husband, Tam, polishes shoes (there are few locals with shoes that suit a polish, but maybe one day…) and sews straps back onto sandals (a thriving business) with needle and fishing line. His wife, Bich, sells a diverse range of goods: French, English, and Vietnamese paperbacks photocopied and neatly bound; chopsticks of ebony-dyed wood; and Tom Thumb–size lacquered pots from a nearby factory. In the evening they prepare rice, harvested by villagers bent low in the flat green glitter of the paddies south of Saigon, and by midnight they lie like three spoons in the grassy postage stamp of a yard tucked safely behind the French-built copy of Paris's Notre-Dame. Phuong informs me proudly that their only child, her best friend, speaks and hears.

Rose, an attractive middle-aged Saigonese with her hair coaxed into a French twist, greets me effusively from her newly built boutique with glass windows and a real door. She is resplendent in embossed silk, hand-loomed and stained golden from a special process using the mud of the Mekong River. Rose, a talented, hardworking seamstress who on my last visit sewed silk in a tawdry shop on this spot, has the funding of a wealthy backer. The Saigonese, the rich and destitute alike, hope Dong Khoi, once the tamarind-lined Fifth Avenue in the Paris of the East, will return to its former glory.

Phuong and I double-back toward the Majestic, passing the Cathedral's spires again. Naively I think how odd it is that Greene was extremely devout. He was a sinner, yes, and if not a saint, at least a staunch defender of the downtrodden and the unpopular cause. My research has Greene pegged as a man with a splinter of ice in his heart, but if so, the ice melted here where he "drained a magic potion, a loving cup which I share with many retired *colons* and officers of the Foreign Legion, whose eyes light up at the mention of Saigon and Hanoi."

A few blocks north of Lam Son Square, exquisite twin angels hover atop the flying buttress of the Municipal Theater, a marble marvel constructed in 1899. I photograph Phuong, who holds up her postcards for my camera's eye. Then it is as if the world is ending and she is the alarm. Her eyes grow as big as saucers and as dark as a soulless night. She cries *"Can sat*—police!"

and thrusts her livelihood, postcards of the wispy-bearded Ho Chi Minh and the bizarre karst formations of Halong Bay, into my hand, then darts behind my crumpled skirt. Her bravado lost, she is a little girl again.

A cavalcade of motorcycles appears unannounced, like the boorish invaders of Vietnam's history. Lolling in an open yellow jeep, armed plainclothes police are followed by armored trucks. "They'll take me," Phuong groans in a whisper, dragging me by the hand toward the side of the theater. There, we crouch behind a bare-breasted alabaster angel the color of seashells.

With a fury born of power, the raid begins and the population scatters, gathering up their child-size plastic chairs in fearful haste, running and pushing hard behind their wheeled *pho* and cigarette stands. Limbless beggars scuttle like crabs into any dark abyss, or streak away on their clever low-wheeled contraptions. Dong Khoi has put its collective finger to its lips. The only sounds are the purring engines of the police vehicles, the clatter and squeak of rickety wheels, and the patter of running feet.

Like a typhoon, the police storm in uninvited and unbridled. Into the prison van they hurl like spent toothpicks the abandoned fold out tables, lacquered chopsticks, lottery tickets, T-shirts, and the ubiquitous GI lighters inscribed: "When I die, I'll go to HEAVEN because I've already been to HELL." Shoved in with the paraphernalia are the people who are too slow to get away, or simply too unlucky. Those who eke out their meager livings without license and sleep in Saigon's doorways and alleys bear the cruel brunt. Wealthy business owners and the Fat Toans grease palms with American dollars or reams of Vietnamese *dong* and stand unscathed. Fat Toan's thick-lipped sneer plays on my memory. Once again I see his yellowed nicotine-wad of spittle as he salivates on his squat fingers, the better to count his ill-gotten gain.

Phuong stifles a protest as the police cart away the deaf woman's makeshift counter. Unable to hear the encroaching menace, Bich has panicked. Abandoned, her tiny lacquered objects are crushed to splinters and gluey dust under the heavy heels of boots polished elsewhere. Copies of *Heaven and Earth* and *The Ugly American* are torn to shreds and flung into the bowels of the van. Then, as quickly as the apocalypse strikes, it is over and Dong Khoi becomes a busy street again.

Phuong is pale. A single tear rolls down her child's curve of cheek, and I brush it away, promising to send her a doll, the only thing she desires. I feel fury, then the heady joy that Graham Greene must have felt so often, for I have experienced pimps and proud *cyclo* drivers, drug lords and small-time hoods. I have walked through Saigon's hot, pumping heart and placed money into the frayed pockets of the wasted whose smiles are sweeter to me than the blessing of any god. I know their house. It is Saigon, a house without walls.

Bicycles in all shapes and sizes are a major form of transport in Ho Chi Minh City, particularly since the only fuel they require is the rider's muscles. Conical hats, as seen here, are only worn by country girls.

Recipes

L'Hôtel Majestic (Ho Chi Minh City)

Saigon Spring Rolls
Miss Saigon
Tomahawk

Hotel Sofitel Metropole (Hanoi)

Duck with Orange Graham Greene
Norwegian Crispy Salmon with *Nuoc Mam* and Passion Fruit in Pumpkin Garden
Graham Greene Martini
Graham Cocktail

Continental Hotel (Ho Chi Minh City)

C&P Cocktail
Pina Colada

Here, L'Hôtel
Majestic, still one
of the grand old
hotels of Southeast
Asia, is shown in
former days
when Vietnam
was French
Indochine.

Courtesy of L'Hôtel
Majestic

Saigon Spring Rolls ∾

Makes four servings.

Main Ingredients

1 package rice-paper wrappers (*banh trang*)
1 lb (500 g) ground pork or chicken (lean pork is best)
½ cup (125 mL) chopped onion
¼ tsp (1 mL) ground black pepper
½ tsp (2 mL) salt, or to taste
1 tsp (5 mL) sugar
1 shredded carrot
1 egg
1 oz (30 g) vermicelli noodles (soaked in hot water for 15 minutes to soften)
2 dried and chopped Chinese mushrooms (soaked in warm water for about 15 minutes)
1 tbsp (15 mL) fish sauce
vegetable oil for frying
1 whole pineapple
toothpicks

Special Hoisin Sauce Ingredients

3 tbsp (45 mL) hoisin sauce
1 tsp (5 mL) finely chopped peanuts

Sweet and Sour Fish Sauce Ingredients

1 finely minced garlic clove
1½ tbsp (23 mL) sugar
1 tbsp (15 mL) lime or lemon juice
¼ cup (65 mL) warm water
3 tbsp (45 mL) fish sauce
¼ tsp (1 mL) ground red chili pepper (optional)

Method

Bring a medium saucepan of water to boil. Boil rice vermicelli three to five minutes, or until al dente, and drain. Chop the noodles into two-inch (five-centimeter) lengths. Mix all the filling ingredients together. Dip the rice-paper wrappers in warm water. Lay out on a flat counter or on a towel. Spoon about two heaping tablespoons (30 milliliters) of filling onto the bottom section of the wrapper. Roll the bottom edge over the filling. Fold the two sides over the filling and then roll up. Repeat with the other wrappers. Pour about two inches (five centimeters) of oil into a wok. Deep-fry the wrappers a few at a time, carefully sliding them into the wok so the oil doesn't splatter. Deep-fry until light brown. Drain the rolls on paper towels. In a small bowl mix the fish sauce, water, lime juice, garlic, sugar, and chili pepper. In another small bowl mix the hoisin sauce and peanuts. Cut spring rolls in half and pierce with toothpicks. Insert spring rolls on toothpicks on sides of uncut pineapple. Arrange each sauce in a separate bowl around the pineapple.

A child hawks baguettes to tourists visiting Hanoi's war museum.

Miss Saigon ❧

Ingredients

2 tbsp (30 mL) rice liqueur
2 tbsp (30 mL) Galliano
1 tbsp (15 mL) lime juice
1 lime slice
1 red maraschino cherry

Method

Shake ingredients with shaved ice, pour into a cocktail glass, and garnish with maraschino cherry and lime slice.

Now part of the Sofitel chain, Hanoi's Hotel Metropole was one of the Orient's gems in the 1920s, as depicted here in this postcard.

Courtesy of Hotel Sofitel Metropol

Tomahawk ☙

Ingredients

1 tbsp (15 mL) gin
1 tbsp (15 mL) white rum
1 tbsp (15 mL) vodka
1 tbsp (15 mL) white crème de menthe
1 tbsp (15 ml) white crème de cacao
1 green maraschino cherry

Method

Mix ingredients, shake with shaven ice, and pour into a cocktail glass. Decorate with the green cherry.

Some Vietnam eateries (but not the venerable Givral Restaurant) specialize in dog, cat, or snake, dishes not for everybody.

Duck with Orange Graham Greene ❦

Makes four to six servings.

Ingredients

1 2 lb (1 kg) boneless duck breast with skin
1 tsp (2 mL) freshly grated orange zest
¼ cup (65 mL) freshly squeezed orange juice
¼ cup (65 mL) mandarin juice
¼ cup (65 mL) soy sauce
¼ cup (65 mL) vegetable oil
2 tbsp (30 mL) honey
1 tbsp (15 mL) white-wine vinegar
¼ tsp (1 mL) salt
⅓ cup (85 mL) water
freshly ground white pepper to taste (optional)

Method

With a sharp knife halve the whole duck breast and score the skin in a quarter-inch (0.6-centimeter) cross-hatch pattern. In a bowl whisk together the zest, orange juice, soy sauce, oil, honey, vinegar, and salt, then pour the marinade over the duck halves in a marinade tray. Let the duck marinate, chilled, turning occasionally overnight. Remove the duck from the marinade, reserving the marinade. Pat the duck halves dry between paper towels and season them with salt and pepper. Heat a skillet over medium to high heat until the skillet is hot. Cook the duck halves, skin side down, in the skillet for five minutes. Pour off the fat, reduce the heat to moderate, and cook the duck, skin side down, for 20 minutes more, adjusting the temperature if necessary for the skin to turn dark brown but not burn. Pour off the fat, turn the duck breasts, and cook them, covered, over moderate heat for eight to 10 minutes more. Transfer the duck to a plate. To the skillet add the water and deglaze over moderate heat. Add the reserved marinade. Bring the liquid to a boil and deglaze the second skillet, scraping up the brown bits. Add any juices that have accumulated on the cutting board and simmer the sauce for two minutes or until it thickens slightly. Strain the sauce through a fine sieve into a small bowl. Cut the duck halves across the grain into thin slices. Arrange the duck on plates and drizzle some sauce around each serving.

A girl in traditional Vietnamese garb sells souvenirs at the site of the famed Cu Chi tunnels, where Vietcong and North Vietnamese Army soldiers hid from U.S. and South Vietnamese forces.

Norwegian Crispy Salmon with Nuoc Mam and Passion Fruit in Pumpkin Garden ❧

Makes two servings.

Main Ingredients

10 oz (280 g) fresh salmon (2 fillets)
4 pieces of rice paper
21 oz (600 g) pumpkin
14 oz (400 g) pumpkin branches
¾ cup (165 mL) olive oil
2 diced cloves of garlic
nuoc mam (fish sauce) to taste
salt to taste
flour as necessary
ground black pepper to taste

Sauce Ingredients

4 passion fruit
3½ oz (100 g) butter
salt and black pepper to taste

Method

Cut salmon fillets by length four to five inches (10 to 12 centimeters), marinate with salt, flour, and pepper, then roll with rice paper and pan-fry medium rare in olive oil. Boil seven ounces (200 grams) of pumpkin, then mash it. Dice rest of pumpkin and sauté with butter, salt, pepper, and *nuoc mam*. Blanch pumpkin branches, then sauté them crispy with garlic, salt, and pepper. Put diced pumpkin in square molds, then pumpkin branches. Cut salmon fillets in two and put on top of molds, then place quenelle of mashed pumpkin next to salmon. Decorate with fried pumpkin leaves. Chop passion fruit; blend thoroughly with butter, salt, and pepper; and heat until warm. Serve as sauce.

Graham Greene Martini ❧

Ingredients

3 tbsp (45 mL) gin
2 tsp (10 mL) dry vermouth
2 tsp (10 mL) crème de cassis

Method

Pour gin, dry vermouth, and crème de cassis into a shaker, then add two or three ice cubes. Shake for 10 seconds, then pour into a glass. Garnish with a green olive and a lime leaf.

Note: The Graham Greene Martini is the signature cocktail of Hotel Sofitel Metropole. It's said that dry vermouth was the favorite alcohol of Greene while he stayed at the Metropole writing *The Quiet American*. Today the Metropole is the only place in Hanoi where martini cocktails are served, and the Graham Greene variety, created in memory of the famous writer, is among the best.

Graham Cocktail ❧

Ingredients

2 tsp (10 mL) dry vermouth
2 tsp (10 mL) crème de cassis
3½ fluid oz (100 mL) champagne
1 strawberry
1 seedless green grape

Method

Pour dry vermouth and crème de cassis into a shaker, then add two or three ice cubes. Shake for 10 seconds. Pour mixture into a champagne glass and add the rest of the champagne. Garnish with strawberry and grape.

C & P Cocktail

Ingredients

2 tbsp (30 mL) rum
2 tsp (10 mL) crème de menthe
1 tsp (5 mL) lime juice
dash of cinnamon
2 tsp (10 mL) simple syrup
1 red maraschino cherry

Method

Mix together well and garnish with cherry.

Pina Colada

Ingredients

2 fluid oz (60 mL) dark rum
2 fluid oz (60 mL) coconut cream
4 fluid oz (120 mL) pineapple juice
2 or 3 ice cubes
1 maraschino cherry

Method

Combine the rum, coconut cream, and pineapple juice in a cocktail shaker and shake vigorously, or whirl briefly in an electric blender. Put the ice cubes in a highball glass, add the liquid, and garnish with the cherry.

The journey from Old Saigon to Angkor Wat decades ago had to be made over a potholed single-lane track.

In Ho Chi Minh City, as in old Saigon, street vendors sell just about everything, including reproductions of Edvard Munch's *The Scream* and other works of art.

The Old Lion and the Young Dictator: when the revolution in Cuba was new, Ernest Hemingway *(left)* and Fidel Castro were friends.

Ernest Hemingway
To Have and Have Not in Cuba

*T*he cayo is attached to the mainland by a narrow yellow tongue lined with weeds and wild grasses. The tongue or Pedraplen, post–Ernest Hemingway, is Fidel Castro's work—17 miles of landfill severing and bridging a daiquiri-frothed sea. The road continues, slicing a man-made swath through mangroves. For the first time, I see pink flamingos picking their way through the green swamp; they remind me of the women of Havana strutting delicately, yet with purpose, across the 16th-century Plaza de Armas. They, too, are birds fishing for their next meal. Clouds of mosquitoes hover, a smoky stain over the shallow green of the water. The salmon-hued bodies and long necks of the flamingos arch and crane, thrusting wavering pink mirror images across the marsh. It seems like a mirage, a hallucination, then the birds spread their wings and it becomes a spectacle hot and sultry like Cuba.

By the mid-1930s, 20 years before he was awarded the Nobel Prize for literature, before his years in Cuba, Ernest Hemingway had made a considerable literary reputation for himself, one illuminated both by his lifestyle and by his larger-than-life presence. His spare, terse prose had been cultivated as a newspaper correspondent, the short sentences finely honed and tightly packed. His emotional suitability for drama was sharpened, too, through unrequited love, the specter of three wars, a difficult childhood (his mother dressed him as a girl) and, when he was

27, his father's suicide. It was when Hemingway became the breadwinner in the family that he nicknamed himself Papa.

Hemingway lived hard, played hard, and wrote hard, bringing a new energy and style to American literature. His method suited America, as did his persona: both embodied the nation's physical brashness and honesty. Already a cult figure in the mid-1930s due to the success of his first novel, *The Sun Also Rises* (1926), Hemingway was the voice of the Lost Generation that roamed Europe aimlessly, disillusioned by the empty aftermath that inevitably follows war.

The Sun Also Rises, with its romantic disenchantment punctuated by splendid heroics, the running of the bulls in Pamplona, and nonchalant banter, was so close to the mood of the period that Hemingway's catchphrase, "Have a drink!" was taken up by youth in Paris, New York City, and even the backwaters of middle America. Everywhere, bright young men emulated Hemingway's heroes, using understatements, talking tough. The novel, based on the author's own wanderings with first wife Hadley Richardson and their friends, was a thinly camouflaged version of people and events that really took place. This would be the course of all his writing.

A Farewell to Arms (1929), his second novel, drew on his experiences as an ambulance driver in World War I, ensuring his reputation as the most powerful chronicler of war America had ever seen. Hemingway was not just a literary influence: each city, town, or country that he brought to life with his carefully chosen words attained instant and permanent star status. But only Cuba, he admitted, attracted him so strongly that he wanted to "stay here forever."

Ernest Miller Hemingway was 33 when he discovered the voluptuous delights of 1932 Havana and the marlin that run like sleek blue torpedoes past Cayo Coco and Cayo Guillermo. These exquisite little islands float like dreams in the blue-green velvet warmth of the Gulf Stream. It is easy to picture Papa here, running naked down the long, pale ribbon of beach, taut muscles visible under tanned skin, his immense feet stamping deep prints into the floury white sand. His hair and mustache are stiff with salt from the sea and from a day of marlin fishing. The darkly handsome author is solid and masculine. He carries his weight, nearly 200 pounds, like an athlete, and although his height is five feet 11 inches, he appears to be taller. His body, toned by boxing and the rigors of deep-sea fishing, is the shade of 10-year-old Havana Club rum.

The *Pilar*, his 38-foot custom-built motor launch, floats alone on an ethereal horizon. White clouds puff languidly by, like tendrils of smoke from his last cheroot. The Gulf Stream is so utterly transparent that the *Pilar's* anchor seems to ripple, a dark cross under the phosphorescent sea. On the beach, the famous Royal portable typewriter awaits Hemingway's touch, the black keys made even darker by the partial shade of a coconut palm.

America's favorite literary son, the heavy drinker, the avid sportsman, the fearless hunter,

Street art can be found everywhere in Havana such as this work in the Plaza de la Catedral, near the city's old cathedral. Che Guevara is still often depicted by curb artists.

the constant womanizer, the immensely talented writer whose lyrical prose cut to the core, made Cuba his own, particularly in the pages of his posthumously published novel *Islands in the Stream* (1970). Cayo Coco and Cayo Guillermo are not only Hemingway's landscape, they are his story: the artist living on an island in the Gulf Stream in the 1930s; the deep-sea fishing, his passion; and the hunt for Nazi U-boats in the translucent waters. More to the point, it was in Cuba that he was to write some of his greatest works and spend most of his last 22 years.

&<>

When Hemingway wasn't on his habitual rounds of traveling, deep-sea fishing in Cuba and the Bahamas, hunting big game in Africa, or a sporting sojourn in Europe (Spain for the bull-fighting, Switzerland for the skiing), he used his home in seedy, unpretentious Key West, Florida, as his writing base from 1929 to 1939. His clapboard house, now a museum, was courtesy of his second wife, the spoiled socialite Pauline Pfeiffer. In 1927 Hemingway married Pfeiffer and converted to Catholicism. A few months before the first of many separations that began in 1932, he left Pauline and their newborn son, Gregory, in Key West and headed for Havana on one of his frequent marlin-fishing trips. At the Hotel Ambos Mundos, he resumed his relationship with 22-year-old Jane Mason. Mrs. M., as she was called, was the wife of Grant Mason—heir to a fortune, part owner of Cubana de Aviación, and a founder and manager of Pan American Airways. Mrs. M., a strawberry-blond, was stunning in every sense.

The Masons were ensconced in the extravagant and decadent lifestyle that Havana and some Third World cities such as Tangier offered. The golden spoon of Spanish and later, American, interests in sugar-rich Cuba hadn't become tarnished yet. Havana was a lifestyle "on a rumba," Hemingway's own phrase for what we used to call "a bender" and youth now call "a rave." It was the dissolute, madcap life that F. Scott Fitzgerald captured in his novels. Hemingway was later to use Mrs. Mason as a model for Helène Bradley, the bottled platinum-blond vixen in his novel *To Have and Have Not* (1937). This violent story of rumrunners smuggling human contraband between Key West and Cuba during Prohibition also details the revolution that overthrew Cuba's tyrannical Machado regime. The 1944 film version of *To Have and Have Not* catapulted new star Lauren Bacall to fame. While filming, Bacall and Humphrey Bogart, her costar, became lovers and went on to become Hollywood's most romantic married couple.

The scene of Papa's and the lovely Mrs. M.'s illicit lovers' tryst was the Hotel Ambos Mundos in the heart of Havana's shabbily sensual La Habana Vieja district. The stunning Spanish architecture in this historic area resonates with the spirit of the *habaneros* and still seems haunted by Hemingway's ghost, although he hasn't walked these streets for nearly 40 years. It was in the midst of this still infinitely physical quarter that Papa was destined to live and work, on and off, for the next five years. The daring Mrs. Mason is reputed to have climbed five floors up the outside of the hotel, through the transom of Hemingway's window, and into his shaded room for a sexual rumba, Havana-style, in Papa's *doble* bed. One daiquiri-swishing evening years later, Hemingway posed this frank question: "What's a man supposed to do when a beautiful woman comes in and he's lying there with a big stiff?"

I arrive in Havana on a hot Sunday in early February and, like Hemingway, head straight for the corner of Calles Obispo and Mercaderes, where the 52-room 1920s Hotel Ambos Mundos still stands. On the sun-splashed intersection, Cubans of both sexes linger, waiting for tourists to chat with, sell a cigar or a factory tour to, or just stroll beside. A mulatto poses, flaunting her physical attributes the way a tropical bird does to attract a mate. Displaying herself against a streetlight like a cliché, she has one bare elbow crooked close to her tiny spandex-covered waist, while her middle and index fingers, elongated and painted, embrace an ebony holder, the burning ember of its cigarillo as hot as she is. Her bare coffee-colored legs stretch to her stop sign of red shorts, one rounded hip thrust saucily, an obvious invitation for wolf whistles. Then a 1948 Buick, its surfaces thick with innumerable coats of barracuda-gray house paint, sidles up to the stone curb, and I'm reminded again of Hemingway, whose own Buick, except for the color, was this very same model.

I insist on a room in the northeast corner of the fifth floor of the Hotel Ambos Mundos, as close as possible to room 511, birthplace of *For Whom the Bell Tolls* (1940), Hemingway's novel of the Spanish Civil War. Between Hemingway's time and mine, the Ambos Mundos functioned as a state hotel for teachers, but it has been recently renovated for tourism.

The young male desk clerk's officious attitude, like Castro's wagging finger, reminds me that this *is* a Communist country and passports must be shown, forms filled out, and bills paid in advance. That done, I ride in the ornate metal cage of the original elevator to what used to be Papa's room, and am delighted to discover that it is just the way he left it.

My room is next door, with the same northern view over red roof tiles of colonial buildings to Havana Bay. As Hemingway described the view, "The rooms on the northeast corner of the Ambos Mundos in Havana look out, to the north, over the old cathedral, the entrance to the harbor, and to the sea, and to the east to Casablanca peninsula, the roofs of all the houses in between and the width of the harbor."

Papa's day in the small hotel room often began with a parched throat brought on by a large

Havana's population is an attractive mix of Spanish, black, and mulatto people.

quota of Papa Dobles, the double-shot frozen daiquiri invented for him at El Floridita. Legend has it that he once drank 16 of them in a single evening.

My room, like Papa's, is small, but the ceiling soars and the double louvered doors open wide onto a facade balcony. Through the pale pink and whitewashed pillars of the balcony, I can see the ruins of Morro Castle and a small strip of blue Caribbean. I hear the emotional strains of *son* music and later the laughter of Creole children backed by the drawl of a freighter's horn. Below, the 16th-century street is under siege by renovators, courtesy of the World Heritage Fund.

La Habana Vieja's subtle odor drifts up to me on the sea's breath. It has swallowed the many kisses of lovers, swallowed the ageless tale of the old fisherman who sits stoically or shares stories with his stubble-faced cronies on the worn wall of the Malecón, Havana's beautiful oceanfront thoroughfare not so far from where I stand. The tangy aroma is a long drink of Russian diesel, Havana cigars, *jineteras*, and perfume, the dust of old rubble, and the choke of new concrete.

The stately columned Spanish palaces lining the Malecón rub noble shoulders. Once the most exclusive and elegant of addresses, the seafront is now a boarded and bitter remnant of a lost era. The narrow two- and three-story structures teem with lonely residents who loiter, jobless, bored, and hungry on rococo balconies that peel *pastillas* of sunburned paint. Empty-eyed, they gaze across the sea toward Miami, where many of their countrymen have gone to escape the economic disaster that plagues them. The Malecón, I remember from a previous visit, is veiled with the sea spray of human tears. Now, looking upward on my hotel balcony, I watch a vulture turn on serrated wing, and somewhere nearby piano music does a Cuban crescendo. Next to me is Papa's balcony, the shutters thrown wide.

When she could bear no more of the small, gloomy hotel room, second wife Pauline Pfeiffer abandoned Papa's double bed for Key West. Third wife Martha Gellhorn, a talented journalist of a more practical bent than her predecessor, perused the classified ads in Havana's newspaper for a solution. She rented Finca Vigía (Lookout Farm) in nearby San Francisco de Paula, a 45-minute drive from the fishing village of Cojímar, where Papa kept the *Pilar*, and nine miles from Havana and the Floridita, his favorite bar.

Hemingway first met the feisty Gellhorn in 1936 at Sloppy Joe's, a bar in Key West. Papa accompanied Joe Russell, the bar's owner, on his rum-running forays during Prohibition, drawing from these experiences when he wrote *To Have and Have Not*. Russell also opened the now-defunct Sloppy Joe's in Havana. A year after Gellhorn and Hemingway met, they became lovers while covering the Spanish Civil War. The blond, attractive Gellhorn, on assignment for *Collier's*, was one of the first female war correspondents.

In 1940, after his divorce from Pfeiffer was official, Hemingway and "Marty" wed, staying on at the Finca. Gellhorn soon grew tired of the writer's refuge she herself had discovered for

Havana is famous for its antique cars and trucks. It's as if time stood still at the moment of Castro's revolution. These automotive relics are often touched up with house paint.

Victoria Brooks

Papa. Back in Europe, World War II raged, and she wanted to cover it. Hemingway, now a familiar fixture in Havana, decided to further the war effort from Cuba with his own heroic scheme.

At Finca Vigía today there is a document that reads:

18 May 1943

To Whom It May Concern:

While engaged in specimen fishing for the American Museum of Natural History, Sr. Ernest Hemingway, on his motor boat PILAR, is making some experiments with radio apparatus which experiments are known to this *Agregado Naval*, and are known to be *arreglado* [arranged] and not subversive in any way.

Hayne D. Boyden
Colonel, U.S. Marine Corps
Agregado Naval de los Estados Unidos, Embajada Americana

This informal authorization, written for Papa's use if the Nazis captured him (an escape hatch of dubious merit), was given to him by the American naval attaché. The U.S. navy issued Hemingway radio direction finders, hand grenades, .50-caliber machine guns, a bazooka, and extra rations of liquor, all for use aboard the *Pilar* while engaged in antisubmarine activities off Cuba's coast. Papa's personal mission was to capture a Nazi submarine with the *Pilar* (now tarted up as a Q-boat but disguised as a fishing vessel), take prisoners, and seize secret codes.

Hemingway never sank or disabled a submarine in the two years the *Pilar* patrolled Cuba's coastal waters, but he and his nine men, including Gregorio Fuentes (at the wheel) and a couple of jai alai players (chosen for their ability to throw grenades down hatchways), sighted one German sub. It got away, though. They also consumed great quantities of raw crabs with lemons. Fuentes, Hemingway's loyal captain of the *Pilar* from 1938 on, was the model for Antonio in *Islands in the Stream*.

Just before embarking on his hunt for U-boats, Papa began a short-lived spy ring he called the Crook Factory. Its secret mission was to infiltrate pro-Nazi organizations in Havana and report traitors to the American embassy. Hemingway, code name Agent 08, financed the project and held covert meetings at the Finca. He recruited during his pleasurable rounds at Havana's

40

Gregorio Fuentes, Ernest Hemingway's Old Man of the Sea, outlived his American friend, dying at the age of 104 in 2002.

bars and the Basque Club. His agents were fisherman, drinking pals, lottery salesmen, a man of the cloth who brought knowledge of machine guns from the war in Spain, an American ambassador, and two intelligence officers—friends with antifascist leanings.

Papa relished playing chief until he tired of the role, then turned his attention to submarine hunting. To Hemingway's latter-day detractors, both efforts smacked of James Wormold and his bumbling, fictitious spy ring in Graham Greene's *Our Man in Havana*. Hemingway was ridiculed as naive and romantic, a playboy who chased submarines off Cuba's coast on a whim. Papa called the *Pilar*'s covert operation "Friendless" after one of his cats.

In late 1943, Gellhorn left Papa and Havana for the battlefields of World War II. She dismissed Hemingway's Secret Service–style contribution to the war effort as a thinly veiled ploy to fish and get extra gasoline rations in wartime.

Gellhorn was replaced in 1946 by Hemingway's fourth and final wife, Mary Welsh, a correspondent for *Time*. Unlike his first three wives, "Miss Mary," as he called her, would remain constant in his heart, just as Finca Vigía and the *Pilar* would.

It was on the grounds of the Finca that one of Hemingway's favorite guests, the beautiful actress Ava Gardner, swam naked on a late September afternoon. While the curvy actress swam, Papa banned his 11 servants (including two Chinese cooks) from the second-floor windows. He alone stood and watched the actress do her paces in the square blue swimming pool surrounded by African orchids.

Gardner is now only a delicious memory, and the pool is empty, but the *Pilar*, Hemingway's beloved boat, sits dry-docked on a wooden throne built on the writer's tennis court. September, the best game-fishing month, brought an endless swarm of friends—bullfighters, Hollywood stars, prizefighters, soldiers, and artists—who came to fish with him in the Gulf Stream and to drink Papa Dobles. Now tourists wander the spacious and shady grounds where Papa bred fighting cocks and dogs.

Hemingway finished *For Whom the Bell Tolls* at the Finca and went on to write *Across the River and into the Trees* (1950), his masterpiece *The Old Man and the Sea* (1952), and *A Moveable Feast* (1964). Papa wrote the drafts in pencil, usually standing up. *The Old Man and the Sea*, a profound story of the struggle between a huge blue marlin and Santiago, a determined old fisherman down on his luck, was set in Cojímar, where Hemingway kept the *Pilar*. The story, inspired by Gregorio Fuentes, helped earn Papa the 1954 Nobel Prize for literature. He dedicated the prize to Nuestra Señora de la Caridad, the virgin patron saint of Cuba's only basilica in nearby Santiago de Cuba.

Now the Museo Hemingway, Finca Vigía was given to the Cuban people by Papa's widow,

Mary Welsh. The one-story Spanish Colonial house is painted a ghostly white. After paying the entrance fee, I wander around the edge of the house, peering through the large wood-framed windows. What I see is pure Hemingway: a hunter's palace, a sportsman's abode, a writer's haven. It is a place of dead things and guns, exactly as he left it.

Except for the kitchen, a cat cemetery, and the cellar, all the rooms are visible through the windows. No one is allowed in to disturb Papa's things: his glasses with the round metal frames, his collection of Nazi daggers, his guns, his fishing rods, his photographs and trophies. The hunting trophies take center stage; a maned lion from his first African safari in 1934 languishes on the tiled floor, its long incisors yellowed in death, its golden coat backed by red felt. A leopard, thick, soft fur the marbled color of my faux tortoiseshell sunglasses, is a souvenir taken by Papa from Kenya's Kimana Swamp in 1953. The taxidermist has artfully shaped the luckless leopard's jaws into a perpetual snarl. Sports magazines and books are strewn on desks and tables. The spines of some 8,000 volumes crowd the floor-to-ceiling bookshelves in a vertical litany of color and type. A wooden stepladder stands ready to access the highest shelves. Two lion skulls watch from a camel-skin bench.

I amble around to the shady side of the house. The cool stone floor I stand on is dappled in the late-afternoon shade of a giant ceiba tree. Papa stood on a lesser kudu rug when he wrote. His bedroom would stay comfortably cool. Now it is neat except for the mail, strewn Hemingway-fashion on his bed. An old issue of *Spectator* and a magazine called *Sports Afield* lie ready for his bedtime reading. A Royal typewriter waits on a polished wood shelf. An hour earlier at the Hotel Ambos Mundos, I saw a young hotel maid in European cap and apron dust a glass case that holds a similar typewriter. One of them must be a replica, but which one?

Around a corner, the dining-room table is laid with white linen. Good china, silver, and crystal are set for Papa's dinner guests. In the living room, next to his chintz-covered and flounced easy chair, is an elbow-height table bar covered with liquor bottles and clean glasses. Hemingway drank while he read, usually in the afternoon. Posters of bullfights and matadors, oils of bulls by Paul Klee and Joan Miró, and a white chalk bull sculpted by Pablo Picasso decorate the walls. More animal hides, kudu and water buffalo, hang beside African trophy heads, dead eyes staring at me. Their bestial mouths gape, yet are perpetually silent. Through the large, clean panes of the Finca's windows, I have a portal on Hemingway's sporty, some say bloodthirsty, soul. Graham Greene once commented dryly, "Don't know how a writer could write surrounded by so many dead animal heads."

Hemingway's incredibly massive size 11 shoes wait beside his bed. They look bigger than life, bigger than any man could possibly fill. On Mary Welsh's last trip to Havana in 1977,

Many of
Havana's
streets are
cavernous and
lined with crumbling
Spanish Colonial
buildings. Often
one gets a glimpse
of a remarkable
edifice such as
the domed
El Capitolio.

she said, "Everything is just where we left it in 1960. But the house is nothing without Ernest." I, too, feel his absence.

৵৵

It is late afternoon in La Habana Vieja, and the sun has stoked the heat to savage intensity on the stone streets outside. In my dim room next to Hemingway's at the Hotel Ambos Mundos, the rhythm of a rumba shakes its Havana hips like maracas through my open window. It is useless to ignore its call. "Have a drink," I say aloud, Papa-style, and prepare to hit the Floridita for a frothed green sea in a glass.

I take the hotel's gray marble staircase down five flights. My hand slides along the smooth, worn wrought-iron balustrade. In my imagination, it's still warm from Papa's large hand. The strains of "Unforgettable You" waft with old-fashioned sweetness from the hotel's public room.

Strolling the short nine blocks up Calle Obispo toward the Plazuela de Albear and another of Papa's shrines, I get hotter and thirstier by the minute. My feet move progressively quicker past a café fragrant with the smell of freshly ground Cuban coffee, past Creole babies, children, and women of all colors, past a museum fronted by a rusted-out Russian Lada. A pedicab, its leather seats shiny with wear, careers around a corner, the muscles in the driver's legs moving like thick snakes under the thin covering of his skin. My feet dodge potholes swimming with construction rubble, a dead cockroach belly-up, cigar ends and wrappers, and unlucky lottery tickets. A small dog yaps from behind an ironclad window, two small children tug at my dress, their mouths open with need—for a dollar, maybe just a kind word. I walk straight up Obispo, shaded from the sun by the tall, yellowed buildings. I am hot on Hemingway's trail and I want a Papa Doble.

A Cuban resplendent in red tuxedo and bow tie greets me at the Floridita. He opens the door with a flourish, and I take my place at the long, dark mahogany bar. The room is as cool as crushed ice. I note the "golden frieze and episcopal drapes" that Gabriel García Márquez describes in his introduction to Norberto Fuentes's book *Hemingway in Cuba*. "There," Márquez writes, "the daiquiri cocktail was created, a happy combination of the diaphanous rum of the island, crushed ice and lemon juice."

I order my first Papa Doble under Hemingway's watchful eye. His bronze bust hangs above me, smiling and carefree. The drink, sans sugar, is capped with froth like Mount Kilimanjaro's snow-covered peak. The liquid glides down my throat. It is the green of the Gulf Stream; it is as heady as the thought of Ava Gardner in Papa's pool. I feel expansive. Although the Papa Doble costs me $6.50, I order a second. It, too, slips down my throat. I am now on my third. It is delicious. I could catch a marlin by his slippery, silvery tail. I am drunk, proud to be on a rumba.

Papa Doble

4 fluid oz (120 mL) of Havana Club rum, or another good Cuban rum if unavailable
2 tsp (10 mL) fresh grapefruit juice
1 tsp (5 mL) grenadine
juice of lime
crushed ice

Shake well, but don't strain.

Old photographs of Hemingway stare at me from the walls: Papa with Gary Cooper, Papa with Errol Flynn, Papa with Spencer Tracy, Papa with his wives, Papa with the circus's Ringling brothers, Papa with Castro. I read the sign across the bar: LA CUNA DEL DAIQUIRI. I float in the liquid embrace of the daiquiri. To me, the cool of the Floridita's air-conditioning is a breeze swept from the sweet curve of Havana Bay. There are no windows in this elegant red room. Nothing exists outside the Floridita's Hemingway-covered walls. My thoughts are as clear as the ice that my good friend Constante has deftly shaken into my Papa-size glass.

I am seized by a thought: maybe Hemingway didn't kill himself with a 12-gauge double-barreled shotgun blast in Ketchum, Idaho, in July 1961. Maybe he's waiting to return to his typewriter in the room next to mine at the Ambos Mundos, or to his writing desk covered with papers at the Finca Vigía. Maybe, like the daring Mrs. M., I'll climb through the transom of Papa's window after dark for a hot and sweaty sexual rumba, Havana-style.

Feeling flushed, I turn my head slowly and marvel at Hemingway's own leather-topped bar stool sectioned off by a polished brass chain. Then, startled, I think I see Papa—a little older than in his photos on the wall behind the bar. A little paunchier, too. I squint through the smoky darkness, my eyes crossing with effort. But, no, of course it isn't Hemingway. It's a look-alike, a German tourist with a white mustache and beard come to pay homage to the legend.

I look around again and notice another Papa, round-faced and mustachioed à la Hemingway. He's wearing the white guayabera I could have sworn hung in Papa's bedroom closet at the Finca. This one looks exactly like the darkly handsome young author (before the neatly trimmed beard, before the gray of age) photographed behind the wooden wheel of the *Pilar*, tanned face shadowed by a long-billed fishing cap. I detect a South African accent and stretch to hear his conversation from across the room, but I needn't strain. I hear him cry Papa's famous incantation in a brazen voice: "Have a drink!" Then I understand. Hemingway is still an influence, still alive in the imagination of the entire world. And these look-alikes, these Papa *dobles* who emulate the author's style and flock to his stool at the famous Floridita are my proof.

So now I know. And there is nothing to do but order my fourth Papa Doble, put my head down on the long, cool bar and, in my rummy stupor, visualize running naked down a sandy beach, my huge size 11 footprints leaving imprints as deep as ditches in the glittering sand. Across a short expanse of water, my trusty blue-eyed Captain Gregorio Fuentes waits silently, patiently, at the *Pilar*'s wheel, the iridescent wake from the boat running behind like the pale green froth of my drink . . .

Ernest Hemingway spent many cheerful days and nights in the El Floridita, cradle of the daiquiri. Here he's enshrined, fittingly, at the bar.

They may not have as many advantages as most children in Canada or the United States, but kids in Havana certainly know how to have fun in the streets.

Recipes

La Terraza de Cojímar

Cóctel Don Gregorio
Cóctel Papa Hemingway

La Zaragozana

Paella La Zaragozana with Salsa Criolla
Daiquiri of La Zaragozana

El Paseo

Capucho de la Langosta

Hotel Ambos Mundos

Hemingway Great Dish with Maître D'Hôtel Sauce

Bodeguita del Medio

Mojito
Roast Pork Rolls
Black Beans
Flat Fried Green Plantains

The bar at the National Hotel in Havana saw many famous movie stars and other celebrities pass through it before Fidel Castro came to power in 1959—everyone from Nat King Cole and Rocky Marciano to Frank Sinatra and Ava Gardner.

Cóctel Don Gregorio ❧

Ingredients

½ tsp (2 mL) sugar or to taste
juice from half a lemon
drop of maraschino liqueur (Triple Sec will do also)
1½ fluid oz (45 mL) white rum
¼ fluid oz (8 mL) Blue Curaçao
ice

Method

Put all the ingredients into a blender and frappé.

Cóctel Papa Hemingway ❧

Ingredients

½ cup (125 mL) grapefruit juice
½ cup (125 mL) lemon juice
3 fluid oz (90 mL) white rum
drop of maraschino liqueur (Triple Sec will do also)
ice

Method

Put all the ingredients into a blender and frappé.

Note: All of Ernest Hemingway's drinks called for a double shot. Enjoy more than two, and you're ready to take on anything, Papa!

Paella La Zaragozana with Salsa Criolla ❧

Makes eight servings.

Main Ingredients

2 cups (500 mL) white rice
1 lb (500 g) shrimp
½ lb (250 g) ham
¾ lb (360 g) squid
1 lb (500 g) cod or halibut
½ lb (250 g) chorizo sausage
1 cup (250 mL) peas
½ cup (125 mL) chopped pimento
parsley or cilantro as garnish

Method

Cook the rice in four cups (one liter) of Salsa Criolla (see below for recipe) for about 20 minutes in a paella pan or similar wide, shallow cooking pan, adding additional sauce as needed to keep the mixture moist. You can also use white wine (traditional) or water. Stir slowly. Add the browned sausage and the ham to the mixture and continue cooking for 10 more minutes. Add the fish, squid, and shrimp and cook five more minutes or until just cooked. Stir in the peas and sprinkle the chopped pimento on top (for color) plus chopped fresh parsley or cilantro and serve. The peas will cook in the heat of the dish. The paella should be moist and creamy, the rice firm.

Salsa Criolla Ingredients

Makes eight cups/two liters (refrigerate or freeze leftover for future use).

½ lb (250 g) salt pork
4 tsp (20 mL) olive oil
6 cups (1½ L) finely chopped onion
4 tbsp (60 mL) finely chopped garlic
8 green peppers, seeded and coarsely chopped
1 lb (500 g) lean boneless ham cut in ½-inch (1.25-centimeter) dices
6 cups (1½ L) chopped drained canned tomatoes (or use fresh)

2 tbsp (30 mL) finely chopped fresh coriander
2 tsp (10 mL) dried oregano
4 tsp (20 mL) salt or to taste
black pepper to taste

Method

Fry salt pork in saucepan until very crisp. Remove and discard. Add the olive oil to the fat in the pan and cook the onions, garlic, and peppers until soft but not brown. Add ham, tomatoes, and spices. Reduce heat to low, cover tightly, and simmer 30 minutes, stirring from time to time to prevent sticking. May be kept in refrigerator for up to a week.

Daiquiri of La Zaragozana ❧

Ingredients

¼ fluid oz (8 mL) lemon juice
½ tsp (2 mL) brown sugar or to taste (Hemingway probably wouldn't have included this)
5 drops of maraschino liqueur or Triple Sec
1½ fluid oz (45 mL) amber or light rum (or double à la Hemingway)
ice cubes

Method

Frappé in a blender and serve in a champagne glass.

In every bar in Havana the sounds of martini shakers and salsa can be heard, particularly in El Floridita.

Capucho de la Langosta ҩ

Makes four servings.

Ingredients

1 lb (500 g) lobster heads
1½ cups (625 mL) fish stock
4 tsp (40 mL) white wine
2 tsp (10 mL) cognac
1 tsp (5 mL) diced carrots
4 tbsp (60 mL) diced onions
2 tbsp (30 mL) diced leeks
1 tsp (5 mL) butter
1 tsp (5 mL) red pepper powder or to taste
2 tbsp (30 mL) tomato paste
2 tsp (10 mL) parsley
1 tsp (5 mL) thyme
1 tsp (5 mL) rosemary
½ tsp (2 mL) black peppercorn
3 tbsp (45 mL) condensed milk
4 tsp (20 mL) amber rum

Method

Break the heads of the lobster (if possible), then fry them in the butter with the diced carrots, onions, leeks, spices, and peppercorn. When all this is fried, add the tomato paste and red pepper powder and fry the mixture once more until the tomato paste is desoured. Then put in the rum and white wine and cook on low for a few minutes, adding the fish stock. Simmer for 90 minutes. Strain off excess liquid and put aside. In another saucepan beat the condensed milk until it starts to thicken, adding cognac slowly. Don't overcook the broth, just simmer it, and don't beat the condensed milk too stiffly. Pour broth on top of dish and serve.

Hemingway Great Dish with Maître D'Hôtel Sauce

Makes four to six servings.

Main Ingredients

1 lb (500 g) shrimp
1 lb (500 g) lobster
1 lb (500 g) cod or halibut
1 chorizo sausage
½ cup (125 mL) Maître D'Hôtel Sauce

Method

Cook the shrimp, lobster, and fish gently and briefly in oil, then set aside. Next cook the sausage. Add the seafood and the Maître D'Hôtel Sauce (see recipe below) and cook for a few more minutes. Don't overcook the seafood. Serve dish with steamed rice and mixed vegetables (see black bean and plantain recipes below).

Maître D'Hôtel Sauce Ingredients

½ cup (125 mL) unsalted or sweet butter
1 tbsp (15 mL) chopped fresh parsley
salt and pepper to taste
6 drops Worcestershire sauce or to taste
2 tbsp (30 mL) lemon juice or to taste

Method

Mix the ingredients very well over low heat. Serve with Hemingway Great Dish above.

Mojito

Ingredients

½ tsp (2 mL) sugar or to taste
¼ fluid oz (8 mL) lemon or lime juice
3 fluid oz (90 mL) soda water
1½ fluid oz (45 mL) amber or light rum
3 fresh mint sprigs (save one as garnish)
ice cubes

Method

Crush the mint. Pour all the ingredients into a tall glass. Stir well to mix sugar.

Note: The *mojito* is a wonderful Cuban creation that Ernest Hemingway loved almost as much as his daiquiri. The Bodeguita del Medio (restaurant/bar in Habana Vieja) claims to have invented this drink. Regardless where it originated, enjoy this excellent libation that Ernest Hemingway made famous. *Salud!* You can also try the above *mojito* recipe with a dash of angostura bitters.

Neon advertises El Floridita, the bar that was immortalized by Ernest Hemingway's posthumously published novel *Islands in the Stream*.

Roast Pork Rolls ❧

Makes four servings.

Ingredients

2 lb (1 kg) pork ribs
1 diced garlic clove
1 tsp (2 mL) sour orange
½ cup (125 mL) lard
salt to taste

Method

Remove bones from pork ribs, then prepare dressing, which is made with the garlic, sour orange, and lard. Marinade the meat with salt and half of the dressing and form into rolls. Roast the meat slowly on low heat in oven for two hours, then take out to cool. Serve on a platter with the remaining heated dressing, pouring it over the rolls.

Black Beans &

Makes four servings.

Ingredients

2 cups (500 mL) black beans
1 diced green pepper
6 diced garlic cloves
1 large diced onion
1 bay leaf
½ tsp (2 mL) cumin
¼ tsp (1 mL) ground pepper
¼ cup (65 mL) sugar
1 cup (250 mL) red wine
1 cup (250 mL) vegetable oil
¼ cup (65 mL) vinegar
salt to taste

Method

Wash the beans and soak them for six hours. Cook the beans in the same water on stove for two hours on low heat, adding garlic, pepper, onion, and the bay leaf. Fry the remaining spices in oil and pour over the beans. Bake the beans for 25 minutes on very low heat (165° F/75° C) in oven. Take out of oven and season with salt and sugar. Add the red wine and simmer on stove for a few minutes.

Flat Fried Green Plantains &

Makes four servings.

Ingredients

3 large green plantains
2½ cups (625 mL) lard (substitute vegetable or peanut oil if desired)

Method

Peel and chop green plantains into three pieces each. Fry in lard. Drain and flatten gently with paper towels. Refry quickly in hot lard and serve at once.

A portrait of Ian Fleming sits on the spy novelist's former desk at Goldeneye, now owned and run as a resort by Chris Blackwell's Island Outpost organization.

Courtesy of Goldeneye/ Island Outpost

Ian Fleming
Seduced by Jamaica's Siren Song

*S*he wears a daring gown, hand-woven with threads spun from sunshine and studded with blue-velvet mountains. Her long hair undulates down her back like sargasso on the waves of a wild storm. When she moves, it is as if she is dancing to the suggestive strains of calypso. Her attraction is legendary. She is the siren Jamaica—birthplace of James Bond.

It was autumn 1944 when Commander Ian Fleming of British naval intelligence was first seduced by Jamaica. The dashing Fleming had not yet created secret agent 007 in his own image. Commander Fleming was on Jamaican shores for an Anglo-American naval conference. He was, as usual, on secret-service business. Security of sea routes during World War II was of paramount importance to Britain, and rumors of Nazi U-boats in Caribbean waters were rampant. Fleming, like his alter ego 007, was a man hell-bent on protecting the free world from dark forces. Consumed by the war effort and no stranger to exotic and foreign settings, Fleming had earlier masterminded Operation Golden Eye, a covert-intelligence operation to be used if the Nazis invaded Gibraltar. Operation Golden Eye would serve to maintain secret and essential communications between Gibraltar and London *and* carry out sabotage. It was never needed.

The naval conference Fleming attended in His Majesty's Service took place in the "hot, vulgar sprawl" of Kingston, as Fleming described Jamaica's capital in a passage from *Dr. No*. But in the evenings, Fleming and a friend who was a secret agent in Canadian spymaster William Stephenson's employ would retire to a "great house" in the lush Blue Mountains that

As this sign for the James Bond Beach Club attests, memories of Ian Fleming's 007 still haunt Jamaica.

soared above the rain-soaked shacks of Kingston and the pounding monsoon night seas that fringe the lush coastline. This same Jamaican mountain manor had played host to Fleming's hero and idol Horatio Nelson when the admiral was a young man. It was here that the man destined to be one of the 20th century's most famous writers became enamored with Jamaica's physical qualities. After a scant three days on Jamaican soil, Fleming made a momentous decision. "When we have won this blasted war," he said, "I am going to live in Jamaica. Just live in Jamaica and lap it up, and swim in the sea and write books."

In 1945, one short year after Jamaica first sang her siren's song to the adventurous Fleming, he returned in civvies, ready to fulfill the promise he'd made to the island and to himself. For 2,000 pounds sterling (approximately US$10,000) Fleming purchased two contiguous plots of land on Jamaica's north shore. The property perched high on a bluff, then tumbled into the translucent turquoise of a secluded bay.

One of these plots was acquired from Blanche Blackwell, famous beauty, socialite, landowner, white-skinned Jamaican, and mother of renowned hotelier, Island Outpost entrepreneur, and music mogul Chris Blackwell. Blackwell was Bob Marley's producer, financier, and promoter, and founded Island Records. In the late years of Fleming's life the same Blanche Blackwell became the spy novelist's fountain of serenity, his escape, his lotus land…his Jamaica in the flesh. The other plot of land was purchased from Irish Jamaican "Busha" Christie Cousins. Busha had used his land as a donkey racetrack, a popular pastime immensely enjoyed by the locals. Together the purchase comprised 30 acres, room enough for Fleming to build the home where he lived from January 15 to March 15 every year for nearly two decades. Fleming christened his Jamaican estate Goldeneye, in honor of his brilliant clandestine wartime operation.

Outside the sleepy tropical banana town of Oracabessa (Golden Head in Spanish) on Jamaica's leafy north coast, Fleming erected the simple stone-and-wood house where at the age of 42 he would write his first novel, *Casino Royale*. The famed concocter of spy thrillers attributed his celebrated creations directly to his surroundings: "Would these books have been born if I hadn't been living in the gorgeous vacuum of a Jamaican holiday? I doubt it."

Fleming lifted the name of his sophisticated hero off the cover of his Bible, *Birds of the West Indies*, by James Bond. The real Bond, a relatively unknown (up until then) American ornithologist, would later remark that his namesake speeded his way through customs when he traveled. In 1966 the real Mrs. James Bond chronicled the "revolutionary" effect Fleming's work had on the couple's life in the 61-page book *How 007 Got His Name*. The cover features a revolver surrounded by bird feathers. On the back is a handwritten inscription: "To the real James

Bond from the thief of his identity." It is signed Ian Fleming. Inside the slim volume are original line drawings of Jamaican birds from *Birds of the West Indies.*

Goldeneye was a modest house centered around a vast living room with large windows open to "Dr. Jamaica," the north coast's cool and refreshing trade winds. Slatted wooden louvers, or jalousies, instead of glass covered the windows. Inspiration spilled into this room with the shafts of Jamaican sunlight that slipped through, throwing their dancehall patterns across the plank floor. Fleming wrote every one of his 14 James Bond thrillers here—books that would go on to inspire one of the most successful movie franchises in Hollywood history and an international cult that shows no sign of waning. Fleming re-created himself and his wartime escapades "with the jalousies closed around me so that I would not be distracted by the birds and the flowers and the sunshine outside until I had completed my daily stint."

After closing his red bulletwood desk and covering his typewriter, Fleming retreated into Jamaica's own Atlantis. Twenty azure-tinted yards from Goldeneye's strand of silver beach a coral reef gleams like a spill of dark ink through transparent waters. Wearing nothing but a snorkel and mask, Fleming languidly studied the reef's inhabitants: long-nosed garfish, neon parrotfish, gold angelfish, glittering barracuda, spiny lobsters, and long-armed octopuses. "I learned about the bottom of the sea from the reefs around my property and that has added a new dimension to my view of the world... I learned about living amongst, and appreciating, coloured people—two very different lessons I would never have absorbed if my life had continued in its

Ian Fleming's red bulletwood desk at his former estate Goldeneye has been lovingly preserved as part of Island Outpost's resort.

pre-Jamaican metropolitan rut," Fleming wrote.

During the Fleming years, Goldeneye became a cradle of inspiration for others, as well. Cecil Beaton, Truman Capote, Graham Greene, and famous playwright and raconteur Noël Coward played and worked at Goldeneye. During Coward's first visit in 1949, he wrote an ode to Fleming's Goldeneye, which he referred to as the "Goldeneye, Nose and Throat [Clinic]." In the poem he complained about the airless bedrooms and the hardness of Fleming's furniture, but ended with "…I was strangely happy in your house./In fact I'm very fond of it." Coward liked Goldeneye so much that he built his own retreat, Firefly (now a historic museum and testament to Coward's life in Jamaica), just a few miles away on a hilltop in St. Mary's where he wrote much of his later music and prose.

Today, of course, the dashing Ian Fleming no longer pens bestsellers at his bulletwood desk. Noël Coward, once resplendent in silk smoking jacket, gripes no more about the discomfort of his friend's chairs. Over martinis, shaken not stirred, the bon vivant creator of *Private Lives* and *Design for Living* no longer addresses his host, sporting bow tie and puffing on black ebonite cigarettes, as "Ian, my dear." The sound of their voices can no longer be heard through the jalousies that have been opened to allow the sweet, seductive scent of Jamaica to drift inside. But life at Goldeneye still inspires and renews. On the house's silver beach Kate Moss, Johnny Depp, Quincy Jones, or Bono of U2 now sip martinis, shaken not stirred, with Jamaica's latest paramour, 21st-century music giant Chris Blackwell. It is their turn to listen and be captivated by Jamaica's siren song.

Playwright Noël Coward wined and dined many celebrities at both Firefly and Blue Harbour, his two houses in Jamaica. Here he poses with Sean Connery, the first film James Bond, whom many still feel was the best.

Courtesy of Blue Harbour

Recipes

Couples Resort (Negril)

Poached Fillet of Salmon with Moroccan Salsa and Roasted Plantain Risotto

Round Hill Hotel and Villas (Montego Bay)

Pan-Seared Sea Bass Wrapped in Rice Paper with Fruit Chutney and Sweet Potato
Jamaican Delight
Spa-Style Sea Scallop Salad with Zucchini Essence

Goldeneye Resort (Oracabessa)

Grilled Lobster Tails
Roast Jerk Snapper
Goldeneye
007 Martini

This English double-decker bus, now parked outside a club in Negril, was used in the filming of the James Bond movie *Live and Let Die*.

Poached Fillet of Salmon with Moroccan Salsa and Roasted Plantain Risotto ❧

Makes four servings.

Main Ingredients

4 pieces fresh salmon (5 oz/150 g each)
salt to taste
black pepper to taste
2 tbsp (30 mL) fresh lime juice or to taste
¾ cup (200 mL) dry white wine
¾ cup (200 mL) water
sprig fresh thyme
10 black peppercorns
½ medium onion (peeled and sliced)
1 bay leaf
½ cup (125 mL) heavy cream
5 oz (150 g) unsalted butter (chilled and cut into small cubes)

Moroccan Salsa Ingredients

1 each red, yellow, and green sweet peppers
1½ oz (50 g) raisins
1 large red onion
salt, sugar, and lime juice to taste
small bunch of fresh cilantro (chopped)
pinch of ground cumin
pinch of cayenne pepper

Roasted Plantain Risotto Ingredients

4 oz (120 g) risotto rice
1 large plantain
4 cups (1 L) chicken stock

¾ cup (200 mL) dry white wine
1 finely diced medium onion
2 oz (60 g) unsalted butter
2 oz (60 g) freshly grated parmesan cheese

Method

Wrap the plantain in aluminum foil and bake for 30 minutes in the oven at 375° F (190° C) until very soft. Remove and peel plantains. Chop into quarter-inch (half-centimeter) cubes. In a heavy saucepan sauté the onions in half of the butter until soft. Add the rice and sauté until rice grains get glossy. Add some of the chicken stock and bring to a boil. Stir constantly and add more stock as it's absorbed by the rice. Keep adding stock until a porridge-like consistency is reached and the rice is cooked. Add the diced plantain. Remove from the heat and cover to keep warm until needed. In the meantime combine the white wine with the water, fresh thyme, onion, peppercorns, and bay leaf in a shallow saucepan. Bring to a boil. Season the salmon with salt, pepper, and lime juice. Place in saucepan and cover with a tight lid. Poach salmon for about five minutes, ensuring that it remains slightly pink in the center. Remove, cover, and keep warm. Reduce the liquid by half. Add the heavy cream and reduce until it thickens (don't boil too much as it might separate). Remove from the heat and add the chilled butter cubes slowly while stirring the sauce constantly. Adjust seasoning with lime juice, salt, and pepper. Pass through a fine strainer. Keep next to the stove until needed. Roast the peppers over a gas flame (or in the oven/grill with strong top heat). The skin will get very black. Place in a plastic bag, close, and leave to sweat for about 10 minutes. Remove the skin. Take out seeds and cut into quarter-inch (half-centimeter) cubes. Cut red onion in quarter-inch (half-centimeter) cubes and quickly sauté in a frying pan with a little butter until soft. Place peppers, onion, and raisins in a bowl. Add lime juice, cayenne pepper, sugar, salt, and cumin to taste. Add freshly chopped cilantro last. Keep by the side of the stove so that it remains warm until needed. If the risotto has thickened too much, add a little more chicken stock, then add the remaining butter and the grated parmesan cheese. Adjust seasoning with salt and black pepper. Place in the middle of the plate. Arrange salmon on top. Cover with Moroccan Salsa and finish with the lime butter sauce. Once the butter has been added to the sauce, it mustn't boil any more as it will separate.

Note: Caribbean people use plantain like potatoes. Substitute sweet potatoes if you can't find plantains.

Pan-Seared Sea Bass Wrapped in Rice Paper with Fruit Chutney and Sweet Potatoes ❧

Makes four servings.

Main Ingredients

4 sea bass fillets (7 oz/200 g each)
2 tsp (10 mL) fresh chopped cilantro
1 tbsp (15 mL) fresh chopped dill
salt and pepper to taste
squeeze of lime juice
4 10-inch-square (25-centimeter-square) sheets of rice paper

Method

Top sea bass fillets with cilantro, dill, salt, and pepper and a squeeze of lime. Marinate for 10 to 15 minutes. Pan-sear fish on both sides until browned. Soak rice paper in cold water and wrap sea bass in rice paper. Refrigerate for one hour. Bake for five minutes in a 325° F (160° C) oven until warm. Do not overcook.

Sweet Potatoes Ingredients

5 sweet potatoes, peeled and cut into ½-inch (1.25-centimeter) pieces
1 tsp (5 mL) honey
½ tsp (2 mL) cumin

Method

Cook potatoes in boiling, salted water until soft. Whisk in mixing bowl with other ingredients.

Fruit Chutney Ingredients

2 tbsp (30 mL) brown sugar
1 oz (30 g) fresh chopped ginger
2 tbsp (30 mL) apple cider vinegar

2 oz (60 g) papaya
2 oz (60 g) cantaloupe
2 oz (60 g) pineapple
pinch of salt, cayenne pepper, and thyme

Method

Combine sugar, ginger, vinegar, cayenne, salt, and thyme in a medium saucepan. Cook over low heat for five minutes until sugar melts. Add fruit. Cover and cook for an additional five minutes. The chutney can be stored in the refrigerator for one to two months. Open the rice-paper package and serve the sea bass topped with two tablespoons (30 milliliters) of chutney and sweet potatoes on the side.

Jamaican Delight ❧

Ingredients

1 tsp (5 mL) sugar or to taste
1½ fluid oz (45 mL) white or amber rum
¾ fluid oz (25 mL) Triple Sec
½ fluid oz (15 mL) apricot brandy
3 fluid oz (90 mL) pineapple juice

Method

Put all ingredients into a shaker and shake with ice, then pour into glass and garnish with maraschino cherry or orange slice.

Spa-Style Sea Scallop Salad with Zucchini Essence ❦

Makes four servings.

Ingredients

4 fresh sea scallops (6 oz/180 g each)
3 tbsp (45 mL) chopped shallots
4 medium zucchini (washed and juiced)
3 tbsp (45 mL) butter
2 handfuls of mesclun (or salad mix) washed dried and cut into 2-inch (5-centimeter) lengths
4 handfuls of red oak lettuce (washed and dried, with root ends discarded)
1½ tbsp (25 mL) olive oil
1½ tbsp (25 mL) sherry vinegar
salt and pepper to taste

Method

Preheat oven to 350° F (180° C). Braise the scallops in oven for seven minutes in the zucchini juice until cooked through and tender. Remove with a slotted spoon and whisk the butter into the remaining juice. Blend the oil, vinegar, salt, and pepper. Toss with the salad greens. Arrange the greens in the center of the plate with the scallops encircling the edge. Pour the zucchini essence over dish.

Note: A colorful mesclun salad mixture can include some or all of the following: baby romaine, arugula, mâche, radicchio, mustard green, blue kale, and Swiss chard.

Grilled Lobster Tails ❧

Makes four servings.

Ingredients

4 lobster tails
salt, pepper, and diced garlic to taste
4 sliced small onions
4 scotch bonnet peppers to taste
4 tsp (20 mL) lemon juice
½ cup (125 mL) butter

Method

Wash and clean lobster tails. Cut each tail in half and devein. Wash and dry. Season with black pepper, salt, and garlic. Set on baking tin. Add sliced onions, scotch bonnet peppers, and a little butter on top. Put under grill until lobster shells become pink and meat gently comes away from the shells. Serve with sauce made from lemon juice, butter, and pinch of salt to taste.

Rose Hall Great House, eight miles east of Montego Bay, was once the home of Annie Palmer, who murdered all three of her husbands and tortured countless slaves in the early 1800s. Today the house is open to the public and available for private parties.

Roast Jerk Snapper &

Makes four servings.

Main Ingredients

4 whole snappers (cleaned, about 1½ lb/750 g each)
juice of two limes
1 lb (500 g) okra

Jerk Sauce Ingredients

15 whole scallions
3 scotch bonnet peppers
3 garlic cloves
1 tbsp (15 mL) Pickapeppa sauce or Worcestershire sauce
1 tbsp (15 mL) soy sauce
½ tsp (2 mL) grated nutmeg
1 tsp (5 mL) dry ginger
½ tsp (2 mL) allspice
1 crushed cinnamon stick
3 tbsp (45 mL) white vinegar
1 tsp (5 mL) salt
3 tbsp (45 mL) water

Method

To make sauce, finely chop and combine scallions, scotch bonnet peppers, and garlic. Add Pickapeppa and soy sauces, nutmeg, ginger, cinnamon, allspice, vinegar, salt, and water and blend. (These can also be ground in a food processor.) Rinse fish, pat dry, rub in juice from limes. Pat dry. Make a few slices in the skin of each fish and rub in jerk sauce on the inside and outside of fish. Place each fish on foil, then put sliced okra on top of fish with a little butter. Wrap each fish in foil. Roast fish on barbecue or in oven at 350° F (180° C) for about 20 to 30 minutes. Serve inside the foil packets with extra Jerk Sauce on the side.

Note: Ian Fleming and Noël Coward often dined together at Goldeneye. Fleming loved Jamaican food, as Andrew Lycett points out in his biography of James Bond's creator: "…Ian discovered the less gainly creatures of the deep, the lobsters and octopuses…wearing nothing but a mask, he spent hours communing with his new neighbours, sometimes wielding a spear which he used to kill lobster for dinner…. Ian made no concessions to his metropolitan guests at mealtimes. He had told Violet [Fleming's cook] that he did not come to Jamaica to eat beef roll. So [his guests] were introduced to the culinary delights of the national dish, ackee and saltfish, to curried goat and to grilled snapper."

Mr. Natural is landscaper, security, and cook at Noël Coward's first Jamaican house, Blue Harbour.

Goldeneye

Ingredients

1 fluid oz (30 mL) lime juice
2 fluid oz (60 mL) simple sugar syrup
3 fluid oz (90 mL) white rum
ice

Method

Blend ingredients with lots of ice. Serve in a standard cocktail glass, piled high, as a frozen drink but with a little liquid around rim of glass, ready for sipping. Decorate with a small fresh orchid.

Note: The signature welcome libation at Goldeneye is the above drink invented there by Chris Blackwell and Clayton Hinds.

007 Martini

Ingredients

3 fluid oz (90 mL) gin
1 fluid oz (30 mL) vodka
½ fluid oz (15 mL) Kina Lillet aperitif

Method

Shake very well with ice until cold, then pour into a martini glass and add a large, thin slice of lemon peel.

The best-selling author of *The Bridges of Madison County* and *Puerto Vallarta Squeeze* has developed a special connection to the Mexican beach resort of Puerto Vallarta.

Robert James Waller
Puerto Vallarta Squeeze

"Happy birthday! You have half your life left."

I flashed an enigmatic smile at my then-husband, Guy, across the feathery shade of the *palapa* that sheltered us from the Mexican sun. Did I really want to be reminded that I'd reached a milestone on my journey through life?

I had hoped to celebrate my birthday on a riverboat in Papua New Guinea, but somehow we ended up in Puerto Vallarta. After recent trips to Sri Lanka and Vietnam, a budget squeeze had prevailed.

Beyond our chichi hotel, The Careyes, the Pacific Ocean's azure tongue lapped in tempo over seashells scattered across the brown sand like tiny ears. The serrated pompadour of coconut palms swayed in the breeze. Steps away, the sea whispered, but it would keep my secret, the exact number of decades that are now both my memories and my past.

Sounds drifted in from the hotel bar. I heard something familiar: "People would be riding on the music, drinking and clapping in flamenco time…. In Puerto Vallarta. In a place called Mama Mia's." I knew those words by heart, and it was an odd coincidence that I should be hearing them at that particular moment. They're from the title track of Willie and Lobo's recording *Puerto Vallarta Squeeze.*

We had come to The Careyes to soak up the sun and sea after a few frenetic nights in Puerto Vallarta. The resort town is associated with a long-ago birthday of the actress Elizabeth Taylor. She and actor Richard Burton played out their tempestuous love affair here and

Destiladeras Beach on the Pacific Ocean coast of Mexico has become a popular destination for sun-seekers.

made the town famous.

Burton discovered the then-simple fishing village in 1963 when filming John Huston's *Night of the Iguana* with screen siren Ava Gardner and nymphet Sue Lyon. The handsome and hard-drinking Burton purchased a love nest for Taylor's 32nd birthday in what is now Old Vallarta. But I had wallowed in the Taylor mystique on previous visits and, like the entire world, have watched the once-exquisite beauty grow fat, unhealthy, and old on the front pages of the tabloids read in the checkout lines at supermarkets. I'd already seen the bigger-than-life statue of Taylor and Burton on a street close by Isla Rio Cuale, the little island that basks like a lazy green lizard in the narrow river of the same name. I had no intention of visiting Taylor's former villa, the oddly named Casa Kimberley again, either, although it's a museum now. I wanted to race as fast as I could to Mama Mia's bar, made legendary by Robert James Waller's adventure novel *Puerto Vallarta Squeeze*.

After we landed at Puerto Vallarta's airport, we strode through the mob of high-season holiday-makers to the car-rental counters. *"Buenos tardes,"* said Maria of Best Car Rental as Guy handed her the confirmation number for the prearranged, four-door, new-model, nonsmoking, American-made vehicle requested. Maria gave Guy the contract for an old-model, two-door, manual-drive, *hecho-en-Mexico* Volkswagen whose drivers had been a fast-fuming line of smokers. "Eet is high season," the woman said, smiling happily as she slapped the keys on the counter. She didn't have to say, "Take it or leave it." Her body language told us that. To be fair, it wasn't just high season; it was also New Year's Eve.

Our VW jounced like a jumping bean down the double-lane cobblestone road past a top-heavy parade of condominiums, luxury hotels, and shopping malls to the Sheraton Hotel, where Guy had booked an ocean-view room on the concierge floor. The clattering of the low chassis and the thin wheels rolling and smacking against the cobbles echoed loudly. When we tried to talk, it was as if we were having a conversation under a volcano.

At the Sheraton I retreated to my room with reasonable expectations. My simple desire was to wake to the sound of the sea. But the concrete box faced another building, and the rush of waves from the curvaceous and blue Bahía de Banderas, Bay of Flags, didn't exist. The constant noise of cars pulling in and out of the parking lot was all we heard. I experienced a niggle of disappointment. The words *high season* and *Puerto Vallarta Squeeze* typed themselves with a *clack-clack-clack* on the screen of the laptop partition located in the right side of my brain.

After my polite request, Guy returned to reception. With a voice that sounded in his own ears as piercing as the one he'd used to be heard above the din produced by the jumping and hiccuping VW, he secured, with difficulty, another "ocean-view" room.

I was anxious to get to Mama Mia's before it was stuffed tighter than a can of flaked Pacific tuna. While I awaited Guy's imminent return from the reception desk, I eagerly pictured the night ahead. Guy and I would perch like coastal birds on the scarred leather barstools at Mama Mia's. We'd sit knee to knee like the fictional down-and-out Danny Pastor, Waller's antihero, and his sensual Mexican girl, Luz Maria. Novelist Waller was inspired by his discovery of Willie and Lobo's fabulous Gypsy flamenco music at Mama Mia's.

We would begin the Technicolor excursion with shots of tequila *anejo*, and blur the intoxicatingly raw kick with sea salt and sucks of fresh lime. Guy and I would drink, clap, and ride high on the music. We'd dance, standing almost still, on the densely packed floor. In between we'd sip refreshing Sangrita, the tomato juice, orange, and jalapeño chaser Mexicans favor when they want a night to remember.

Guy, bellhop in tow, interrupted my daydream. We moved to room 809. It, too, had the charm of a concrete box, the air-conditioning was out of order, and the lower mattress was covered with ripped plastic. But at least the ocean might be just visible in the morning *if* I strained my eyes across the huge expanse of swimming pools and over the gardens. Guy doubted we'd hear the surge of the sea at all. And then he told me his bad news. He'd checked with the concierge, and Mama Mia's no longer existed. Mama Mia's, made famous by *Puerto Vallarta Squeeze*, had been closed down.

Abandoning the rented VW for a cab, we sped to Puerto Vallarta's crowded oceanfront strip, the Malecón. We wandered aimlessly, dodging the throngs of drunken tourist revelers and resort touts in black net undershirts and Reeboks. The neighborhood was as frenzied as Mexico City's Zona Rosa at midnight. It was in the Zona Rosa at an outdoor café that I'd first discovered tequila and the tasty chaser Sangrita, and while imbibing saw two baby owls, impossibly downy and big-eyed. They had been taken from the Sierra Madre. Sadly they were being offered for sale.

Sharp-edged memories like that bloom perennially in my memory, while I easily forget omnipresent chain hotels and tourist traps that could be anywhere.

Guy and I pressed our way past Puerto Vallarta's trendy Carlos O'Brian's, Senior Frogs, and Hard Rock Café. Past red-roofed shops with T-shirts and tequila displayed behind glass windows, past ceramics painted with flowers, past straight-legged Mexican dolls with striped ponchos and soft hair that reminded me of the baby owls I'd seen in Mexico City.

Each establishment had a lengthy lineup at the door. We were about to give up in despair when a second-story bar, reached by a set of side stairs, caught our weary gazes. One tiny table was available, close by the entrance to the bathroom and too far from the wide-open shutters

This oasis-like pool at Puerto Vallarta's Hotel Quinta Real is the perfect place for guests to cool their heels after a night of dancing at the frenetic bars on the Malecón.

to feel or see the action on the hyper Malecón playing itself out against the serenity of the evening sky. Seating ourselves, we called for tequila—there was no Sangrita—and hoped for the best.

The other patrons who had found their way up the stairs were sedate Mexican couples on vacation. And the music, though not the exciting Gypsy flamenco depicted so arousingly in *Puerto Vallarta Squeeze,* was at least not the disc-jockey disco that blared into the street from the clubs on the Malecón. The lone "bohemian-style guitarist" sang folksongs in Spanish to the low-key audience.

Outside, we knew people were lingering and mingling on the pale strip of beach as the Mexican night pranced in polished shoes toward morning. The sky was a silk scarf decorated with stars. A shy moon peeked, then receded behind a cloud that reminded me of a child watching a party from a darkened stairway. And then, at the exact moment when Guy kissed me to mark my own new year—my new decade, the second half of my life—something happened. The patrons who sat in the windows over the Malecón began to ooh and ah and dance and cheer.

Guy and I ran to the tables by the open windows to look, our eyes, filled with the spectacle, rounder than tortillas. The sky above the bay had turned to mercury. Lit like a wild changeling in a kaleidoscope, the heavens exploded, sighed, shrieked, and spouted fountains of sparks. Shooting stars rained down, creating amoeba shapes seen only in fantasies 10,000 leagues beneath an inky sea. Tangerine and chartreuse blazed. Molten ingots glittered. Trinkets and teardrops of silver dripped. Ruby streaks of brimstone slid in crazy rivers to drown beneath dark waters.

The Mexican couples, sedate and aloof when we arrived, welcomed us, the strangers, with embraces. A young Mexican woman, who had appeared charmless earlier, took castanets from some secret place and danced the flamenco. Her name could have been Luz Marie. I saw the fireworks mirrored in Luz's shiny raven eyes. Luz twirled round and round like quicksilver, her skirts frothing sea foam above brown knees. The crowd, too, began to clap and dance with abandon to the hot light generated by her dance, to the explosive brilliance of the fireworks over the night-draped bay. The evening rode high and wild…and I heard Robert James Waller's words: "People would be riding on the music, drinking and clapping in flamenco time…. In Puerto Vallarta. In a place…" In a place I shall always call Mama Mia's.

Something is always happening in Puerto Vallarta, like a police motorcycle procession before a parade.

84

Recipes

Willie Royal

Willie's Italiano Chicken

Casa Las Brisas

Cream of Poblano Chili Soup

Mama Mia's

Mama Mia's Special

Hotel Quinta Real

Quinta Real Tropical Refresher

Wolfgang Fink

Bavarian Pork Roast with Potato Dumplings and Cucumber Salad

Willie and Lobo's old haunt, Mama Mia's, has moved to San Miguel de Allende, but the performers can still be found in Puerto Vallarta at places like the River Café.

Willie's Italiano Chicken ❧

Makes four servings.

Ingredients

1 whole free-range skinned chicken
4 baking potatoes
12 garlic cloves
6 small onions
2 bell peppers
¼ lb (125 g) string beans
3 stalks of celery
1 large can of whole peeled tomatoes (28 fluid oz/795 mL)
8 bay leaves
salt and pepper to taste
3 or 4 pinches of oregano
sprinkling of capers

Method

Cut up and skin chicken and put into four-quart-deep (4.5-liter-deep) casserole dish with cover. Cut each potato into three pieces and put them in with chicken. Cut onions in half and spread throughout. Cut garlic cloves in half and spread throughout. Slice up celery and bell peppers and add along with string beans throughout. Then add salt, pepper, and oregano. Add capers if desired. It's important to add all the ingredients so that they're evenly distributed in the casserole dish. Add the can of tomatoes with juice over the whole dish, cover, and bake at 375° F (190° C) for one hour and 15 minutes.

Cream of Poblano Chili Soup ✷

Makes two to three servings.

Ingredients

6 roasted, peeled, seeded, and sliced poblano chilies
3 minced garlic cloves
1 large minced yellow or white onion
1 tbsp (15 mL) olive oil
2 cups (500 mL) chicken broth
½ lb (250 g) softened cream-style cheese
½ cup (125 mL) milk or cream

Method

Sauté onions and garlic in olive oil in a pan until translucent. Add sliced chilies and chicken broth and heat thoroughly. Then put entire mixture into a blender with cream cheese and blend until smooth, adding milk or cream as needed for desired thickness. Reheat as necessary and serve.

Mama Mia's Special ❧

Ingredients

1 fluid oz (30 mL) vodka
2 fluid oz (60 mL) coconut milk
splash of grenadine
2 fluid oz (60 mL) pineapple juice
½ banana
1 fluid oz (30 mL) Baileys liqueur
crushed ice

Method

Put all ingredients in the blender and liquify. Pour into cocktail glass and garnish with pineapple slice and maraschino cherry.

Agave plants in the Mexican state of Oaxaca are grown to be processed into tequila.

Quinta Real Tropical Refresher ❧

Ingredients

2 fluid oz (60 mL) orange juice
2 fluid oz (60 mL) pineapple juice
2 fluid oz (60 mL) mango juice
sparkling mineral water
touch of grenadine (if desired)
ice
lime slice

Method

Pour orange, pineapple, and mango juices over ice into a tall glass, then top with mineral water. If desired, finish with a touch of grenadine, allowing it to run down the inside of the glass and settle at the bottom. Garnish with a lime slice.

Note: If alcohol is desired, add an equal part of rum, tequila, or vodka.

Wall paintings are a common feature in all Mexican towns and cities, including Puerto Vallarta.

Bavarian Pork Roast with Potato Dumplings and Cucumber Salad ❧

Makes six to eight servings.

Ingredients

3 lb (1½ kg) pork (rear leg or upper thigh, boneless)
7 oz (200 g) butter
5 garlic cloves
1 medium onion
2 tbsp (30 mL) caraway seeds
4 small dried chili peppers
salt and ground black peppercorns to taste (for pork)
2 or 3 bay leaves
12 fluid oz (340 mL) flat beer
3 lb (1½ kg) potatoes
5 midsize cucumbers
salt and pepper to taste (for cucumber salad)

Method

Wash the boneless pork well. Dry it off and poke one-and-a-half-inch-deep (3.75-centimeter-deep) holes into the meat (about eight holes} with a sharp pointed knife. Insert little garlic spears into the holes (cut a good-size garlic clove into thin spears), then rub salt all over the meat. Next, bring the butter to a frying point in a big skillet. Put the pork in the skillet, add a couple of bay leaves, and sear the meat golden brown on every side, making sure you seal the pores and conserve the juices. Make certain during the whole browning process that the butter doesn't turn black (focus on heat control). After the pork turns golden brown and looks sealed all around, remove it with all the sizzling butter and transfer it to a big pot (preferably stoneware or an ovenproof dish). Cover this pot with an appropriate lid and place it in a preheated oven (450° F/230° C) for approximately 20 minutes.

While you're waiting, chop the medium-size onion (preferably yellow) and the remaining four garlic cloves. After the pork has been in the oven for 20 minutes, take it out and distribute the chopped onions and garlic around the sizzling meat. Now add the crushed dried chili peppers, some ground black peppercorns (to taste), and the caraway seeds. Then put the pot back in the oven for another 20 minutes. When those 20 minutes are up, take the pork out again, pour the flat beer over it, and put the pot back in the oven. After another 10 minutes, add water equal to the amount of beer and reduce heat to 350° F (180° C). Leave the pork in the oven for approximately two more hours with continuous supervision of color (nothing should turn black) and add more liquid (you want to have plenty of sauce from this meat). Make sure you bathe the meat every once in a while with the drippings to keep the meat moist. (If you add more liquid, you should add more water rather than beer, because if you use too much beer, the juices could become bitter.) Now you can leave the kitchen for a while and attend a conga jam in the living room to balance the aura of the pork roast (just kidding).

Next step: the potato dumplings. Peel half of the potatoes and boil them until they're soft. Take them off the stove, pour the water off, and let them cool. Peel the remaining half of the potatoes and grate them raw into a big bowl of water. (You have to grate them into water; if you don't, they'll turn black from oxidation.) Next, take a big white cotton cloth, pour in the grated potatoes, close the cloth around them, and squeeze until totally dry (you need lots of strength for this). Now take the cold boiled potatoes, mash them well, and mix them with the raw grated ones. Meanwhile bring a large pot of water, slightly salted, to a boil. Moisten the palms of your hands, form tennis-ball-size dumplings, and submerge them in the boiling water. They'll sink to the bottom of the pot, so make sure you turn the heat lower, keeping it barely boiling for about 40 minutes. (When the dumplings are ready, they'll float to the surface.) Watch the pot carefully and make sure the dumplings are completely covered with water at all times. Don't put a lid on the pot.

Last step: the cucumber salad. Wash the cucumbers and grate them very fine into a large bowl (don't peel them), then add salt and pepper to your liking and mix everything together. When the pork is done (golden brown, fabulous smell, et cetera), take it out of the oven, slice it, and put it on a plate. Then take a dumpling out of the water, cut it into small pieces, put it on the plate, and pour a couple of spoons of the roast juice over it. Next, put a couple of spoons of the cucumber salad in another corner of the plate. Serve the plate with a mug of Bavarian beer and enjoy!

In Puerto Vallarta, accordion in hand and Stetson on head, a street minstrel delights tourists for a few pesos a song.

The author in his element: Sir Arthur C. Clarke relaxes while his constant companion, the one-eyed Chihuahua Pepsi, peeks out from his shirt.

Sir Arthur C. Clarke
Sri Lanka's Sahib of Serendipity

I was introduced to science-fiction grandmaster Sir Arthur C. Clarke's adopted home-land on the long, wet tongue of Sri Lanka's seemingly endless political monsoon. Like watching my first screening of a subtitled Sinhalese film, the experience performed a cacophonous dervish on my senses that threw me into a state from which I fear I may never quite recover, and will certainly never forget.

∽

A few miles from where I rest in my elegantly shabby Galle Face Hotel room, a baby cuckoo falls from its nest, landing, as luck and serendipitous occurrences would have it, in the well-tended Colombo tropical garden of noted futurist and writer Sir Arthur C. Clarke. Winner of science fiction's three highest tributes and author of some 80 books, including *2001: A Space Odyssey* and *Childhood's End*, Sri Lanka's most famous resident is also a science writer, adventurer and adventure writer, treasure-seeker and collector, entrepreneur and philanthropist.

I arrive in Colombo only a few hours before sunup, in torrid heat, to endure a 22-mile taxi ride from Bandaranaike International Airport, a ride that bumps and jounces over pock-marked streets and is disrupted further by mandatory and makeshift checkpoints padded with sandbags and manned by air force, army, navy, and antiterrorist commandoes, their faces annihilated by night shadows. All are armed with flashlights, flack jackets, and rifles.

They are checking identification papers—hunting for Tigers.

Far to the east, in Yala National Park, leopards stretch and fret and growl. They while away the late afternoon on smooth, high rocks that bask like dark pools in the flickering light, or glitter like oil beneath falling rain. Once lions roamed this diverse and beautiful island, but now the great golden beast that represents Sri Lanka's Sinhalese is extinct and only visible on sunset-colored billboards emblazoned with Lion Lager's audacious slogan: PUT A LION IN YOU.

ॐ

There are no tigers in Sri Lanka except for the Liberation Tigers of Tamil Eelam. The LTTE or Tigers have terrorized Sri Lanka since 1983 when the southeast trade winds conveyed on their dank breath an anti-Tamil government-fueled pogrom that devastated Colombo's Tamil areas. Sri Lanka's majority ethnic group, the Sinhalese, backed by government troops, have been battling these shadowy separatist guerrillas ever since. Their methods are extreme: suicide bombers and surprise attacks. Their weaponry is modern: T-56 rifles, grenades, and rocket launchers. The Tigers fight ferociously in this ethnic civil war for a separate and independent homeland in the north and east where they are based. They accuse the majority Sinhalese of widespread discrimination against Tamils. More than 60,000 people have died in the conflict so far.

The 3.2 million predominantly Hindu Tamils are a minority in Sri Lanka's 18.6-million population. The country's Sinhalese, the ruling majority at 69 percent, follow the teachings of Buddha, the government-approved religion. Buddhism has thrived in Sri Lanka for millennia except for a brief 75-year period in the late 10th and 11th centuries when it was suppressed by a Hindu dynasty from nearby Tamil Nadu.

To my untrained eye there seems little, if any, difference between the physical appearance of a Tamil and a Sinhalese. They are all Sri Lankans, renowned worldwide for their physical beauty. Beauty or not, for nearly two decades Colombo has been in a continual state of emergency.

By the time I arrive to see Arthur C. Clarke, the Tigers and the government troops have begun battling it out at Elephant Pass, the narrow land bridge that leads to the hotly contested Jaffna Peninsula and the Tamil city of Jaffna. The area is a Dry Zone; War Zone now. The off-limits north lies 125 miles up Highway A-12, a desolate journey north of Anuradhapura, Sri Lanka's ancient capital 2,500 years ago and the apex of Sri Lanka's cultural triangle. Anuradhapura is also the partial setting for Clarke's novel *The Deep Range* (1957), one of whose characters is a Buddhist monk.

Another bleak, meandering road leads 72 miles east to the port of Tricomalee, a favored diving spot that intrepid voyageurs like Clarke can no longer explore. In 1970 Clarke and his company Underwater Safaris introduced the three *Apollo 12* astronauts to those fecund depths—after the astronauts returned from the moon's barren landscape.

&

As I look out at Colombo's famous Galle Face Green, all thoughts of civil war fade. I admire two young men, lean and brown-muscled in white cotton boxers and scoop-necked undershirts, stretching under a fast, light sky shot through with orgies of marigold-stained clouds. In Sri Lanka there are two seasons: the Siberian High with its northeast trades, and then the May-to-September Mascarene High. It is very near May now, and the southeast trades churn the island's waters off the south and west coasts, the areas still open to travelers.

My choice of hotel was determined months earlier when Clarke, in his forward-thinking way, e-mailed me with the message: "You must definitely stay in the Galle Face Hotel." During an electricity blackout in 1996, Clarke moved into the hotel to write *3001: The Final Odyssey*. He was one of a long line of illustrious people who have stayed at the hotel and whose photos line the walls of the office once occupied by the late Cyril Gardiner, the hotel's manager. Among the famous faces are those of Winston Churchill, Queen Elizabeth II, a youthful Prince Philip, and Indian leaders Indira Gandhi and her son, Rajiv, the last assassinated in 1991 by a Tamil Tiger suicide bomb. An oil painting of Clarke is mounted among the photos.

Three floors below my room is the 132-year-old high-ceilinged, open-air lobby with two tiny square pools cut into the floor. These ponds are fragrant with jasmine, a tree that cartwheels with pink, blood-red, or velvety white blooms on Colombo's already leafy boulevards. A glass-encased bronze bust of Clarke, the great leveler himself, stands near the ponds. Clarke is credited with bringing science to the masses and science fiction into the realm of literature.

Sri Lanka, a name that means "hallowed island," was known as Ceylon until the Democratic Socialist Republic was formed in 1972. Before it was called Ceylon by the British, Muslim traders referred to it as the Land of Serendip. Still earlier, the ancient Greeks and Romans dubbed it Taprobane.

Clarke's journey to Sri Lanka was more indirect and far more enduring than my own. Back in 1943, a bespectacled, tall, and gangly 28-year-old officer and instructor of the No. 9 Radio School (Yatesbury) in the British Royal Air Force packed his bags and raincoat for an assignment to a foggy airfield at the southern tip of England. In seclusion he worked with the young

American physicist Luis Alvarez, inventor of the ground-controlled approach (GCA) talk-down system, a radar device that could bring down an aircraft, in Clarke's words, "in one piece, instead of several." Clarke credits that mysterious assignment with allowing him the time away from the war to work out the principles of communications satellites (Comsats).

In the spring of 1945, Clarke wrote a four-page memo on "The Space Station: Its Radio Applications." In it he predicted—one could say invented—the radical idea that radio transmitters carried by an artificial satellite could provide low-cost communication around the world. He suggested the exact longitudes and conditions (the Clarke Orbit) for the station's placement. The paper was published in the October 1945 issue of *Wireless World*—and the planet has looked up to space and to Clarke ever since.

Clarke's scientific ideas were published 12 years before the Russians launched *Sputnik*, the first artificial communications satellite carrying a radio transmitter; 17 years before Telstar, the first communications satellite; and 30 years before the first experimental broadcasting satellites—each proving Clarke's predictions exactly.

It is 5:45 in the morning Colombo time. I unlatch the massive casement of my windows, pushing them wide to the sea-heavy air, to the sounds of gulls and crows swooping past my balcony. The sun commences its habitual yet perpetually seductive ascent. It is a moving masterpiece of special effects reminiscent of the 1968 film *2001: A Space Odyssey*, the classic collaboration between Clarke and the ingenious director Stanley Kubrick.

Elephants at Yala West National Park in Sri Lanka attempt to cool down with a bath. The park also boasts a small population of leopards.

By noon Clarke's Colombo will be an inferno of heat and seething traffic led by shoeless *bajaj* drivers tooting and threading through a mélange of suited businessmen and half-naked beggars, bicycles, trucks, motorcycles, cattle, and cars. But now, on Galle Face Green, the expansive yellow square that sleeps peacefully beside the restless Indian Ocean, a lone driver grabs at a few last dreams in the breezy back seat of his Jetson-like three-wheeled taxi. A length of Indian madras covers him. The soles of his feet are callused and bare.

I have risen early to watch the city stir into life and to go through my notes. I am excited as well as nervous about meeting this amazing man, sometimes referred to by his legions of fans as ACC. After being knighted in Colombo by Prince Philip (New Year's Honours List) in early 1999 for "Services to Literature," Clarke remarked in his tongue-in-cheek Internet Ego-gram: "I regarded this as a compliment to the entire genre of science fiction as much as to myself. The Eng. Lit mandarins could put this piece of news in their pipes and smoke it!"

Later I will learn that Sir Arthur also awakened early on the morning of my arrival. After rising, he is dressed by Wickie, his valet, and begins his daily routine. The morning is fresh and he has not yet gone to his computer (a gift from CNN for live cybercasts) to open his 50-odd morning e-mails, answer calls from old friends like Rupert Murdoch and Walter Cronkite, or glance out his window to see a baby cuckoo fall from its nest. That incident causes him to think about the odd habits of the cuckoo and how it makes its home in another bird's nest. Letting out a short burst of laughter, he realizes he and the cuckoo have something in common.

Throughout the day he will work on some 30 projects in various stages of completion. His routine is broken only on Sundays when he is chauffeured around Sri Lanka's capital in his beautiful red Mercedes, imported duty-free under the Clarke Act. This clever bit of legislation, passed in 1976, made him Sri Lanka's first Resident Guest and was a move to save him from paying killer local income tax and not be double-dipped elsewhere. In his autobiographical *The View from Serendip* (1967), Clarke wrote in frustration: "Yet I still had to spend at least six months in every year out of Ceylon (now Sri Lanka), otherwise the local tax laws would have ruined me."

Weekends for Clarke are a time to gallivant: to an important gallery opening, or to a convocation at Sri Lanka's Arthur Clarke Institute for Modern Technologies at the University of Moratuwa, where he has acted as chancellor for more than 20 years and been reappointed by successive governments of various political stripes. He might attend an embassy luncheon; visit Colombo's hospital for soldiers wounded in conflict, an institution that counts him among its patrons; or stop at the Animal Welfare Association. On most Sundays for the past half century, he has made his way to Otter's Aquatic Club to enjoy a soft drink and a rousing game of table tennis.

Clarke's bid to make Sri Lanka his home wasn't easy. As well as having to deal with the volatile nature of Sri Lankan politics and tax laws, he experienced financial difficulties brought on by the uncertain income derived from his diving business Submarine Safaris and by the shortcomings of his then-partner, the now-deceased Mike Wilson, who was hopeless at accounting.

A Buddhist monk out for a walk poses for the camera. Buddhists monks are a common sight throughout Sri Lanka.

The word *serendipity,* according to Horace Walpole's 18th-century fairy tale *The Three Princes of Serendip,* means making an important discovery while searching for something completely different. It was serendipity, coupled with an all-consuming fascination with space, that brought Clarke to his adopted island nation.

By the late 1940s he had purchased his first snorkel and flippers. As he once described it, they were a "cheap and simple way to experience the weightlessness of space travel—or something very close to it."

Clarke was on his way to Australia's Great Barrier Reef to meet Mike Wilson for a diving expedition when he discovered Sri Lanka. The year was 1955. He later wrote: "The Great Barrier Reef had been my objective when, almost by accident, I paused at Serendip for a single afternoon! Even when, a year later I returned to write *The Reefs of Taprobane* (1957), I still did not know what I had discovered, for the excitements and distractions of the outside world (indeed, outside *worlds)* clouded my eyes."

Wilson and Clarke endeavored to stay on, lured by the spectacular underwater reefs, the temperate climes, the culture, and a rich sense of the past. (Clarke collaborated with the British-born Wilson on five works of nonfiction based on their underwater adventures.) Sometime later Clarke recalled: "Though I became steadily more involved with the country, returning as a tourist at least once a year, it was not until the late sixties that I found it more and more painful to say goodbye, and felt completely happy nowhere else on earth."

In 1962, not long after Clarke's first brush with ill health, the science-fiction writer and his partner raised a cache of shining Arabian coins of pure silver from beneath the treacherous Great Basses Reef on Sri Lanka's south coast. The feat was chronicled in Clarke's 1964 out-of-print book *The Treasure of the Great Reef.*

Now, at 83, Sir Arthur's daring encounters with sea creatures and sharks, "great beasts cruising, gills opening and closing like vast venetian blinds," and his watery meandering through skeletons of shipwrecks, appear to be over. With style and vigor, Clarke continues to play a winning game of Ping-Pong, although in 1999 he was diagnosed with post-polio syndrome and is confined to a wheelchair. Today he must play propped up against the table—a position that forces him into a slightly illegal serve.

There *are* Tigers in Sri Lanka.

North of my window and Galle Face Green, the Fort area awaits the day, and with it the crowded omnibus of humanity that will enter Colombo's rather lackluster commercial center with its boxy office towers; Hilton, Galadari (formerly the Marriott), Oberoi, and Taj Samudra hotels; and indoor shopping mall. Few reminders remain of the Portuguese, Dutch, and British colonial periods. But tragic events continue to occur.

In October 1997, in the rheumy eye of the Siberian High, the time when brief, intense rainfalls deluge the narrow streets, when tourists and locals scurry for shelter in buildings and under doorways, Tiger bombs blasted Colombo's three international hotels, killing 15 people and wounding more than 100. After a relative lull in 1998, there has been a resumption of terrorist attacks.

I recall the warning posted on the British embassy Web site before my trip: "It is recommended that travel within the Fort area only be undertaken on urgent business." But here I am, and Sir Arthur, too. Clarke is accustomed to the threat that plagues this gorgeous little island that hangs like a fallen tear off Mother India's face. He is no stranger to danger, nor is the specter of death brought on by disease alien to him. In the Fort's 545-square-yard heart beats the Pettah (outer fort). Here, remnants of Colombo's past glory as a cinnamon port for Arab traders flutter like tattered flags in the tiny, crowded shops and maze of narrow lanes. The Pettah has always been cursed with pickpockets, but more recently the danger quotient has risen. On April 21, 1987, a bomb at Pettah's central bus station blew through the bazaar, killing 120 and injuring 298—all civilians.

While shopping in the Pettah's bazaar in February 1962, Sir Arthur walked into physical danger of another kind. In *The Treasure of the Great Reef*, he deadpans: "I conducted an unsuccessful experiment to see if two objects could occupy the same space at the same time. One was a doorway and the other my head." The next day he was completely paralyzed and barely able to breathe. The prognosis from Colombo physicians was spinal injury. A full recovery was uncertain.

Eventually, though, he was able to sit propped up in a chair, and there, in excruciatingly slow squiggles, he penciled an adventure novel for juveniles and adults. *Dolphin Island* (1963) drew on his exploits on Australia's Great Barrier Reef and on Ceylon's teeming coast. "When it was finished I felt rather sad," he told Neil McAleer, his biographer, who quoted him in *Arthur C. Clarke: The Authorized Biography*. "I could not help thinking it was my farewell to the sea," he added.

It was a year before Clarke completely recovered, but he found the strength to travel to India to accept the Kalinga Prize for science writing, a prestigious award administered by

UNESCO. By the following year, the unstoppable Clarke was back in the sea engaging in what every child and adult has dreamed of doing: raising sunken treasure.

I am expected at Barnes Place. An automatic gate à la James Bond opens with an electronic whir as I approach the door marked ARTHUR C. CLARKE. The exterior of the large house is stucco with much glass. The Iraqi embassy is next door. The Norwegian embassy is barely three blocks away. The Norwegians are involved in peace talks between the Sri Lankan government and the Tamil Tigers. This district, too, is rife with danger. As I climb a narrow indoor staircase that leads to Sir Arthur, I notice, and remember later with protective satisfaction (for Clarke), an electric wire running up the window of his office.

Wickie ushers me into Sir Arthur's inner office where I find the author at work. He has just completed directing a small humanitarian effort: the tiny cuckoo he witnessed fall earlier this morning has been returned to its adopted nest. After he tells me about this odd incident, he says, "The most important things in life are pure chance and coincidence, it seems to me." That is his life philosophy.

To Sir Arthur's right is the computer that bleeps constantly, signaling that another e-mail message has arrived. I present Sir Arthur with my token gifts: maple syrup and British Columbia smoked salmon, a reminder of the underwater world he has written about so enchantingly.

I am instantly charmed. Sir Arthur sports a sky-blue short-sleeved shirt, unbuttoned from his collar almost to the gentle rise of his stomach. (He *is* human and makes reference to his caloric battle in *Greetings, Carbon-Based Bipeds: Collected Essays 1934–1998*.) A plaid cotton sarong is wound around hips that sit snugly between the handles of his wheelchair. The cloth covers his legs and bare feet. Both shirt and sarong are clean and pressed, and by their softness I know they must be his daily favorites.

Underneath his shirt and snuggled to his pale chest is a one-eyed Chihuahua, a dog that fits in a teacup. Sir Arthur pets the nine-year-old Chihuahua's short coat with gentle fondness. "I brought the little character from Singapore as a present for my adopted nieces," he offers in his animated, gravelly voice, the words delivered in elegantly accented English.

The one-eyed Pepsi resembles the miniature dogs sold in the back pages of comic books during my own childhood. Clarke read more substantive material when he was growing up. He sparked his superior intellect with the science-fiction magazine *Astounding Stories of Super-Science*. He credits that publication with teaching him about the multidimensional world and the concept of expanding the universe, among other scientific theories.

Sir Arthur's blue eyes dazzle behind the lenses of his metal-framed glasses. His eyes and open smile are effervescent, and he laughs frequently with boyish pleasure. When I ask him what he attributes his great success to, he answers gleefully, "A careful choice of parents and a lot of luck."

With talk about family, I am sent to meet the Ekanayakes, his self-chosen extended family. On the way I quickly pass the Yorkshire terrier that took little Pepsi's eye out in a jealous rage over Sir Arthur's affections. The terrier is banished to the main floor while the Chihuahua enjoys Sir Arthur's spacious upstairs office. If the civil war wasn't such a serious matter, I would be tempted to make a few jocular comparisons about ethnic squabbles.

The interior of the house the Ekanayake family shares with Clarke feels very much like the tropical interiors immortalized by Somerset Maugham. The curved backs of the chiseled teak couch and chairs are inset with woven rattan, pale and breezy. Ceiling fans rotate like tops and purr like well-tended electric kittens. The decor is graced by the touch of Valerie, Hector Ekanayake's attractive Australian wife and mother of Sir Arthur's three almost grown "nieces."

Hector is Sir Arthur's right arm and, since 1973, he's been an associate in the writer's renamed diving company, Underwater Safaris. That was the year Clarke's earlier partner, Mike Wilson, went off the rails, left his wife to become a monk, got into drugs, and died of an

Boats bob tranquilly on the beach at Hikkaduwa where Clarke owns a beach shack.

overdose. The details remain fuzzy, even to those who knew the freewheeling and financially irresponsible Wilson.

A former boxer, Hector has a strong jaw that is visible under his neatly trimmed beard rivered with the silver that comes with age and responsibility. I am not surprised when he tells me he was the youngest flyweight ever and went on to win Ceylon's championship in that class in 1956. Like Muhammad Ali, with whom Hector has been photographed, he stung like a bee and floated like a butterfly. Hector and Sir Arthur struck up a friendship a year after the championship bout when the young Sinhalese worked at a U.S.-sponsored agricultural show in Colombo. Over the years, Hector became indispensable, helping Clarke with projects, accompanying Clarke and Wilson on diving expeditions, and eventually learning the diving business.

In 1986, while attending an H. G. Wells symposium, Clarke was stricken once again by illness. London's National Hospital for Nervous Diseases diagnosed Lou Gehrig's disease, a degenerative motor-neuron affliction of the brain and spinal cord. The physicians gave Sir Arthur 18 months to live. Hector, ever Sir Arthur's bulwark against adversity, took him home to Barnes Place and, with physiotherapy and massive vitamin intake, Sir Arthur proved the physicians wrong. These same physicians have diagnosed post-polio syndrome, not the spinal injury sustained while shopping at Pettah in the 1960s, as the source of his current debilitation.

After my visit with the amicable Ekanayake family, I am whisked back to Sir Arthur who, even with his boundless energy, can only speak for short periods before he becomes breathless. With a pleasant guffaw, he shows me the printed replies he has ready for his mountain of mail—the "Kindly drop dead" letter or the more polite "You may resume breathing" version. He does few interviews and has made a point of not writing forewords or introductions to books. As we speak, he decides to turn down the offer to be namesake to a science-fiction magazine: "Don't want to take away Isaac Asimov's thunder." The late Asimov was one of Clarke's dearest friends and is often in his thoughts. Unlike the once-peripatetic Clarke, Asimov had a fear of flying and never visited Sri Lanka, but he did pen this limerick:

Old Arthur C. Clarke of Sri Lanka
Now sits in the sun sipping Sanka
Enjoying his ease
Excepting when he's
Receiving pleased notes from his banker.

Our amiable conversation is punctuated by e-mail messages, telephone calls, mail delivery, and the constant comings and goings of Clarke's eight Sri Lankan secretaries. I soon realize Sir Arthur is no recluse, nor typical expatriate writer. He is a happy and sociable man if ever I've seen one. The whole world keeps in touch with him: Walter Cronkite ("I cohosted with Cronkite on CBS during the *Apollo* missions"), Rupert Murdoch ("The poor guy has prostate cancer"), Buzz Aldrin ("Visited me in hospital at Baltimore…"), and other famous and not-so-famous friends.

Sir Arthur returns a call to Elizabeth Taylor in London. She, he informs me, is also in a wheelchair. Taylor starred in the 1954 movie *Elephant Walk* after Vivien Leigh had a nervous breakdown attributed to watching a Sri Lankan spirit dance while she was on location here. Leigh believed she was possessed.

The lovely Taylor never set foot in Sri Lanka. Her scenes were filmed on a London set. While I was with Sir Arthur, I didn't feel I was in Sri Lanka, either. I could have been on a studio set with all his stars milling around, walking on the moon with the astronauts, planning the colonization of Mars, or just wheeling about in Clarke's soaring and limitless imagination— one that oddly, to me, is solidly grounded in scientific fact.

Sir Arthur directs me to his walls: they are thick with photographic memorabilia. I marvel at happy photos of him with *Apollo 11*'s Buzz Aldrin; with Stanley Kubrick, taken in 1966 on the *2001* set; with his close friend the late science-fiction writer Robert Heinlein and his wife, Ginny, in 1980 at Sir Arthur's Colombo home; and with his adopted "daughter-in-law," Valerie Ekanayake, Steven Spielberg, and Harrison Ford, arms draped around one another's shoulders. In another photo, Sir Arthur is resplendent in a collarless Nehru-style suit at the 1984 Hollywood premiere of *2010* with Ray Bradbury and Gene Roddenberry. And then, the happiest photo of them all, Sir Arthur with the youngest Ekanayake, Melinda, on his lap. On his right is his Rock of Gibraltar, Hector Ekanayake, and behind the two patriarchs are the almost-grown girls, Cherene and Tamara, and their mother, Valerie. This "family" portrait was taken in 1992 on a visit to Minehead-by-the-Sea, where Sir Arthur was born in 1917 under an auspicious star.

"What do you love most?" I ask the mythmaker, trying to ground us in Sri Lanka. "And what keeps you here?"

"The Ekanayakes," he replies, not hesitating.

The conversation bounces back to space, and he wonders aloud why he was knighted for services to literature rather than for his invention. "My communications satellite paper is much more important," he says. "It is by far the most important thing I ever wrote." Clarke

On the island of Taprobane, a younger Clarke taped the 1989 video documentary *Arthur C. Clarke's Mysterious Universe.*

Courtesy of
Sir Arthur C. Clarke

then remarks modestly, "Someone else would have done so very shortly after if I wouldn't have." I can't help but be astounded at the breadth and scope of his achievements—accomplishments he attributes to coincidence and luck.

❧

Tigers *can* swim (the Palk Straits to India).

It was 1988, hardly a year after Sir Arthur's battle with Lou Gehrig's disease when, at the late Indian Prime Minister Rajiv Gandhi's initiative, the Indian Peace Keeping Force arrived in Sri Lanka and became embroiled in the Sinhalese government's battle against the Tigers; 1,200 Indian soldiers lost their lives. Due to Sinhalese resentment against foreign intervention, a new terrorist organization came into being. The Sinhalese JVP (People's Liberation Front), founded to combat the rebel Tigers, began a terrifying round of indiscriminate killing, even slaughtering physicians as they treated their patients. In the midst of this new threat, Clarke was honored with a CBE (Commander of the British Empire) in recognition of British cultural interests in Sri Lanka. At one point in our breakneck conversation, Sir Arthur says to me as an aside: "Religion exacerbates wars."

For the most part, though, Clarke wants to talk about science, space, and the stars, not religion or his adopted country. In fact, he dazzles me with science, something I confess with acute embarrassment I know little about. When I pose questions on Sri Lanka, he tells me it's all in his books and directs my attention to an inscribed photo: "To Arthur C. Clarke. My idol. You opened my mind to the possibilities of space travel. Stan Golden [NASA's administrator]."

When another sarong-clad secretary is captured in Sir Arthur's orbit, he introduces me to him, simply saying, "Meet Tyron." Then he checks his e-mail again, only to discover that his computer has crashed. Oops—the communications guru has been cut off, and we both laugh like mad things at the irony. At his polite request I open the clip of the microphone I've attached to the collar of his shirt. "Even opening a clip taxes my strength," he admits with stoic acceptance, then turns back to his resurrected computer and 50 brand-new e-mails. The man who developed the concept of satellite communications is understandably addicted to communication, and I am on my own.

❧

I am like Pepsi, a dog that must have its bone. I think about Sir Arthur and *The Fountains of Paradise*, his science-fiction novel set in Sri Lanka. He takes real places in Sri Lanka and imaginatively infuses them with his science-based fiction. The plot is shot through with mythology and inspired by the sacred Adam's Peak, a green-clad mountain once visible to Sir Arthur from his Barnes Place office window, but now obscured by a ticktacktoe of buildings. In *The Fountains of Paradise*, he writes: "I saw the spectacle for which the peak is famous. As the sun rose, the perfectly triangular shadow of the mountain was cast on the clouds below, stretching for perhaps 50 kilometers [30 miles] into the west."

For more than a thousand years, Adam's Peak—where the Bible's Adam supposedly first set foot on Earth after being cast from heaven—has been the object of countless Christian, Hindu, and Buddhist pilgrimages. It is here that the Hindu god Shiva allegedly left his giant three-foot-long fossilized footprint when he danced creation. Buddhists call the 7,297-foot peak Sri Pada (Sacred Footprint) and claim it as their own. It is the Stairway to Heaven. Earlier, when I asked Sir Arthur if he believed in an afterlife, he replied, "If there is, it would be too crowded there."

I have left the brilliant, brave, indefatigable, elusive man, armed with generously offered and priceless souvenirs. Safely tucked away is a signed reprint of his paper on satellite technology published in *Wireless World*. I have photocopied images of satellites and celebrities, including one of the stunning Elizabeth Taylor.

After stopping to fix Sir Arthur's home in my mind, I walk slowly through the searing heat and down the empty afternoon road. In front of the Iraqi embassy I pass an itinerant male. His bare upper body and face are smeared with dirt, his *lungi* (sarong) is abysmally tattered. He is pushing a homemade wheelbarrow heaped with garbage. It crosses my mind that it could contain a bomb. We eye each other with mutual distrust and then look away.

Back on the main road I hail a *bajaj* to ride the few miles to one of Colombo's two indoor shopping centers. I haggle like an old hand with the young driver before getting in. He asks for 70 rupees. I have been told 50 is fair. We settle on 60. It seems to me that the amount is a good compromise. The driver's bare foot hits the accelerator, and the velocity-generated wind cools me like a delicious ocean breeze. The speed and shake of the little cab changes my mood. I remember Sir Arthur's earnest words: "My vision for the world and for Sri Lanka, of course, is one of peace." There is nothing more important to him. He also said with deep sadness that Sri Lanka's situation was getting worse.

The driver interrupts my thoughts. "I like the color of your skin." His eyes flash at me in his miniature rearview mirror.

I respond simply and without thinking, "Thank you."

After minimal conversation, he says, "I love you. I want to have sex with you."

I am aghast. I think he is joking. I see he is young, smooth-faced, and handsome. I try to end the conversation. "I am married and have a son your age."

"Only 20 minutes in your hotel room," he says.

I am not flattered, just surprised. I expect next he'll ask *me* for money.

"I love you," he says again, and I get out as fast as I can.

I wander on Galle Face Green. The sun is a juicy tangerine that slips beneath the blue froth of the adjacent sea. I relax to the sight of pretty dark-eyed children with gleaming smiles running fast in the wind, trailing paper kites across the sky. Men in plaid sarongs offer pony rides, and a snake charmer waltzes with two coiling, iridescent cobras he has taken from a woven yellow basket as round as the setting sun. Guy, my husband, is coming tonight, and I think how I'll tell him what a nice place Colombo is—with its seething traffic, pounding waves, and parades of freighters like silent dragonflies alight on the sea. I think of Sir Arthur's ongoing dedication to the Ekanayake family, and they to him. And I know he is right: it is people who make the place.

Guy goes out to rent us a Toyota Bluebird and I, as directed by Clarke himself, go to his books. The next day we are let loose on Arthur C. Clarke's Sri Lanka. We forsake the city for the south coast with its pale sand bays set against glittering waters made choppy by the monsoon sea. Our little car swoops and lunges down Galle Road, past bare-chested men in rainbow sarongs fastened tight over slim hips by origami-like twists; past dark women in cotton-candy-hued silks with hourglass figures worthy of the 1940s Hollywood siren Dorothy Lamour. There are saris and sarongs everywhere, all under the cover of parasols that sway like giant sunflowers above human stalks.

We fly beside Sir Arthur's beloved ocean to fabled Unawatuna Bay, the setting of his 1976 science-fiction novel *Imperial Earth*. It is the year 2276 and man has colonized Mars. In *The View from Serendip*, Clarke also speaks of the magnetically scenic Unawatuna Bay and plays with serendipitous events, science, and the great Indian Sanskrit epic, the *Ramayana*. As in person, his words are steeped with high spirits and grounded in science. He asks: "Did something *really* fall down, centuries or a millennia ago, at Unawatuna Bay?" Then he speculates: "A meteorite would be the obvious explanation: it must have been a big one for the legend to have lasted down the ages."

The 2,000-year-old epic he refers to lives on in the garishly hued statues worshiped in Hindu temples and sometimes even in Buddhist shrines. We spend time in so many we become inured to the cloying fragrance of incense, the jolt of bold colors, and the shock of almost air-conditioned cool the temples offer to worshipers and travelers.

Daily I hunt for newspapers, then wish I hadn't found them. "More roads closed in Kandy," I read. Kandy, the island's cultural heart, is next on our itinerary. "Bodies returned home," I read on. And then a headline pounces on my personal paranoia: TIGERS THREATEN TO HIJACK INTERNATIONAL FLIGHT.

We pass through the seaside village of Dickwella, where Sir Arthur's beach shack sits boarded against the season. Here I learn in the newspapers that TIGERS TROUNCE GOVERNMENT FORCES and INDIA CALLED ON FOR SUPPORT. The next day we discover that "India refuses."

I study civilian faces in the markets, on the road. I search for the glaze of fear in the eyes of soldiers tightly holding battered AK-47s while manning roadblocks and stop checks. I see only bravery and am reminded of Sir Arthur. The entire Sri Lankan experience offers itself, just as Sir Arthur does to the entire planet, with positive energy and the highest of spirits in the face of incredible adversity.

At Clarke's beloved Unawatuna the day is overcast. The beach is deserted. The sand is sluiced pink with the powder of rubies mined in nearby Ratnapura. Crumpled plastic bottles and wrinkled bags, byproducts of tourism and poor infrastructure, drift in the warm sea and then die like old jellyfish on the exquisitely tinted sand. I read in the newspaper *The Island* that "All reports on military affairs subject to censorship under Emergency Regulations proclaimed." And I see that my hunt for news is as desolate as the view before me.

We move on to Dondra Head, where the sea stretches to Antarctica. Here the ocean speaks in a rushing tongue to whoever will listen. It whispers the secrets of the universe as it has for billions of years. It whispers long and clear, and behind the sound I imagine Sir Arthur's ready guffaw of joy. I go to his books and read: "For politicians and governments and social systems come and go; the land and the sun and the sea remain in exquisite proportions."

Soon we are off to Yala where leopards bask on high rocks. Then it's upcountry, past Adam's Peak, which we are unable to climb because it is not the season. Here we discover the revered temple that contains Buddha's Tooth (bombed in 1998 and surrounded with guards like some inside-out prison). Next comes Sigiriya, the site of a brooding rock fortress built high in the clouds. Then, finally, we head back to Colombo for a flight away from Sir Arthur's adopted land, with its palatable threat of all-out war and death to the unlucky by suicide bombers.

Since the early 1980s, Sri Lanka's minority Hindu Tamils have been at increasing odds with the majority Sinhalese Buddhists. Here a Hindu child waits for his mother.

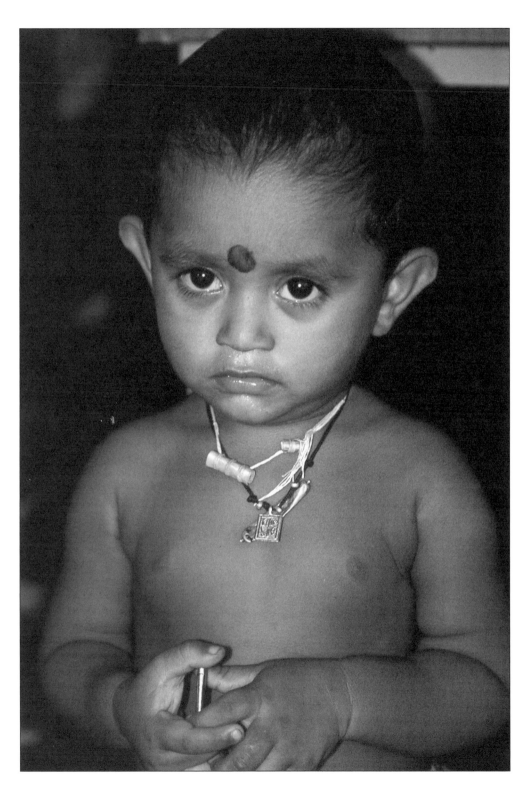

The 12-foot-high electric gate that surrounds Sir Arthur and the Ekanayake residence/offices opens with a scientific whir. Sir Arthur is expecting Jean-Michel Jarre, known to audiophiles as "The Master of Synthesizers." Wickie ushers us into Clarke's office.

"Darn," Sir Arthur says, lifting his gaze from the computer screen and snapping his fingers in disappointment. "Jarre isn't coming. The American embassy issued a travel warning." And then with a cheery wave he returns to his computer and his multitude of projects and important communications, all delivered in a flash of science and borne from his personal genius.

The ensuing midnight ride to Colombo's Bandaranaike International Airport is marred by sporadic security checks manned by antiterrorist air-force commandos in sky-blue jumpsuits patterned with flying black eagles. On Airport Road the stops and starts become a somber conga line of commotion—air-force vehicles block the road, identification is rechecked by armed soldiers, cars and passengers are searched, and metal detectors are spun like mini-spaceships under the chassis of each vehicle. They are searching for bombs. Hunting down Tigers. It is now near dawn. I hold on tightly to my boarding pass, marked May 14. It is crumpled and wet with my sweat and fear.

Peering out the Boeing 747's convex window, I glance down, down, down at a riff of dark clouds. The cloud cover has annihilated Colombo and the isle they once called Serendip. Then, before my sleepy eyes, the floor of cloud parts. Fathoms below I see dim lights. Looking closer, I focus on lines that I know are roads. I notice squares and swoops of green. It is obvious they are Sri Lanka's famous tanks, the ancient man-made lakes. To the west is a constant of color—the Indian Ocean, maybe the sea of Serendip. And then, just as the day is resurrected and the sun, a flamboyant blaze, starts its seductive climb, there is a serendipitous occurrence. Adam's Peak has become a full-blown spectacle, casting its otherworldly triangular shadow, the proverbial Stairway to Heaven, on an ethereal swath of the palest cloud. It is an amazing vision—and with its appearance, all imagined and real fears of death and dying fly from my thoughts.

I doze and dream. Or maybe it is déjà vu. I am with Sir Arthur in his localeless, office on Barnes Place. The past and the future seem like foreign countries. Sir Arthur relates to me once again, in his upbeat and optimistic way, his belief that our lives are largely a matter of luck and coincidence. Then I understand: life is an uncharted adventure. The concept is perfect in its simplicity, and I hold it protectively to my chest with affectionate acceptance as he does with Pepsi, his tiny one-eyed dog.

"But there is more," Sir Arthur says, and my déjà vu refuses to end. "Go to my books," he directs, and he reads from *The View from Serendip* in a voice that encompasses the entire awe of the cosmos. "The island of Ceylon is a small universe…if you are interested in people, history, nature, and art—the things that *really* matter—you may find, as I have, that a lifetime is not enough." He directs my attention to a recent photo of his adopted family, the Ekanayakes. Sir Arthur's face is wreathed with smiles, he holds the smallest girl on his lap, his cornerstone, Hector, stands protectively behind—and then I see the biggest picture of all.

Sri Lanka is blessed with photogenic children, like this delightful girl who eagerly posed for the author's camera.

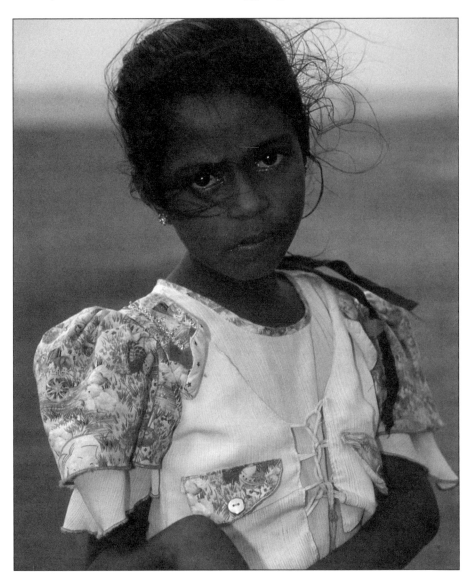

Letters from Sir Arthur C. Clarke to Victoria Brooks ✍

19 March 2003

Dear Victoria,

I've never been really interested in food—and would be quite happy if I could live on a couple of pills every day, washed down with a glass of milk. However, there are some things that I enjoy—during my lecture-touring days in the U.S., I practically lived on liver pâté and Cadbury's milk chocolate (a nice balanced diet…). I'm also rather fond of Harvey's Bristol Cream—a sweet sherry—which my serious drinking friends always referred to disparagingly as cough syrup…

Oh, yes, I like strawberry ice cream and, best of all, real strawberries with clotted Somerset cream! Used to enjoy steak and kidney pie, but it's seldom available here. Also sardines and sole.

Think that's about it. Now halfway through my final novel, *The Last Theorem*.

Love,

Arthur

20 March 2003

Dear Victoria,

How could I have forgotten—distracted by news, probably…?

My favorite meal—and the only one I've ever prepared myself—is Welsh rarebit, a kind of cheese omelet on toast.

Love,

Arthur

In Sri Lanka it's not uncommon to encounter men in traditional garb such as this fellow sporting a jeweled headdress.

Recipes

Galle Face Hotel

Grilled Fillet of Lamb
Smoked Salmon, Potato, and Iceberg Salad
Prawn and Lemon Grass Kebabs

Kandalama Hotel

Pan-Fried Darne of Seer Fish with Orange Caper Sauce
Roast Chicken with Orange and Chili Glaze
Kohila Temperadu—Tempered Yams
Sri Lanka Sunrise

Earl's Regency Hotel

Gotu Kola Tempered and Boiled Jackfruit Seeds
Pork Spareribs with Tomato and Honey
Regency Breeze
Arthur C. Clarke's Steak and Kidney Pie

A coconut vendor's daughter plays near the road to Clarke's beach shack at Hikkaduwa. Coconuts and their milk are frequent ingredients in Sri Lankan cuisine.

Grilled Fillet of Lamb &

Complemented with rosemary-and-red-wine reduction, fried camembert wedges, leek mash, and marked fresh vegetables.

Makes four servings.

Ingredients

1¼ lb (600 g) lamb fillets
½ tsp (2 mL) rosemary
3 fluid oz (80 mL) red wine
3½ fluid oz (100 mL) demi-glaze
2 fluid oz (60 mL) olive oil
chopped parsley
7 oz (200 g) broccoli florets
3½ oz (100 g) yellow bell pepper wedges
3½ oz (100 g) red bell pepper wedges
8 baby carrots
1¾ oz (50 g) small trimmed oyster mushrooms
1¾ oz (50 g) diced leeks
½ lb (250 g) mashed potatoes
1¾ fluid oz (50 mL) cream
¼ lb (125 g) camembert cheese (nine wedges)
1½ oz (40 g) white breadcrumbs

Method

Marinate the lamb with half of the red wine, rosemary, and olive oil, then let stand for about two hours. Boil the broccoli and carrots, and grill the bell peppers and mushrooms in olive oil with some oregano. Sauté the leeks in olive oil, add the mashed potatoes and cream, and cook to a smooth paste. Heat a frying pan, add the lamb fillets, and cook till medium done. Add the red wine, reduce, add the demi-glaze, and take off the heat. Rest the fillet for 30 minutes and slice. Arrange the creamed potatoes on the center of a plate and then place the slices of lamb in the center and the vegetables around. Pour the sauce over and sprinkle with chopped parsley.

Note: Various demi-glazes are available in gourmet stores, or you can make your own. Combine one part beef stock with one part brown sauce and cook until the mixture is reduced by half. Add a little sherry or Madeira for good measure.

Smoked Salmon, Potato, and Iceberg Salad

Makes four servings.

Ingredients

7 oz (200 g) smoked salmon (cut into strips)
3½ oz (100 g) diced potatoes
5¼ oz (150 g) iceberg lettuce
1½ oz (40 g) chopped onions
1½ oz (40 g) horseradish cream
1½ oz (40 g) chopped capers
3½ fluid oz (100 mL) mayonnaise
2 oz (60 g) julienned yellow bell pepper
2 oz (60 g) julienned tomatoes
2 oz (60 g) chopped bacon
pinch of salt
1 oz (30 g) caviar

Method

Mix the mayonnaise, horseradish cream, onions, capers, and chopped bacon together. Toss all the ingredients just before serving and garnish with caviar.

Prawn and Lemon Grass Kebabs ❧

Served with green curry sauce, steamed rice, and petit tomato and bean sprout salad.

Makes four servings.

Main Ingredients

1 lb (500 g) prawns (31 to 40 peeled and deveined)
1 cup (250 mL) basmati rice
8 lemon grass stalks
1 tsp (5 mL) honey
1 tsp (5 mL) lemon juice
¾ tsp (3 mL) paprika
½ tsp (2 mL) salt

Ingredients for Green Curry Sauce

3½ fluid oz (100 mL) coconut milk
1 tsp (5 mL) green curry paste
3½ fluid oz (100 mL) chicken stock
1 tsp (5 mL) sugar
1 tsp (5 mL) fish sauce
½ tsp (2 mL) ajinamoto (or MSG, optional)
lemon grass to taste
citrus leaves to taste

Ingredients for Salad

2 cups (500 mL) bean sprouts
8 small chopped tomatoes
salad dressing (1 tbsp [15 mL] each of vegetable oil, sesame oil, vinegar, soy sauce, and chili oil)

Method

Marinate the prawns with paprika, salt, and lemon juice. Cut the lemon grass stalks on the slant and thread the prawns. Grill the prawns while glazing with the marinade. Make the Green Curry Sauce by boiling the chicken stock and all the other ingredients except coconut milk, then simmer for two to three minutes. Add the coconut milk to sauce and stir until thick. Arrange a timbale of steamed rice in the center of a large plate. Place the grilled kebabs on either side. Pour sauce over the kebabs and serve with bean sprout and tomato salad.

Note: Ajinamoto is akin to MSG. Wooden skewers can be substituted for lemon grass stalks. A timbale is a presentation mold to shape rice.

In the evenings Colombo's Galle Face Green is a carnival of snake charmers, donkey rides, and fruit sellers. Here you'll also find the shabbily elegant Galle Face Hotel.

Pan-Fried Darne of Seer Fish with Orange Caper Sauce

Makes four servings.

Main Ingredients

4 darnes of seer fish (Spanish mackerel)
salt
pepper
juice of 1 lime

Method

Season four slices of darne of seer fish with salt, pepper, and lime juice. Pass through seasoned flour (half cup [125 milliliters] of flour and half teaspoon [two milliliters] each of salt, pepper, oregano, basil, and thyme) and shallow-fry in clarified butter until brown. Serve with orange caper sauce (see below for ingredients and method).

Ingredients for Orange Caper Sauce

1¼ cups (315 mL) orange juice
1 tbsp (15 mL) soy sauce
1 tbsp (15 mL) olive oil
2 tbsp (30 mL) butter
1 tbsp (15 mL) capers
1 tbsp (15 mL) chopped parsley

Method

Make a reduction using the first three ingredients. Add the rest of the ingredients and take off heat.

Note: Seer fish is another name for Spanish mackerel. A darne is a thick slice or steak cut from the center of the fish.

Roast Chicken with Orange and Chili Glaze ❧

Makes four servings.

Main Ingredient

4 boneless whole chicken legs with skin

Ingredients for Orange and Chili Glaze

1 tbsp (15 mL) chopped onion
½ tsp (2 mL) chopped garlic
1 tbsp (15 mL) vegetable oil
1 tsp (5 mL) chili pieces
1 tsp (5 mL) crushed coriander seeds
4 tsp (20 mL) chili powder
2 tsp (10 mL) cumin powder
1 cup (250 mL) orange juice
1 cup (250 mL) chicken stock
1 tbsp (15 mL) vinegar
salt to taste
crushed pepper to taste
1 tbsp (15 mL) cornstarch

Method

Season chicken legs with the following: salt, pepper, orange juice, white wine, olive oil, and coarsely ground chili pieces. Keep for four hours. To make Orange and Chili Glaze, heat vegetable oil in frying pan and sauté onion and garlic. Combine with red chili pieces, coriander, cumin, crushed pepper, and chili powder and fry well. Add vinegar, orange juice, and chicken stock and bring briefly to a boil. Thicken with a mix of three tablespoons (45 milliliters) of cold water and one tablespoon (15 milliliters) of cornstarch drizzled in. Brush chicken with glaze. Roast chicken in a roasting tray in the oven. Baste frequently. Serve with leftover glaze.

Kohila Temperadu— Tempered Yams ⁊

Ingredients

½ tbsp (8 mL) vegetable oil
3½ oz (100 g) chopped onion
1 oz (30 g) chopped garlic
2 chopped green chilies
curry leaves to taste
2 tsp (10 mL) powdered mustard
1 lb (500 g) kohila (yams)
2 tsp (10 mL) fenugreek
2 tsp (10 mL) chili powder
4 tsp (20 mL) curry powder
2 tsp (10 mL) turmeric
1 large chopped tomato
2 gamboges
2 cups (500 mL) coconut milk
1 tsp (5 mL) salt

Method

Heat oil in a frying pan and sauté onion, garlic, green chili, and curry leaves. Add mustard and fry. Then add the kohila (yams) and all the other ingredients except coconut milk. Fry for a few minutes. Add coconut milk, bring to a boil, and simmer until yams are tender. Remove from heat and serve hot with basmati rice.

Note: Fenugreek is a common ingredient of curry powder and should be available at Indian or Chinese specialty stores. Gamboge is an acidic fruit from Sri Lanka. The fresh fruit is bright orange-yellow and the size of an orange. When dried, it's black. Tamarind or limes can be used as a substitute for gamboge to get the same acidic taste.

Sri Lanka Sunrise ∂

Ingredients

1¾ fluid oz (50 mL) Sri Lanka arrack
1 fluid oz (30 mL) passion fruit juice
1 fluid oz (30 mL) lime juice
½ fluid oz (15 mL) lemon grass juice
soda

Method

Shake together and top with soda.

Note: Sri Lankans tend to make arrack from the fermenting sap of the coconut flower. However, arrack can be made from rice or dates.

Gotu Kola Tempered and Boiled Jackfruit Seeds ෨

Ingredients

7 oz (200 g) skinned boiled jackfruit seeds
1 bundle roughly cut gotu kola (pennywort)
1¾ oz (50 g) roughly cut red pepper
1¾ oz (50 g) roughly cut seedless tomatoes
1 oz (30 g) finely chopped garlic
1 oz (30 g) finely chopped onion
½ tsp (2 mL) chili powder or to taste
½ tsp (2 mL) curry powder or to taste
¼ tsp (1 mL) turmeric powder or to taste
black pepper powder to taste
salt to taste
½ cup (125 mL) thick coconut milk
¾ oz (20 g) Maldive fish
¾ oz (20 g) butter

Method

Boil jackfruit seeds and break into small pieces. Melt butter in saucepan. Sauté onion and garlic. Add Maldive fish, tomato, and half of the jackfruit seeds, then sauté. Add chili and curry powders and turmeric and cook. Add coconut milk. Add gotu kola and cook, maintaining color. Add salt and pepper to taste. Take off heat and garnish with the rest of the jackfruit-seed pieces.

Note: Jackfruit is the largest tree-borne fruit in the world and can weigh up to 100 pounds (45 kilograms). If you can't locate fresh jackfruit, you should be able to find it in cans in most supermarkets. Gotu kola, better known as pennywort, is sold in Vietnamese shops or in plant nurseries. It has a slightly bitter tang, so you might want to substitute arugula. Gotu kola is a slender creeping plant that grows in swampy areas of Sri Lanka. It's known in the West as a nerve tonic and for its ability to promote relaxation and enhance memory. Maldive fish is Sri Lanka's answer to fish sauce or shrimp paste. The fish comes dried and is as hard as rock. It keeps indefinitely. In the old days it was pounded at home with a pestle and mortar. Now Maldive fish usually comes splintered and powdered in small bags. It acts as a thickening agent and a flavor and protein additive for vegetable dishes.

Pork Spareribs with Tomato and Honey ❧

Makes four servings.

Ingredients

1 fluid oz (30 mL) sunflower oil
1 oz (30 g) butter
8 pork spareribs
1 finely chopped medium onion
1 clove chopped garlic
chopped ginger to taste
¼ tsp (1 mL) cinnamon or to taste
2 lb (1 kg) chopped tomatoes
1 fluid oz (30 mL) Kithul honey
1¾ oz (50 g) blanched cashews
½ oz (15 g) sesame seeds
salt and ground black pepper to taste

Method

Heat sunflower oil and butter in frying pan. Add pork spareribs. Cook until light brown. Add onion, garlic, ginger, cinnamon, seasoning, and tomato. Cook until tomato is soft. Cover and simmer gently for an hour until ribs are properly cooked. Transfer ribs to plate. Cook tomato mixture, stirring frequently until thick puree. Stir in the honey and cook for a minute. Return ribs to frying pan and cook thoroughly. Fry the cashews and sesame seeds. Add to sauce. Serve with crusty bread.

Note: Kithul honey is produced from the Kithul palm. Sri Lankans also use the syrup from the Kithul palm to make treacle and sugar. For the above recipe substitute regular honey.

Regency Breeze ❧

Ingredients

1 fluid oz (30 mL) white rum
1 fluid oz (30 mL) brandy
5¼ fluid oz (150 mL) orange juice
14 fluid oz (400 mL) pineapple juice
1 cup (250 mL) blended banana
dash of sugar syrup

Method

To make simple sugar syrup add two parts sugar and one part water, then boil for five minutes (refrigerate syrup and use as needed). Shake ingredients of drink and pour into cocktail glasses.

Fruit and vegetable stands dot the road to Kandy where the Temple of the Tooth is said to house a relic purported to be Buddha's Tooth. The fabulous Earl's Regency Hotel is an excellent base for experiencing Kandy's cultural offerings.

Arthur C. Clarke's Steak and Kidney Pie ❧

Makes five servings.

Ingredients

½ lb (250 g) puff pastry or short-crust pastry
1½ lb (750 g) steak cubes
¾ lb (375 g) kidney cubes
¼ lb (125 g) butter
½ lb (250 g) chopped onion
3½ oz (100 g) chopped garlic
1 bay leaf
1 cup (250 mL) beef stock
salt and pepper to taste
2½ oz (75 g) tomato paste

Method

Cut the steak and kidney into cubes. Boil the kidney first and keep separate. Heat butter and sauté onion and garlic until brown. Add steak and kidney cubes and cook until half done. Add beef stock and simmer. When the beef is cooked, season to taste and add tomato paste. Arrange in a casserole dish. Cover with puff-pastry dough. Egg-wash and bake until golden brown in an oven at 375° F. (190° C.) for 45 minutes. Cover the pastry with foil to prevent overbrowning.

Note: On discovering that Sir Arthur C. Clarke enjoys Steak and Kidney Pie, the Earl's Regency Hotel agreed to cook a couple and send them to him as a Sri Lankan New Year's gift. Sri Lanka's New Year's Day is April 14.

For centuries tea has been a major Sri Lankan export, and verdant green tea fields such as this one are a familiar sight on the island.

Dick Francis now lives alone after the death of his beloved wife, Mary, and says he has no plans to continue writing his ever-popular mystery novels.

Dick Francis
Dead Cert on Grand Cayman

> The first law for a secret agent is to get his geography right…
> —Ian Fleming, *The Man with the Golden Gun*

I hold in my hand Dick Francis's latest thriller *Shattered*. As I observe my surroundings, I scc that my fcllow travelers are butchering the boredom of our long plane flight to the Caribbean with paperback escapism. Mystery, crime, stories of spies and lies, thrillers. Novels of dark journeys and razor escapes. It's entertainment, yet some of the best travel writing is found in this genre.

I'm on my way to the champion-jockey-turned-bestselling-author Dick Francis and the tax-free haven of Grand Cayman in the Cayman Islands where the Welsh-born 83-year-old makes his home. My mission is to persuade him to pen the foreword for *Mystery Trips: Following in the Footsteps of Fame*, a travel anthology I intend to publish. Unlike Dashiell Hammett who was a private detective with Pinkerton, or Ian Fleming who was recruited as an operative in Britain's SIS during World War II, Francis had no prior experience in the dark currency of spying or crime, yet the jockey who became a thriller writer is one of popular fiction's greatest success stories. So far he's produced 39 novels that have been translated into 35 languages. His works are usually set in his milieu, British racecourses, but his hardboiled heroes venture to Scandinavia, Australia, New Zealand, and Canada, and his books have sold more than 60 million copies.

Born in 1920 in South Wales, Francis was a keen horseman from the time he could walk. He won "best boy rider" awards at all the major horse shows between the wars and attracted the personal attention of British royalty. Although he disliked his studies, he was the child star of the English riding world.

When World War II began, Francis was turned down by the cavalry. He decided to join the Royal Air Force, with the idea of training to be a pilot, but was tricked into signing on as an airframe fitter. Francis was told he should acquire a trade and remuster for flying later. In his 1957 autobiography *The Sport of Queens*, he admits it was his first experience of the "easy callous lying of the forces, and I did not recognize it…"

Through sheer perseverance, a trait of both Francis and his protagonists, he finished the war as a Lancaster bomber. Upon demobilization, he returned to racing and became a champion steeplechase jockey. At the pinnacle of his career he rode Her Majesty Queen Elizabeth the Queen Mother's horse Devon Loch in the 1956 Grand National. His luckless mount mysteriously collapsed just 40 yards from the winning post, and in the lead. Devon Loch's failure and the heartbreak of the near victory made Francis even more famous. Not long after that, he ended his jockey life and, with the help of his wife, Mary, transformed himself into a racing journalist for the *Sunday Express*. From there he turned to fiction writing and became, like the title of his first thriller, a dead cert. He was 36.

Grand Cayman is flat and featureless with a complaint of luxury hotels and condominiums that crowd Seven Mile Beach. The condos boast endless glass and four-car garages. Tiffany's and a dazzle of duty-free jewelers, English pubs and restaurants, including an Outback Steak House and the American chain eatery Ruth Chris, rub shoulders on West Bay Road. The traffic snarls as the well-heeled geriatric set push grocery carts on the sidewalk near the high-priced supermarket. The imported Mercedeses and SUVs are driven on the left-hand side of the road, which is expected, since Grand Cayman is still a British crown colony. When I look at the sea, it's surprisingly the color of blue milk.

The island is made to order for the wealthy. It boasts a dizzying array of banks, nearly 600. George Town, the tiny and uninspiring capital, welcomes a lineup of cruise ships whose passengers tumble out, then rush in tight formation down the streets as if propelled by a current of cash. Homosexuality is illegal, and the island made itself a reputation by turning away a cruise ship that catered to gay passengers. You'd think the tax advantages and financial secrecy would create a shady island of money-laundering mafiosi and political criminals, but only the wealth is obvious. Boringly so. To me, Grand Cayman is someone else's idea of the perfect escape. It calls to mind Patrick McGoohan's cult TV series *The Prisoner* in which the title character can't escape his isolated seaside surroundings. I wonder why Dick Francis, a mystery writer, would choose such a simulated place.

The US$350 per night "villa" where I bide time is one of a collection of rambling beach cabins from the 1970s. Sadly their time is up. They're scheduled for demolition and will too soon be replaced by an expensive, spaceless square of condos.

On my patio I peruse the island's paper, the *Caymanian Compass*. The weather report synopsis predicts "no significant features." The police report reads: "A 72-year-old woman was rescued Monday after getting into difficulty while snorkeling." I know that Francis, who suffers from arthritis inflicted by riding accidents, swims daily. I know, too, that the windows of his living room afford him a similar view.

The flat blue of the sea is illuminated by the sun's unhurried demise—from azure to pink, then the finale of blood-red. I retreat inside my villa, pointedly ignoring the signage on the wall that warns: OUR GUESTS ARE OUR MOST PRECIOUS POSSESSIONS. PLEASE CLOSE AND LOCK ALL WINDOWS BEFORE RETIRING.

Almost nodding off, jet lag fanned by the breeze, I feel as if I'm in a somnambulistic haze as I get ready to leave for my interview with Francis, only to be brought up short when I notice

A fishing trawler shimmers like a mirage off Grand Cayman at dusk, making this tropical paradise even more alluring.

two items missing: my sunglasses, necessary in the sunny bankers' paradise, and the note with the mystery writer's name and address. Nothing else is missing. My purse and its contents, a surfeit of dollar bills needed for tips and my credit cards, are untouched. Did someone squeeze through the child-size window and abscond with my sunglasses and the note?

In my bleary state I think back, now certain that I placed the note and the sunglasses beside a copy of *Second Wind* and Francis's latest thriller, *Shattered*, both partially set on Grand Cayman. A siren shrieks, jarring me, drawing my eyes to the window. I've heard of sneak thieves in Thailand who come up through toilets to rob houses. I know there are gangs that use children and monkeys to steal. A child, a monkey, yes, someone or something must have squeezed through my open window. Maybe the culprit knows the famous name and has gone to Francis's condominium to rob him, but Francis, a fearless type like the heroes in his thrillers, surprises the thief. Perhaps...Dick Francis has been...murdered!

It's my fault. I opened my big mouth at the bar the previous night, bragged I was going to meet the celebrated jockey and author. On a barstool in the sand I talked and, in response, saw a greedy flicker in the bartender's bloodshot eyes. I know that behind the wealth here there's an underclass of poorly paid immigrants. My own tired eyes open wide as I shake myself out of a reverie that could be the beginning of a...mystery.

❧

A thoroughly alive Dick Francis greets me at the door of his opulent condominium, appropriately christened The Sovereign. He's trim, tanned, and neat in salmon golf shirt and matching shorts. He shuffles when he walks, a legacy from innumerable racing injuries. He doesn't weigh much more than he did as a steeplechaser—110 pounds. The dapper scribe is charming and affable: "When I'm writing about a place, I go there. When I wrote *Blood Sport*, I went to America, out west. There was an internal air strike, and so Mary and I bused to Albuquerque. You get more detail. You can look behind people's eyes."

Francis speaks in well-modulated British tones, then stops, apologizes, and leaves the room to change the batteries in his hearing aid. His creed is: Do your best, take what fate dishes out, and don't complain.

Felix Francis, the mystery author's business manager and youngest son, sits in the open kitchen doing accounts and answering the telephone. When Francis returns, he says, "People will say to me, 'You write mysteries.' But I call them adventure stories. They don't always have a murder in them."

Dick Francis still swims twice daily on his beautiful beach in front of his luxurious condo on Grand Cayman.

Francis relates his schedule. This evening he's signing copies of *Shattered* at a local restaurant for 200 visiting conventioneers. Yesterday there was an emergency trip to the dentist. Soon he'll fly to Washington, D.C., and from there he'll be back in the air on a transatlantic flight to attend the Grand National at Aintree racecourse. After that he'll return to Grand Cayman.

Later he writes in a fax to me: "The only blot on my visit to England was, of course, the death of the Queen Mother." Francis goes on to say that her timing was "in a way most considerate of Her Majesty, otherwise I would have had to make another special visit." I know that the Queen Mother would have understood Francis's statement and sympathized, since the flight is a long and tedious one at any age. After all, she knew Francis as a boy, then as her royal jockey, and for years he was the Queen Mum's favorite author. In fact, he personally presented her with a new novel every year.

Francis gestures at his floor-to-ceiling glass window and the timeless sea with its array of promenading bathers. He says, "We saw Hemingway's house in Key West, and how could anyone write in there with no light." It isn't a question. Where we sit in his favorite room, the reflected light through the glass and the holiday aura is a tonic. Francis calls over to Felix, "Fee, who wrote Bulldog Drummond?"

"Sapper," Felix answers after checking his veracity on his computer. Francis's favorite writers are Edgar Wallace, who penned a number of thrillers with racing settings; John Buchan, author of *The Thirty-Nine Steps*; and, more modernly, Ed McBain and P. D. James. Felix can recite the first lines of his father's books and does so, to my delight. The father/son relationship is close.

I recall that a Francis hero is an honest man who risks everything for his family. Francis readily admits that his protagonists are partially autobiographical. He's acknowledged that Mary, to whom he was married for 53 years, was an integral part of the writing of the books. No mystery for the analysts there, though Graham Lord's Dick Francis biography *A Racing Life* touts itself as a who-really-wrote the-Francis-thrillers tell-all. Francis has perennially been candid in interviews, saying he would have liked to have Mary's name on the books alongside his own, but she preferred not.

"I'm not writing any more novels," Francis informs me with a wry grin. "I'm struggling on a tribute to my wife." Although he speaks of his loss, he accepts it. Felix is with him, for now. I know that Mary's final resting place is close by in their double plot in West Bay Cemetery. Francis has had COME ON, MY DARLING inscribed on her tombstone. The man's warm humor is evident even when he deals with grief. Mary would always make a quick trip to the loo before their outings, and Francis would call to her each time, "Come on, my darling."

My hour disappears and Francis escorts me to the door with his painful shuffling gait. Felix waves a cheery goodbye from the kitchen table. Outside, the Grand Cayman breeze strokes my skin. I think of how Francis will return to his naturally illuminated room facing the startlingly tinted sea, a milky blue that hides the depths below, just as old eyes do. And beyond his great pane of glass, the size of Saks Fifth Avenue, he'll be entertained by tourists strutting across the sand. He'll call out, "Fee…" to jog a memory of racing, writing, or royalty mislaid somewhere on his journey from his bright past. Francis wrote in his autobiography that even as a child on his rocking horse he dreamed of jumping the fences at Liverpool and "their names have an even stronger evocative power, for I remember them with a more intense pleasure than ever I imagined them."

I think again of *The Prisoner* with its striped umbrellas and round ball that captured McGoohan's character when he attempted to flee his false paradise. And then I realize the false paradise isn't this island made in the image of the wealthy, but age. From that there's no escape for anyone, only the wait for the final destination, not unlike the ultimate suspense before the denouement of a thriller.

Letter from Dick Francis to Victoria Brooks ∽

July 22, 2003

Dear Victoria,

In reply to your fax, since Mary died, I'm afraid I am not much of a gourmet. I tend to get myself the necessities of life, such as bacon and eggs, steak, macaroni-cheese, sausages, etc., etc. For drinking I'm always very partial to red wine, and sometimes Chianti and fizzy lemonade. However, I do enjoy desserts, especially, apple pie, apple tart, pineapple pie or tart, and particularly most blends of ice cream. To all these desserts I like to add a touch of runny cream.

One particular dessert I much enjoy is lemon meringue pie…

Regarding photos of me when young, I regret that I have none of these left. Mary was always the family photographer, as well as being the librarian, and consequently, having satisfied all those who have requested them since she died, I've therefore not got any left. Very sorry.

Sorry I can't give you a better description of what I generally eat and enjoy.

Love and best wishes,

Yours ever,

Dick Francis

White sand leads to an exclusive Grand Cayman hotel where no doubt a superb meal can be had.

Recipes

Dick Francis

Dick Francis's Lemon Meringue Pie

Bella Capri

Fettuccine Alfredo
Sautéed Dover Sole with White-Wine Lemon Sauce
Coconut Cream Pie
Cayman Mama Drink
Mud Slide Drink
Snapper Cayman-Style

Pappagallo Restaurant

Lobster and Shrimp in Tarragon Cream Sauce with Frazzled Leek (Aragosta di Buba)
Long Shot

Neptune Restaurant

Cayman Lemonade

Dick Francis's Lemon Meringue Pie ❧

Ingredients

3 tbsp (45 mL) cornstarch
1¼ cups (375 mL) warm water
juice of 1 lemon and grated rind
1 cup (250 mL) granulated sugar
1 cup (250 mL) water
3 eggs, separated
1 tsp (5 mL) vanilla
1 baked pie shell
pinch of cream of tartar

Method

Mix the cornstarch with sugar (except for three tablespoons), then add the beaten egg yolks, warm water, lemon juice, and rind. Cook in a pan over hot water until thick to avoid burning filling. Cool and pour into baked pie shell. Beat egg whites until stiff, adding three tablespoons (45 milliliters) of sugar and the vanilla. (One can put a pinch of cream of tartar in egg whites when one starts beating.) Top pie with beaten egg whites. Brown in oven (350° F/180° C) for 10 minutes, turn off heat, and leave in oven with door open until cool. If you bring it out to room temperature too quickly, the egg whites are apt to fall.

Fettuccine Alfredo ❧

Makes four servings.

Ingredients

1 cup (250 mL) cream
½ cup (125 mL) grated parmesan
3 tbsp (45 mL) finely chopped garlic
couple of dashes of nutmeg
2 chopped green onions
¾ lb (375 g) fettuccine noodles (cooked)
2 tbsp (30 mL) olive oil
salt and pepper to taste

Method

Sauté garlic in a pan with the olive oil. Add cream and simmer for three or four minutes. Add parmesan and nutmeg and simmer for five more minutes. In boiling water with salt, cook pasta until al dente. Drain pasta and add to sauce with green onions, salt, and pepper.

Note: Bella Capri is a traditional Italian restaurant and a favorite haunt of Dick Francis.

Sautéed Dover Sole with White-Wine Lemon Sauce ᘕ

Makes eight servings.

Ingredients

2 fluid oz (60 mL) vegetable oil
8 cleaned whole Dover sole (12 oz/340 g each)
2 oz (60 g) butter
½ cup (125 mL) white wine
1 tsp (5 mL) chopped garlic
2 lemon slices
1 cup (250 mL) vegetable stock
salt and pepper to taste
½ cup (125 mL) flour

Method

Cook the whole sole dredged in flour in a hot frying pan with oil until golden brown. Flip the sole around and add garlic, lemon slices, white wine, and butter with vegetable stock. Then add salt and pepper to taste. Bake for 10 to 15 minutes at 500° F (250° C).

Coconut Cream Pie ❧

Ingredients

⅔ cup (165 mL) sugar
5 tbsp (75 mL) cornstarch
½ tsp (2 mL) salt
3 cups (750 mL) milk
3 egg yolks
1 tbsp (15 mL) butter
1½ tsp (7 mL) vanilla
2 tbsp (30 mL) coconut rum
1 cup (250 mL) fresh shredded coconut
2 tbsp (30 mL) toasted coconut
whipped cream

Method

Combine sugar, cornstarch, salt, and milk in a saucepan and cook over medium heat. Stir consistently until the mixture thickens and boils. Boil for one minute. Gradually stir half of the hot mixture into the slightly beaten yolks and blend into remaining mixture in the saucepan. Boil for one minute, stirring constantly. Remove from heat and add butter, vanilla, coconut rum, and shredded coconut. Pour into baked pie shell and chill. Top with whipped cream and sprinkle with toasted coconut. May also be made with graham-cracker crust.

Cayman Mama Drink ❧

Ingredients

1½ fluid oz (45 mL) amber rum
1 fluid oz (30 mL) Kahlúa
½ fluid oz (15 mL) amaretto
1½ fluid oz (45 mL) pineapple juice
1 fluid oz (30 mL) orange juice
splash grenadine syrup
ice

Method

Mix ingredients, pour into a glass, and garnish with a maraschino cherry and orange slice.

Mud Slide Drink ❧

Ingredients

1 fluid oz (30 mL) vodka
1 fluid oz (30 mL) Kahlúa
1 fluid oz (30 mL) crème de cacao
1 fluid oz (30 mL) Baileys liqueur
½ fluid oz (15 mL) chocolate syrup
1 scoop of vanilla ice cream

Method

Blend with ice, pour into a cocktail glass, and garnish with cocoa powder.

Snapper Cayman-Style ❧

Makes four servings.

Ingredients

4 snapper fillets
¼ red bell pepper
½ medium onion
1 tomato
1 tbsp (15 mL) olive oil
½ tsp (2 mL) chopped garlic
¼ scotch bonnet pepper
1 dash Worcestershire sauce
1½ cups (375 mL) white wine
flour
salt and pepper to taste

Method

Julienne the vegetables. Flour and season the fish with salt and pepper. Sauté the snapper fillets for two to three minutes in a hot pan with olive oil on both sides, add all the vegetables, then add the white wine and the Worcestershire sauce and continue cooking for eight to 10 minutes.

Lobster and Shrimp in Tarragon Cream Sauce with Frazzled Leek (Aragosta di Buba) ❧

Makes four servings.

Main Ingredients

1 lb (500 g) lobster tail meat cut into 1-inch (2.5-centimeter) chunks
1 lb (500 g) medium-size shrimp
1 cup (250 mL) sliced button mushrooms
2 tbsp (30 mL) sliced scallions
½ tsp (2 mL) finely chopped garlic
¼ cup (60 mL) brandy
½ tsp (2 mL) dried tarragon
½ tsp (2 mL) tomato paste
1 cup (250 mL) diced tomatoes
3 cups (750 mL) heavy cream
vegetable oil
salt, black pepper, and cayenne pepper to taste

Frazzled Leek Ingredients

1 finely julienned leek
½ cup (125 mL) milk
1 cup (250 mL) all-purpose flour (as needed)
vegetable oil for frying

Method

Season the lobster and shrimp with salt, black pepper, and cayenne pepper and sauté in a hot pan until nicely seared on the outside. Add mushrooms and garlic and flame with brandy. Add tarragon, tomato paste, and heavy cream and bring to a boil. Cook on low heat until the seafood is cooked and the cream is reduced to a sauce consistency. Finish by adding diced tomatoes and scallions. This delicious seafood dish is served at Pappagallo with a generous helping of pasta sautéed in butter, tomatoes, and scallions and topped with frazzled leek. Moisten the leek with milk and dredge in flour and fry immediately in hot oil until crispy and golden brown. Season with salt and pepper.

Note: Situated on a 14-acre (5.7-hectare) bird sanctuary overlooking a natural saltwater lagoon, the area surrounding Pappagallo is so rich in natural wildlife that most of the book *Birds of the Cayman Islands* by Patricia Bradley and Yves Jacques Ray Millet was researched and photographed here. Pappagallo's oldest employee is Humphrey Bogart, the African gray parrot who greets patrons at the doorway. Chef Steve Wagner has developed a loyal following, many of whom sometimes ask for one of the chef's original creations—Aragosta di Buba. In telling the story of the naming of this lobster-and-cream-sauce delicacy, Steve explained that Pappagallo owner Vico often brought his infant son, Michael, into the restaurant. As Michael babbled in his "baby-talk," he once looked at Steve and exclaimed, "Goo-goo, buba," after which "Uncle Buba" was coined. As Michael grew older, Steve's nickname was shortened to "Buba"—and a legend was born!

All sorts of exotic vegetation bloom in the West Indies heat of the Cayman Islands, including this splendid hibiscus.

For decades Vietnamese leader Ho Chi Minh, seen here in his youth, struggled against one occupying nation after another, but died before seeing his North Vietnamese forces finally drive out the Americans in 1975.

A boat plies the placid waters of Vietnam's Halong Bay where the French movie *Indochine* was filmed.

A girl
with a sun
umbrella strolls
the cobblestoned
streets of Havana's
Habana Vieja.

In Havana street musicians often play for as little as one American dollar per set.

The Havana restaurant/bar
La Bodeguita del Medio is
said to have the best
mojito in Cuba.

A Havana artist
paints in an apartment
across from Hotel Ambos
Mundos in Habana Vieja.

A "patriotic" Jamaican girl sports a hand-knit cap featuring the colors of her Caribbean home.

An old man peers through a bakery window in Negril, Jamaica, where *Roots* author Alex Haley once hung out.

Everywhere one goes in Jamaica one discovers vibrant art on walls; more often than not, it depicts food.

A flamenco dancer struts her stuff in the former Puerto Vallarta location of Mama Mia.

Note the Pickapeppa and scotch bonnet sauces in the middle of the colorful table at Jamaica's Rock House Resort.

Tamils from
southern India
were brought to
Sri Lanka to pick
tea during British
Colonial times.

This beach
at Taprobane
in Sri Lanka is
one of Sir Arthur C.
Clarke's favorites.

Grand Cayman's Seven Mile Beach can hold its own with the world's beaches when it comes to sunsets.

On the outskirts of Tangier a tribesman and camel share a smooch.

A mother and child rest against a wall in Fez, Paul Bowles's favorite medieval city.

A staired
street leads to
Hôtel El Muniria,
the small hostelry
in Tangiers's Ville
Nouvelle where
William Burroughs
wrote *Naked
Lunch*.

Neon illuminates
the night along
Nanjing Road
in Shanghai.

Doorways, such
as this one at a medicinal
shop in Beijing, often lead
to interesting discoveries.

A girl poses for the author's camera at a gift shop near Beijing's Forbidden City.

In China
the traditional
continually jostles
against the modern,
as seen in the face
of this woman in a
store on one of
Beijing's busiest
shopping streets.

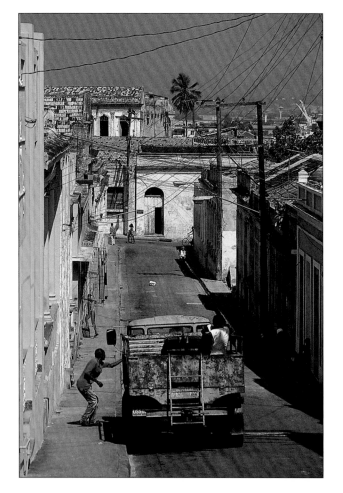

A truck
makes its
way down a
dusty road in
Cuba's second city,
Santiago de Cuba.

In Havana
a boy takes a
break from playing
marbles to smile
for the camera.

Unfortunately
many families live
in derelict housing
in Havana, the City
of Broken Dreams.

Goldeneye   Jake's   Strawberry Hill   The Caves   Marlin

Pink Sands   Cuckoo's Nest

www.islandoutpost.com

Long Shot ❧

Ingredients

1 fluid oz (30 mL) Campari
½ fluid oz (15 mL) dry vermouth
½ fluid oz (15 mL) vodka
touch of Grand Marnier to taste

Method

Shake all the ingredients and pour into a sugar-rimmed old-fashioned glass over a few ice cubes. Garnish with an orange slice and fresh mint if available.

Cayman Lemonade ❧

Ingredients

1½ fluid oz (45 mL) vodka
½ fluid oz (15 mL) peach schnapps
1 fluid oz (30 mL) lemon juice
3 fluid oz (90 mL) cranberry juice

Method

Shake all the ingredients and pour into a cocktail glass.

Many have come and gone, the famous and infamous, but Paul Bowles endured in Tangier for more than 50 years until his death at 88 in 1999.

Paul Bowles
Dreaming in Tangier

It is a balmy night. A night of 1,001 stars. Outside her suite overlooking the mosque is a sitting room shaped like a cupola. She has thrown the windows wide to the sounds of the ancient Medina, to the drums of the women, to the ancient and reverent song of the muezzins—to her dreams. When the 4:00 a.m. call of the muezzins comes, she dreams of a young man who invites her to a concert held in a large, timeless garden edged with sunset splashes of fragrant mimosa and purple bougainvillea. The garden is shaded by date palms that sway like belly dancers and is flanked by high walls washed in white. Above, the sky is a sea of shimmering blue.

The young man in her dream is well spoken and elegant. He exudes brilliance as if it were a hot white light. She wonders if he is the actor Steve McQueen. She knows he is famous. His words to her evoke mystery and promise, maybe even wisdom. As he speaks, the garden becomes a yellow desert filled with the sound of flutes and drums. He speaks gently of his passions: travel, music, literature, and Morocco. She gazes at him, marveling at the oceanic depth of his teal eyes, his gaze as profound and entrancing as an Arabian sheikh's. Moving closer, he gently kisses her mouth.

She awakens. The experience has begun.

Just a 20-minute walk from Place de France in Tangier, Morocco, is Paul Bowles's three-and-a-half-room flat, located in a nondescript suburban four-story building. The apartments sit atop a convenience store stocked with detergent, Coca-Cola, and plastic bottles of Sidi Ali and Olmos mineral water. Today the store is closed and the cheap goods are protected by rolling aluminum shutters. The entrance to the building is in the rear. The small metal elevator that brings visitors and pilgrims to Bowles's door creaks as it ascends. The safe, middle-class street outside is empty, except for a few neighborhood children playing jacks. Bowles lives alone, looked after by a trusted manservant. Born in 1910, the dreamer will soon be 89. His blue eyes are as cloudy as milky tea, but his memories are vivid.

When I first see the author, I find him wrapped in an old brown housecoat and woolen blankets on his monastic single bed. Around him are the items usually found in a sickroom: Kleenex, aspirins, sinus medicine, a glass with a straw, books and papers he can no longer see. Outside his comfortable, lived-in apartment, tall palms housing twittering birds shudder slightly in the cool Atlantic air of spring, much as his lungs do when he breathes. In his still-agile spectator's mind, he is aware of the details of life beyond his window. He was, is, the ultimate dreamer—a transcendent creator, a wizard of the written word. His brilliance remains untouched by the heavy cloak of age he is forced to wear. His brilliance is still a hot white light that pierces the veneer of humanity.

At Port de Tangier, just a few miles from where the old dreamer rests, a ferry opens its white painted metal mouth to expel trucks, cars, campers, Land Rovers, workers, and passengers. Waiting like an expectant horde of mosquitoes are the touts. Ragged and unshaven, they loll and wait and smoke, stubbing their cigarettes on the litter-strewn ground. The ferry made no sound as it slid through the Strait of Gibraltar, but they know it has arrived. The knowledge

Paul Bowles's living room in his apartment in Tangier was cluttered with music and books, the essentials of his life.

coils them like springs. The tourists have arrived. The litany of the touts begins.

"Come with me. Come with me," one cries.

"You will lose your way. You may be robbed," another shouts.

Like barracuda, they follow the tourists warily but aggressively with their hungry, shifty eyes. "A room at a good hotel, first-class, clean, cheap," several cajole.

"I will guide you through the Casbah," others promise. "Come with me. Come with me."

This is Port de Tangier, where the ferries arrive from Algeciras, Spain, where touts slouch and wait, where crumpled Marvel and Gitane cigarette packs cover the customs house floor just as they did when Nelson Dyar, Paul Bowles's protagonist in the nightmarish novel *Let It Come Down*, first arrived.

❧

It is a humid late-summer day in 1947. A parade of porters, dressed like poor physicians in stained blue cotton, carry the traveler's burden through the tight knots of touts to a fleet of ancient, beatup Mercedes, Citroën, and Renault cabs. In the cavernous boots of the old-fashioned taxis, the sweating porters deposit 13 trunks, one of which is a makeshift library heavy with books. The others are treasure chests stuffed with elegant clothes: a few pale tropical suits of silk and linen; a straw hat woven in Panama, still in its narrow wooden box; and, for lounging, a striped silk-and-cotton djellaba purchased by the dreamer in a market in Fez, where he had spent most of that summer. Carefully wrapped in the clothes is a heavy tape recorder, along with notebooks and pens for writing. The dreamer has truly arrived. He is young and handsome, blond and blue-eyed, slim and elegant. He is the still-youthful Paul Bowles.

The dreamer gropes in his pockets for coins for the porters. He looks up and admires the whiteness of the sky. It is like the inside of an oyster shell, like the painted houses of Tangier that are capped by ceramic-tiled roofs whose color and shape mimic the waves and hue of the sea.

❧

From 1923 to 1956, Tangier was an international zone, a twilight one-night stand that danced with naked abandon to the dubious tune of resident diplomatic agents from nine nations: France, Spain, Britain, Portugal, Sweden, Holland, Belgium, Italy, and the United States. Its special status meant it was a free-money market and almost no one was denied entry. It was an anything-goes town. It was what author William Burroughs called the "Interzone." Its wide-open nature attracted the wealthy and the louche, the artist and the exile. And some were all of these.

Paul Bowles was lured to Morocco by a vivid dream on a balmy New York City evening in 1947, the smell of spring, of change itself, tangible in the air. It was a dream that took him back to Tangier where he had spent a deliciously exotic summer 16 years earlier in 1931 with composer Aaron Copland, his friend and mentor. The dream had been launched in France on the advice of novelist Gertrude Stein, who had told Bowles, "Go to Tangier." Nearly 70 years later, Bowles says to me in his apartment, "It was to be a lark, a one-summer stand."

Bowles had purchased passage for Copland and himself from Marseilles to Tangier, but just before they sailed, the captain of the *Iméréthie II* announced an itinerary change to Ceuta, a Spanish possession in Morocco on a peninsula that juts into the Mediterranean Sea 75 miles northeast of Tangier. The 20-year-old Bowles stood alone on the ferry's planked deck at dawn, imagining the summer heat of Tangier "like a Turkish bath" as he leaned against the salt-sprayed rail deep in thought. His sharp young eyes were trained on the rugged scribble of the mountains of Algeria, and he was filled with a sense of excitement. Then, as he writes in his autobiography *Without Stopping*, his dreamer's vision turned inside out as he gave form to his "unreasoned conviction that certain areas of the earth's surface contained more magic than others." This conviction, this view of himself, initiated his self-exile in Tangier. To Bowles, his flight was akin to escaping from a prison whose bars were the conventions and confines of the Western world.

On that first trip in 1931, Bowles and Copland disembarked for their summer lark in Ceuta with so much luggage that they needed a small detachment of porters. As soon as they could, the pair boarded a narrow-gauge train for Tangier. On arrival they booked into El Minzah, a new deluxe hotel, when they couldn't get a room at the Grand Hôtel Villa de France, which Gertrude Stein had recommended.

To this day, Bowles wonders about the reason for the change in the ship's itinerary. "It's still unknown to me," he tells me with a shake of his head, his old eyes misted with the past and the mystery of the unknown.

The change in destination did nothing to transform his destiny, however. Bowles's initial look at the North African landscape became the first few strokes on a paper canvas that was soon sealed and signed with the indelible ink of his existence in Tangier and his travels throughout Morocco. The first time he saw Tangier, he says, "I loved it more than any place I'd seen in my life."

Still, it wasn't until 1947 that Bowles was able to settle in Tangier. He had already gained

Burka-clad women promenade down a dusty street in Tangier's Casbah.

a considerable reputation as a stage composer, having written scores for Tennessee Williams's *The Glass Menagerie* and *Summer and Smoke*; William Saroyan's *Love's Old Sweet Song*; Lillian Hellman's *The Watch on the Rhine*; and *Horse Eats Hat*, directed by Orson Welles for the Federal Theater Project.

His short story "A Distant Episode" had been published by the *Partisan Review* in January 1947 and was critically acclaimed. The story tells of a condescending American linguistics professor whose tongue is cut out by nomads when he wanders off the tourist path. The professor becomes a captive and is paraded through the North African desert, miming obscene gestures taught to him by those he once thought he was superior to. It is a tale that renders the so-called civilized world and all its intellectual trappings meaningless, an account of the perils that may face Westerners who stray into uncharted territories. Tangier was, and is, such a place. The central conceit of "A Distant Episode" is Bowles's recurring theme, his trademark and his warning.

After his talent was recognized, Bowles was offered an advance by the U.S. publisher Doubleday for a yet-to-be-written novel that he would eventually title *The Sheltering Sky*. On the brink of literary success, he booked a one-way passage in June 1947 from New York to Morocco. The writer Jane Auer Bowles, his wife since 1938, was to follow in six months. She was a lesbian, he a homosexual.

But it wasn't only the Bowleses who were enticed by the exotic allure of Tangier. European émigrés, American expatriates, and literary renegades of every stripe descended on the sybaritic city where anything could be had for very little money, where homosexuality was accepted, where use of the local *kif* (cannabis and tobacco) and *majoun* (hashish jam) were commonplace, where the lifestyle was decadently delicious, sometimes even depraved.

As Bowles notes in *Without Stopping*, Tangier struck him as a dream city: "Its topography was rich in prototypal dream scenes: covered streets like corridors . . . hidden terraces high above the sea, streets consisting only of steps . . . as well as the classical dream equipment of tunnels, ramparts, ruins, dungeons and cliffs."

Bowles wrote as he traveled in Morocco, constructing his first novel from within his soul, layering it with the details and textures of North Africa. Much of his writing was done while lying in French pension beds. But in the autumn of 1947 he purchased a villa in Tangier for $500 and settled down to complete *The Sheltering Sky*.

Paul and Jane Bowles would always travel often and far, but their hearts would remain caught in the gossamer web of Morocco. The dreamer's talented and tempestuous wife often flitted like a nervous butterfly from Connecticut or New York and back, following her whims and women (New York ladies and Berber country girls). In between she practiced her craft (the novel *Two Serious Ladies*, the play *In the Summer House*, and a short-story collection *Plain Pleasures*). Jane Bowles, too, belonged to Tangier. After a long illness, though, she died of a stroke in 1973 at the age of 56.

Cecil Beaton, Truman Capote, Gore Vidal, James Baldwin, and Tennessee Williams all visited Tangier during Bowles's first few years in the city. David Herbert, second son of the Earl of Pembroke, who was once described by guest Ian Fleming as the "Queen Mother of Tangier," and Woolworth heiress Barbara Hutton held court in the city, where expatriates were nicknamed *tangerinos* and natives were dubbed *tanjawis*.

After her third divorce in 1946, Hutton purchased a stone palace inside the Casbah, the fortress that stands within the walls of the old Arab quarter known as the Medina. Hutton threw parties featuring camels, snake charmers, belly dancers, and "blue men" brought in from Morocco's High Atlas Mountains. The blue men are a tribe of tall, handsome nomads whose skin is stained indigo from the dye in their turbans and flowing desert robes. The "poor little rich girl" entertained like a nomad queen in a Hollywood extravaganza, wearing glittering Moroccan caftans while seated on a throne. When not in a party mood, she retired to her bedchamber, and disappointed guests went in search of pleasure elsewhere.

More than a half century later, Bowles shares a memory of her with me: "Barbara Hutton

One can still imagine Paul Bowles and his minder on this road in Tangier where they once took their daily exercise strolls.

was so weak from reducing and pills she had to be carried through the streets of the Medina when she left her palace." He "was not impressed with her dramatics," her messy life, and preferred to distance himself from the decadent fray. Over the years, his desire for solitude has been frequently interrupted by the parade of socialites, artists, exiles, and escape artists who have passed through Tangier's revolving door and thrust Bowles into the role of the city's unofficial, often reluctant ambassador.

In the 1950s, a motley crew of literary renegades, including Beat writers Allen Ginsberg and Jack Kerouac and their godfather William Burroughs, made the scene. In 1954 Burroughs followed Bowles to Tangier after reading *The Sheltering Sky*, a novel written in a dazzling, visionary stream-of-consciousness style with more than a few echoes of the work of Albert Camus and Edgar Allan Poe, the authors Bowles most admired. Bowles's masterpiece of three American postwar travelers adrift on an emotional voyage in the desolate yet beautiful North African Sahara explores their creator's powerful theme: the dream/nightmare that awaits the culturally and morally estranged.

Doubleday, which had already paid Bowles an advance, refused to accept the book "for not being a novel," so the manuscript began a yearlong journey across publishers' desks before its release in September 1949 by the English publisher John Lehmann. A month later an American edition was put out by New Directions, and soon after the novel became an international bestseller and received powerful critical praise. In 1959 Norman Mailer wrote in *Advertisements for Myself*: "Paul Bowles opened the world of Hip. He let in the murder, the drugs, the incest, the death of the Square . . . the call of the orgy, the end of civilization; he invited all of us to these themes."

The Sheltering Sky's mystique was heightened by the fact that Bowles had put himself into a *majoun*-induced state to write his character Port Moresby's grippingly horrific death scene. Local drugs were often used by the Tangier literary set to tap into their subconscious minds and write in the "proper style."

Burroughs, whom the locals called El Hombre Invisible, lived in Tangier for four years. In a small room in the city's Hôtel El Muniria, he wrote his hallucinatory satire *Naked Lunch*, a fictional rendering of his own descent into the hellish world of the heroin addict. Later, when Bowles and I rendezvous on the outskirts of Tangier, he conjures up an image of Burroughs: "He was always dressed to his fingertips in black, with black gloves that he would slowly and theatrically peel off, one finger at a time, like an undertaker." In the beginning, Bowles was aloof with Burroughs, but later, he admits, he came to "admire his humor."

In *Let It Come Down*, Bowles writes that "If a man was not on his way anywhere . . . then the best thing for him to do is sit back and be." The literary, the louche, and the loaded followed his vision of flickering light and shadow, pounding drums, shifting desert sands, and Moroccan keyhole doors that lead into the dark recesses of the human mind. Over mint tea, sherry, *kif*, and Marlboroughs, sybarites and eccentrics reclined low in the scuffed brown leather chairs of the Café de Paris on Place de France, basking in the intense light of Bowles's oracle.

Now, outside the café, I watch the continuing pageant in Rue de la Liberté: beggars with outstretched, unwashed palms etched with want; darkly handsome men, both young and old, in brightly hued pantaloons or tassel-hooded djellabas; Berber women with round peasant faces obscured by the shade of their wide-brimmed straw hats, black pom-poms dancing to the soft beating of their bare feet as they walk their wares to the souks; and Arab women swaddled from shining midnight eyes to pale toes in voluptuous white cotton. It's an ageless procession of Arab commerce and culture, and all of it unfolds just as it did in Bowles's heyday. During one of our meetings, he told me gnomically: "If we weren't eccentrics, we wouldn't have been here." And now I see what he meant. All around me are shopkeepers selling faux antiques, boxes of camel bones from the Sahara encrusted with amber and silver, and leather slippers from Fez as soft and yellow as butter. The shopkeepers are entirely men, and they place their carved wooden chairs strategically on the street, vying for attention among the beggars in cheap Western garb and old men in fezzes and stained caftans.

A street
artist in
Tangier's
Grand Socco
plies his trade
outside the
Medina.

161

The Tangier of past and present become one, then separate. The hours still pass as if in a dream, but today the Café de Paris is no longer an appropriated salon where the Bowleses and the literary renegades discuss their muses. These days it brims with gloomy unemployed Arab men who hover over mint tea in glasses that are stormy with milk.

The renegades, infidels, and exiles took everything they could from Tangier. And when the Moroccan oasis no longer offered the free status of an international zone, they scattered. For them it was a place to use like a cheap, exciting prostitute, a place to take selfish pleasure for a night, a year, or until the thrill was gone. But Bowles stayed, and he, and the City of the Dream, still mesmerize.

Yes, the Master remained, centered in his own vision, to write more novels and stories and to translate the works of talented Moroccan authors, continuing to offer his revelations to the world, his rare gift wrapped in sunlight and shadow, extreme beauty and disturbing discovery.

She dreams again. This time she lies sleeping in Tangier's famous Hôtel El Minzah in a suite overlooking the waters of the Strait of Gibraltar and the sleek ferries from Algeciras that slide into the harbor like a hallucination from Paul Bowles's world.

The experience has begun. It is Sunday. She dreams she is riding in an aged Mercedes taxi down Boulevard Pasteur, down a long, empty avenue lined with bougainvillea and palms, the outstretched, sun-baked fronds of the latter reaching heavenward as if seeking Allah's benediction. Her driver is named Ali. The sun shines high and clear. The sky is as translucent and white as a pearl. Abruptly she tells Ali to stop.

She has spotted the old dreamer perched on a folding stool at the side of the deserted road. Leaving the taxi and approaching him, she sits beside his stool: she, a child, a convert, a pilgrim; he, her oracle. Birds chirp discreetly in the trees, while on a distant hill a herd of goats bleat, the sounds fading away like old memories.

He regales her with his travels to Sri Lanka, Santiago de Cuba, Panama, Berlin, Mexico, and Central America. He tells her of New York and his dislike of large cities, then, when she asks him what wisdom he has acquired during his decades in Tangier, he replies, "Patience." Then he adds, "This is as good a place as any. It has been good to me."

He is elegant, even more so than when she dreamt about him as Steve McQueen. His eyes are as deep and mysterious as his soul, as entrancing as a sheikh's. He has wisdom, charm, humor. She loves him. He is Paul Bowles. She knows she is blessed just by sitting near him. She puts her hand over his. He rises with difficulty, then walks in the sunlight like some old god, stopping to rest on the folding stool when he tires. Too soon the manservant notes his master's exhaustion and tells her they must go.

She gives Bowles a gentle lover's kiss on his soft old mouth. As she watches his battered gray Citroën drive slowly away, she vaguely remembers something important he once wrote in Without Stopping: *"I had always been vaguely certain that sometime during my life I should come into a magic place which, in disclosing its secrets, would give me wisdom and ecstasy, perhaps even death."*

She raises her eyes to the pale horizon and sees Tangier like a scrawl of mauve ink on a page of his dream. It is his Tangier, refracted like a diamond through her veil of tears.

(Note: A few weeks before his 89th birthday, Paul Bowles died on November 18, 1999, of heart failure in the Italian Hospital in Tangier. I had planned to return to Morocco to present him with a copy of *Literary Trips*, the book this story first appeared in. If only I could have sat by his narrow bed and held his gnarled old hand one last time.)

For decades
Paul Bowles
lived in a three-
and-a-half room
flat in this Tangier
apartment building
near Place de
France.

Recipes

Le Chablis (Marrakech)

Breast of Duck with Seasonal Fruit

Dar Jamai (Fez)

Aubergine Salad

L'Anmbra (Fez)

Chicken Kebabs

Le Douira—Hôtel Le Royal Mansour (Casablanca)

Harira Soup

El Korsan Restaurant—Hôtel El Minzah (Tangier)

Lamb Tajine with Prunes
Moroccan Mint Tea

Palm trees line the pool at Hôtel La Mamounia in Marrakech.

Breast of Duck with Seasonal Fruit ❧

Makes four servings.

Ingredients

2 duck breasts
3 oz (80 g) honey
1 cup (250 mL) bullion stock
¼ lb (125 g) butter
4 pears, quartered (cook with syrup)
3 apples, peeled, cored, and sautéed
½ lb (250 g) chopped spinach
2 tsp (10 mL) balsamic vinegar
salt and pepper to taste

Method

Place the fruit and cut-up vegetables on a plate and keep warm. Fry duck for 15 minutes on medium heat. Remove duck and keep warm, then drain grease and deglaze pan with balsamic vinegar and honey. Caramelize, stir in bullion, and reduce. Incorporate butter and pour over the duck with fruit and vegetables on the side. Serve immediately and hot.

Aubergine Salad ҉

Makes four to six servings.

Ingredients

2 lb (1 kg) eggplant (aubergine)
1 lb (500 g) seeded, peeled and crushed tomatoes
1 sprig of parsley
4 finely chopped garlic cloves
½ tsp (2 mL) chili peppers or hot sauce (or to taste)
½ tsp (125 mL) cumin
½ cup (125 mL) oil
½ tsp (2 mL) salt

Method

Cut eggplant into one-inch (2.5-centimeter) cubes. Steam for 10 to 15 minutes until tender. Put the remaining ingredients in a frying pan and simmer for 10 to 15 minutes. Stir occasionally, finally adding the cubed eggplant. Continue cooking until the juices are absorbed. Can be served hot or cold.

Ancient Tangier has all the classic trademarks of a Mediterranean city: a bluer-than-blue sky and bone-white buildings.

Chicken Kebabs ❧

Makes four to six servings.

Ingredients

2 lb (1 kg) chicken breasts
2 tbsp (30 mL) olive oil
1 tbsp (15 mL) paprika
1 tsp (5 mL) hot pepper or to taste
1 tsp (5 mL) cumin
½ tsp (2 mL) salt
1 chopped sprig of parsley
2 crushed garlic cloves

Method

Skin and remove the bone from chicken breasts. Cut into one-inch (2.5-centimeter) cubes. Mix the rest of the ingredients and place chicken in them. Return to refrigerator and marinate for four to six hours. Thread on wooden skewers that have been soaked in water and grill over very hot barbecue. Do not overcook.

Harira Soup ✑

Makes four servings.

Ingredients

1 cup (250 mL) chickpeas/garbanzo beans (soaked overnight if using dried beans)
1 cup (250 mL) lentils (soaked overnight if using dried lentils)
1 cup (250 mL) dried, peeled fava beans (soaked overnight)
1½ cup (375 mL) white flour
½ cup (125 mL) oil
½ cup (125 mL) rice
½ cup (125 mL) vermicelli
2 tbsp (30 mL) tomato paste
1 lb (500 g) peeled plum tomatoes (or canned)
1 large to medium-large onion
1 bunch fresh coriander
1 small bunch parsley
2 sticks celery
6 cups (1½ L) water (you may need to add more as the dish cooks)
½ tsp (2 mL) black pepper
½ tsp (2 mL) cumin
½ tsp (2 mL) turmeric
1 tbsp (15 mL) salt
2 garlic cloves
2 tsp (10 mL) lemon juice
1 egg

Method

Cut all the ingredients finely and put them into a large pot. Save the vermicelli, the flour, and the egg for the last stage. Boil for 40 minutes. When chickpeas are cooked, it's time to add the vermicelli and mix the flour in a bowl with warm water until it's liquid and there are no lumps in the bowl. Add some of the lemon juice and pour into the pot very slowly while stirring with a large spoon or any other wooden spoon. You should have a thickish soup (it must not be too thick, nor too watery; if it's too watery, you may want to add some flour). Just before serving, beat egg with a little lemon juice in a small bowl and add to the soup, stirring with a long wooden spoon until mixture forms strands. Serve in bowls and enjoy.

170

A Bedouin walks along a street in the market close to where Paul Bowles once lived.

Lamb Tajine with Prunes

Makes four to six servings.

Ingredients

2 lb (1 kg) lamb meat cut into bite-size pieces
1 lb (500 g) prunes
2 onions
½ cup (125 mL) oil
1 cup (250 mL) sugar
¼ cup (65 mL) rose-flower water
1 tsp (5 mL) salt
1 tsp (5 mL) white pepper
1 tsp (5 mL) shredded ginger
2 pinches of saffron
3 crushed garlic cloves
1 sprig each parsley and coriander
1 cinnamon stick
2 tbsp (30 mL) toasted sesame seeds
4 oz (115 g) toasted almonds

Method

Mix ingredients (except for prunes, sugar, cinnamon stick, rose-flower water, sesame seeds, and almonds) and let stand for a few minutes. Add four cups (one liter) of water. Cook lamb mixture in a covered pan over medium heat for one hour. During cooking, take the prunes (which have been soaked in salted water for two hours) and drain, stone, and mash them with a fork. Add to prune pulp: cinnamon stick, rose-flower water, one teaspoon (five milliliters) of oil, and sugar. Place prune-pulp mixture in frying pan and caramelize. Then add to the lamb and continue cooking for 10 minutes. Just before serving, add sesame seeds and almonds.

Moroccan Mint Tea ❧

10 sprigs fresh mint, plus extra for garnish
1 tbsp (15 mL) green tea
3 tbsp (45 mL) sugar (or more to taste)
4 cups (1 L) water

Method

Boil a fresh pot of water and pour a small amount in the teapot, swishing it around to warm the pot. Combine the mint, green tea, and sugar in the teapot, then fill it with the rest of the hot water. Let the tea brew for three minutes. Set out small glasses for the tea (a shot glass is very similar to the glasses used in Morocco). Fill just one glass with the tea, then pour it back in the pot (this helps dissolve the sugar). Repeat. Pour the tea. You want a nice foam on the tea, so always pour with the teapot high above the glasses. If you don't have at least a little foam on top of the first glass, then pour it back into the teapot and try again until the tea starts to foam nicely. Garnish with the remaining sprigs of mint.

Note: Paul Bowles didn't drink alcohol. Mint tea is the drink of choice in Morocco. It's usually made sickly sweet. Tea is served in glasses rather than cups as a welcome drink and is ubiquitous at every meal.

Roadside tables selling food, as depicted here, are a common sight in Morocco's Atlas Mountains.

A pop
superstar
by 1971, Bob
Marley died all too
soon of cancer at
the age of 36
in 1981.

Bob Marley
Everything Is Everything in Jamaica

*W*henever I hear the recorded reggae cry of *"Rastafarrr!"* in rain-soaked Vancouver, in sultry Havana, in romantic Prague, in polluted Beijing, anywhere, I'm taken out of my world and transported to what I've come to think of as "mi yard"—Jamaica, political tinderbox, artist's muse, beauty spot, and birthplace and home of Robert Nesta Marley.

Son of a striking 18-year-old black girl and a 50-year-old white quartermaster attached to the British West Indian Regiment, Marley was born in 1945. After an almost fatherless childhood in the rural pastures of St. Ann's Parish on Jamaica's sinuous north coast, he moved with his mother into the grinding poverty of Kingston's Trench Town. Marley was barely into his teens. His friends were other street youths who were also impatient with British racism, the disparity between rich and poor, and the broken promise of Kingston's lure as a place of opportunity.

On a hot summer evening in Kingston I sit quietly in a rental car. The night is close, and though I've locked the doors, my window is open. As I drink in the street scene, a rasping voice whispers almost in my ear, "Money fo' medicine." The voice belongs to a dark-faced Rasta. He peers at me, his age-streaked locks filling the window like white lightning.

"No," I respond, clutching my purse.

"Yah mun," the Rastaman says, looking me straight in the eye. "Sorry mi scare you. Respect." And with those words he withdraws.

Rolling the window up as a barrier against the Jamaican capital city's dark beat, I find my attention drawn to the outside again. A youth whirls like a dervish in the middle of the thoroughfare. His baggy pants Hula-Hoop his knees, and his penis leads like a divining rod as he twirls.

Marley cut his first vinyl with the track "Judge Not" in 1962 at the age of 19. He recorded it with friends Winston Hubert MacIntosh ("Peter Tosh") and Neville O'Reilly Livingston ("Bunny Wailer") as the vocal trio the Wailers for Kingston record producer Sir Coxsone Dodd on the hip (in Jamaica) Coxsone label. The Wailers explored inner-city themes, identifying with the Rude Boys street rebels in Kingston's slums. Although they recorded regularly with Dodd, one of Jamaica's finest sound-system men, economic success eluded them, and three other members of the group went their own way to search for more immediate financial gratification.

In 1966 Marley's mother, Cedella, remarried and sent her son an air ticket. Marley followed her to the United States with the idea of finding work to finance his music. A few months later the island's magnetic pull and the lure of a woman, the young singer Rita Anderson whom Marley had just met and would eventually marry, proved too much to resist and he returned to Jamaica. Marley's homecoming was on the heels of a state visit by Ethiopian Emperor Haile Selassie, who brought with him renewed credence and excitement for the Rastafarian movement in an island always searching for answers.

Rastafarianism, a religious form of the African Jamaican's protest against a society pressured

Rastafarianism is at the heart of Bob Marley's music, and Jamaican Rasta men such as this fellow constitute its soul.

by poverty, got its start in the 1950s and was inspired by charismatic Jamaican preacher and entrepreneur Marcus Garvey's revelation: "Look to Africa for the crowning of a Black King. He shall be the Redeemer." Referred to as Jah, the movement's Messiah was identified as the revered Haile Selassie (real name Ras Tafari) who, among his other achievements, was a key architect of and player in the Organization of African Unity (OAU) in the early 1960s.

Marley's growing commitment to Rastafarianism and his philosophical maturity changed his persona as well as his musical attitude. The tough urban stance in his lyrics was replaced by what would become his trademark: an uplifting spiritual and social ideology. Jamaican music, too, had progressed, the effervescent ska swapped for a slower, more sensual rhythm that suited Marley's emotionally tender melodies and socially conscious, often marijuana-infused lyrics. The Wailers, with the compelling Marley as leader, would become the first reggae artists to achieve international success.

Smoking marijuana is a Rastafarian rite. The right of the tourist to indulge in "de herb" is a given in Jamaica, and at concerts, as elsewhere, the pungent smell of ganja perfumes the air. As I sit in my rental car, I think about my imminent attendance at the yearly Tribute to Bob Marley, held at the simple concert venue MXIII in the lovely seaside resort town of Negril. Every year cutting-edge Jamaican musicians like Capleton, Baju Banton, Ziggy Marley, and Toots and the Maytals show up at MXIII to play to a motley bunch of tourists and locals who can ante up the cover charge of 500 Jamaican dollars (US$8.50).

Eventually I make my way to Negril where at MXIII I stand shoulder to shoulder with a local friend, leaning over a low wall on a second-floor viewing area made of concrete and perfectly placed for seeing the stage and the crowd below. The stars wink above the dimly lit scene like fireflies, and the mob dances sensuously to Everton Blender, the opening act of a DJ's dancehall-style reggae. The drill is up-tempo reggae talked or sung over computerized rhythm tracks. It's akin to Jamaican street talk, the musical patois, on speed. Dancehall reggae has been vilified by politicians and church leaders since its inception in the late 1980s for glorifying violence, drugs, and crime. The artists maintain that the music represents the voice of the people and mirrors Jamaican society. The controversy was escalated by a former police commissioner who attempted to ban DJ lyrics that promoted violence in a throwback to the Rude Boys era of the 1960s when the government actively censored the music. The ballyhoo peaked in the mid-1990s when some dancehall reggae musicians imbued the songs with a cultural flavor and added acoustic instruments.

Looking down from our perch, I watch the men milling, their dreadlocks zigzagging wildly. Others have shaven their heads, and their brown skulls glow with cocoa butter. The faces are mostly black, though there are a few white ones. Rastas with skinny legs and ragamuffin clothing wander through the crowd, hawking red-and-blue packages of American cigarettes and island-picked peanuts in tiny hand-tied plastic bags. A makeshift bar does a brisk trade selling rum punch, bottled Red Stripe beer, island-bottled Heineken, and the stronger Dragon Stout. A contingent of Jamaicans, youths in Marley's heyday, have come from all over the island to see Bunny Wailer, the lead and last act. These men are tall, as most Jamaicans are, and they're elegantly attired in African caftans. Their ladies, curvaceous in form, wear brightly patterned frocks. Their hair is wrapped in high turbans Erykah Badu–style. While their heads remain still, their generous hips twitch, shake, and shiver like metronomes keeping time in an earthquake. Jamaicans are sexy at every age.

I spy a joint being passed at the edge of my little crowd. "Pass the jo"—a refrain from a lyric on popular dancehall artist Sean Paul's CD *Dutty Rock* flits through my brain. Impulsively I reach for the spliff, pursing my lips and inhaling. I draw in the smoke deep, knowing the pleasurable feeling that marijuana brings. Ganja hones the senses. It's a known fact that all manners of sensual pleasures are heightened. I pass the joint on and then pass out. When I come to, I'm lying on the concrete with an array of concerned faces gazing down at me. I can't hear anything, and the people seem like faraway *duppys*, or spirits, edged in primary colors, as in a Haitian painting. Then slowly my senses return and I discern voices and glimpse movements, only to pass out again. Later, when I've recovered from my odd collapse, I'm told I must have smoked what the locals refer to as a "seasoned spliff," marijuana laced with coke or crack, drugs that are cheap and prevalent in Jamaica, drugs I would never knowingly take and am not accustomed to. My local friend is beside himself, and in typical Jamaican style lectures me with variations on "Never take nuting from stranger. No even food, no drink, and specially no spliff." Eventually I'm transported back to my hotel and put to bed, causing my friend to miss the appearance of Bunny Wailer without complaint.

Marley and the Wailers defined the direction of reggae with classic tracks such as "Soul Rebel," "Duppy Conqueror," "400 Years," and "Small Axe," but only survived financially as songwriters for a company associated with Johnny Nash, who had an international hit with Marley's "Stir It Up." In 1971 Marley accompanied the American singer to Europe and secured a recording contract with Columbia Records. Marley and the Wailers cut their own Columbia single "Reggae on Broadway" but found themselves poorly promoted, then stranded and broke, the track unsuccessful in London.

As the last hard throw in a sidewalk crap shoot, Marley walked into Chris Blackwell's Basing Street Studios. Blackwell's company, Island Records, was the major mover behind the

Chris Blackwell, music impresario and resort specialist, was a key figure in the ascendancy of Bob Marley and reggae. Today his Island Outpost organization owns Goldeneye, Ian Fleming's former home, and The Caves.

Courtesy Island Outpost/ Copyright © by Cookie Kinkead

invasion of Jamaican music in Britain. He'd launched Island in the 1950s in Jamaica and relocated to London in 1962, realizing he could represent his Jamaican rivals in Britain. Jamaica's ska rhythm of the time was so danceable it scored high, not just with Britain's numerous expat Jamaicans centered in London and Birmingham, but with the entire Mod culture. In 1964 Blackwell produced "My Boy Lollipop," a pop/ska hit by Jamaican singer Millie. As well as being the source of Jamaican music, his company represented white rock, with premier artists such as Cat Stevens, Jethro Tull, and Fairport Convention.

Marley and the Wailers, through Blackwell, were connected to the hottest independent recording company in the world at that time. The Wailers' first album, *Catch a Fire*, was produced, packaged, and properly promoted. By the age of 26, Marley was a superstar. In 1981, a mere decade later, cancer claimed the ascetic, mystical musician and composer.

After selling Island Records to Polygram in 1989, Blackwell started Island Outpost, turning his talent to the hotel-and-resort industry and opening exclusive boutique hotels that attract musicians and music lovers. And that's where I go now—to a hideaway far from the mainstream in the West End of Negril where the vibe remains. Where I have found that in the 20 years I've been visiting the island nothing seriously changes. Or, as a Jamaican would say, "Everything is everything."

In the first decade of the new millennium, a time feathered with tragedy and tarred with terrorism, I've found there's still no place on the entire planet as seductive as West End Negril, and no small hotel there as fittingly musical as Chris Blackwell's The Caves. The West End is a six-mile stretch of spectacular limestone cliffs that plunge into the turquoise Caribbean. It's a far cry from the ghettos of Kingston, from the hurly-burly, all-inclusive, resort-fat Montego Bay, even from Negril's own spectacular seven-mile beach with its luxury hotels just minutes to the east by car and where author Alex Haley wrote for a while from a beach shack in the 1970s. Haley also discovered what would become another Blackwell property—Jakes, a few hours away by car on the south coast—and wrote his epic book *Roots* there.

On the cliffs, brand-name hotels and properties with more than 30 rooms don't exist in this small stretch of village, rock, and sea where I often come to write. When I'm ensconced with my laptop on the shady balcony of my room, my only distractions are the melodies of the birds and the sea, and I'm once more reminded of Ian Fleming's writing method in relation to Jamaica's effects on the senses. The ex-spy and creator of James Bond wrote "with the jalousies closed around me so that I would not be distracted by the birds and the flowers and the sunshine outside until I had completed my daily stint."

At the western tip of Negril's meandering West End Road, just past the working light-

Tensing Pen, a small luxurious hotel co-owned by Richard Murray, has a marvelous cliff-side view from Negril's West End Road.

house, is the periwinkle-blue stone gate simply marked THE CAVES. The heavy entrance doors are shut tight against the outside. But like Aladdin's cave, it opens wide with a knock and words that have become a Jamaican mantra—"Chris Blackwell, Chris Blackwell, Chris Blackwell." Besides being Jamaica's music scion, Blackwell is the son of landowner and society dame Blanche Blackwell. Rumor has it that the dashing Ian Fleming had a love affair with the young, ravishing Blanche. Goldeneye, another Blackwell property and once Fleming's 30-acre home, is now back in the hands of the family it came from, bearing out the truth in a Marley song: "what goes around comes around."

Like all the small resorts on Negril's West End Road, Chris Blackwell's Caves was built over limestone sea caves. The wood-shuttered windows of the cabins let in fresh breezes and the sounds of the sea; on stormy nights the boom of the waves in the inky ocean grottos below recalls the bass of a reggae tune reverberating through natural speakers, island-style.

Musicians and artists of all stripes are particularly attracted to The Caves. Irish singer Bono of U2 and Senegalese artist Baaba Maal often jam here. Jimmy Buffet flies in on his seaplane to visit. Hollywood actor Harrison Ford once threw a birthday bash that lasted until dawn.

Sharing the same view with The Caves are two other luxurious boutique hotels I frequent: the delightful Tensing Pen, run perfectly by talented management and named by English co-owner Richard Murray after a Himalayan Sherpa; and closer to the roundabout, the well-managed, Australian-owned gem, Rock House. A gaggle of other properties with descriptive names such as Citronella, Xtabi on the Cliffs, and Banana Shout are simultaneously picturesque and ramshackle—quaint, but certainly not for the sophisticated. All except The Caves are landmarks from long-ago hippie days, and they flaunt their colorful pasts from seductive roosts right over the ocean.

The properties on Negril's West End Road are intimate clusters of palm-roofed cabins clad in Walt Disney sunset pink or butterfly blue. Balconies of brightly painted planked wood or stone sit high atop the sea. Their balustrades mirror nature—hand-carved with sunsets, birds, lizards, and flowers. Statuesque green palms, heavy with brown-skinned coconuts, and sea grape adorned with tendrils of cloud-white jasmine, provide atmosphere, shade, and privacy. Stairways carved into the cliff side connect to natural sunbathing areas of flat, smooth rock and look as though they were painted by Salvador Dalí on a canvas of azure sea.

The unusual hideaway character of West End Negril and the stunning cliffs are priceless in a world where beauty, privacy, individualism, and creativity are highly valued. Swimsuits are optional—a hedonist's dream. Fleming snorkeled nude daily on his private curve of beach at Goldeneye. None of the small hotels in the West End have beaches, but who needs sand when the warm Caribbean becomes your own private pool, complete with ladder? Below the granite of the jagged cliffs, the warm Caribbean, the color of old-fashioned green ink, is so transparent the reefs underneath are visible. Flying fish, dolphins, and needle-nosed garfish flash silvery on the surface, while barracudas lurk in the coral. On the cliffs the swimming is without peer, as are the dramatic beauty of nature and the visual tapestry of Jamaican village life. The cozy West End village captures the look of a primitive painting with all its charm and outward naivete.

On the road, Rastas, Gorgon-locked, ready to connect and willing to exchange philosophies, lope leanly down the sun-drenched street, chatting, strutting, singing Bob Marley tunes and hawking carvings, tours to Mayfield Falls, and drugs for U.S. dollars. Everywhere Marley's inspirational and quintessentially Jamaican music emanates from road stalls and tiny open-air restaurants lining the road.

One evening, when the jet-black night is particularly pregnant with the warm, salty spray of the sea, I leave my room and stroll West End Road toward the Marley-memorabilia-bedecked Anne Beer and Joint for jerk chicken, Red Stripe beer, and chat time with Merton, the owner, waiter, and jerk cook extraordinaire. I navigate the quiet street alone until a youth on a bicycle keeps pace with me. We strike up a conversation, and I discover that Daniel is an upbeat 18. He tells me he's jobless and visiting from the dusty market town of Savanna La

Little roadside shops such as this one in Negril are an integral feature of Jamaican life.

Mar, referred to by locals as Sav. Our talk in the shared darkness is punctured by reality when we notice a police car, door ominously hanging wide, in a seemingly empty lot. I advise my new friend, "When you see something dangerous, don't stop to stare. Just keep going."

The youth asks, "What you think mi do if mi see dem rob you wit gun?"

I study the boy's eyes for clues to his meaning, then conclude I've nothing to fear from him. "What *would* you do?" I venture.

"I'd rescue you. I'd risk mi life for you."

At that stage in our odd palaver we round the bend to the tumbling click of a crap game, and spot Anne Beer and Joint in fairy light that also illuminates a mangy visiting dog and two picnic tables in the grass. Merton greets me from his place outside by the scarred kettle-drum barbecue. His dreadlocks are held up from his back by sticks, a fashionable touch. He flashes me a toothless grin and hugs me to his bony chest. I enter Merton's immaculately kept house to use the bathroom, and as I sit on the toilet I hear a high-pitched voice calling through the thin walls. "You bring me cigarettes?" the voice pleads, childlike. "You promise."

The words belong to Pretty, a mentally challenged albino in midlife. I know he's harmless and stays in his room around the clock. Merton and his wife, Anne, take care of him. I hand Pretty, who stands waiting in the hall in his boxer shorts, two single cigarettes, expecting this to satisfy him.

"You bring me rum now," he insists.

"No," I say, and hightail it out of the house and back to Merton. Not to my surprise, Merton is playing "Survivor," a Marley tune, and mouthing the lyrics.

When I eat my fill of Merton's chicken, served hot from the scarred drum on makeshift plates of tinfoil, when I'm satiated by Merton's music, talk, and positive vibes, I return to my hotel and sleep under the mosquito netting to the tune of nature's concert. The sea's waves sing through their stone grotto microphone outside, and I dream of Bob Marley and his powerful lyrics that speak of dangers in the deeps of Jamaica itself.

The next morning I rise and take another walk along West End Road. Snatches of Marley's fiercely political "Get Up, Stand Up" emanate from the boom box of a dilapidated red taxi careening down the street. Ahead of me a bicyclist in tie-dyed Marley T-shirt swoons to the seductive emotion he puts into his own rendition of "Is This Love?" I remember my banter with an acquaintance the previous evening at Anne Beer and Joint. The young man was a successful drug dealer, with all the cars and women he wanted sweetened with real clout. But eventually a policeman came to him and said, "We're going to take you down." My acquaintance said that night he had a revelation in a dream: it was time to "get up, stand up." He owned a large house in Negril and decided to divide it into rooms to rent to tourists. That way he could quit selling drugs and save his skin.

Through my lucky time on the island and thanks to Marley's lyrics, I've come to feel the helplessness of Jamaica's people in the poverty-stricken alleys of Negril as well as in the yards of Kingston. Yet I'm repeatedly filled with hope by the reggae master's intuitive lyrics about overcoming adversity, and often heed his messages in my own life. To me, Bob Marley's music is an expression of private truths. He's revealed a secret to me. When I can't travel to Jamaica, the swoop of his guitar and the reedy tenor of his vocals transform my mindset and transport me to Negril's familiar West End where I swim in the sea, sit in "mi yard," and am uplifted.

Recipes

Idle Awhilc Resort (Negril)

Ital Stew

Goldeneye (Oracabessa)

Curried Goat
Desi's Rum Punch

The Caves (Negril)

Pan-Seared Grouper
Carrot Ginger Sauce
Mashed Sweet Potatoes
Creamed Callaloo
Jamaican Curried Mutton
Pumpkin Rice

Tensing Pen Hotel (Negril)

Roasted Plantain and Pumpkin Soup

Caristy, the Rasta chef at Negril's Idle Awhile, prepares the tastiest of vegan feasts.

Ital Stew ❧

Makes four servings.

Ingredients

2 dry coconuts
1 lb (500 g) spinach
½ lb (250 g) beans (kidney, broad, black-eyed, or lima)
½ lb (250 g) carrots
½ lb (250 g) squash
½ lb (250 g) potatoes
1 tin ackee (optional)
¼ lb (125 g) string beans (optional)
1½ onions
3 scallion stalks
5 garlic cloves
1 thyme stalk
½ chopped tomato

Method

Either grate coconuts or cut into small cubes and run through a blender with approximately one cup (250 milliliters) of water added. Strain and squeeze milk extract from the grated coconut. Place a third of this milk into a saucepan and boil until oily. Add beans and boil for 15 minutes, then add carrots and potatoes long enough to parboil them. Next, add half a chopped onion, one scallion stalk, and two chopped garlic cloves and boil for another five minutes. Add thyme stalk for the last three minutes, then remove the twig. Place the second third of the coconut milk extract in another saucepan and boil until it turns to oil. Add spinach and a third of the remaining chopped onion with chopped tomatoes and steam over low heat for 10 minutes. Put the remaining third of the coconut milk extract in a third saucepan and boil until it turns to oil again, then add the rest of the onion, garlic, and scallion stalk. Steam for approximately five minutes, then add ackee and steam for another six to seven minutes. Serve these together with any type of rice or rice and peas. As garnish (and a good food combination), serve with slices of tomatoes and shredded raw carrots and cabbage.

Note: Ackee is the national fruit of Jamaica. When cooked, ackee has the consistency of scrambled eggs. Eating underripe ackee or the pink portion of ripe ackee can cause vomiting or, in extreme cases, even death. It's advisable to skip ackee entirely in this dish.

Curried Goat ❧

Makes six servings.

2 lb (1 kg) goat meat
juice of 1 lime
1 tbsp (15 mL) salt
1 tbsp (15 mL) black pepper
1 scotch bonnet pepper
½ tsp (2 mL) thyme
½ tsp (2 mL) allspice
3 tbsp (45 mL) curry powder
2 whole scallions
1 onion
3 garlic cloves
¼ cup (65 mL) vegetable oil
3 tomatoes
7 cups (1¾ L) water

Method

Wash meat and rub it all over with half the lime juice. Put in large bowl, add salt, black pepper, scotch bonnet pepper, thyme, allspice, curry powder, scallions, onion, and garlic. Leave to marinate in refrigerator for at least two hours. Heat oil in a large skillet over medium heat until very hot. Add meat, reserving the seasoning mixture, and cook until golden brown—approximately six minutes. Add seasoning and cook, stirring for two minutes. Add tomatoes and cook for another three minutes. Add water and bring to a boil. Reduce heat to low, cover skillet, and cook until tender (about another two hours). Stir in remaining lime juice and serve with a chutney, fried plantain, and white rice.

Desi's Rum Punch

Ingredients

1 fluid oz (30 mL) fresh lime juice
2 fluid oz (60 mL) simple syrup
1 fluid oz (30 mL) white Jamaican rum
2 fluid oz (60 mL) amber Jamaican rum
ice

Method

Blend and serve in a rock-crystal glass. Add a tiny drop of bitters. Garnish with lime slice.

Eating and drinking are two pastimes dear to the hearts of Jamaicans and are frequently depicted in the colorful wall art of the island.

Pan-Seared Grouper ❧

Makes six servings.

Ingredients

2 lb (1 kg) grouper fillets
1 tbsp (15 mL) olive oil
juice of 1 lemon
1 tbsp (15 mL) vinegar
1 tsp (5 mL) Dijon mustard
1 tbsp (15 mL) honey
¼ cup (65 mL) chopped green onions
1 tsp (2 mL) ground ginger

Method

Rinse grouper under cold water and pat dry. In a shallow bowl mix olive oil, lemon juice, vinegar, mustard, honey, green onions, and ginger. Heat a nonstick skillet over medium heat. Dip grouper fillets in marinade to coat both sides and place in skillet. Cook for two to three minutes on each side. Pour remaining marinade into skillet. Reduce heat and simmer for two to three minutes or until fish flakes easily with a fork.

Carrot Ginger Sauce ❧

Makes six servings.

Ingredients

1½ lb (750 g) carrots
2 tbsp (30 mL) ginger, peeled and grated finely
1 small onion
1 tbsp (15 mL) butter
1 tbsp (15 mL) soy sauce
3 tbsp (45 mL) olive oil

Method

Cook carrots and onion on stove until tender. In a blender make a smooth puree of the carrot, onion, and ginger. Combine puree, soy sauce, and butter in a saucepan. Bring to a boil and simmer for seven to 10 minutes. Whisk olive oil into sauce in a slow stream.

Mashed Sweet Potatoes ❧

Makes eight servings.

Ingredients

8 medium sweet potatoes (about 4 lb/2 kg)
2 tsp (10 mL) salt
2 tbsp (30 mL) brown sugar
½ tsp (2 mL) salt
¼ tsp (1 mL) white pepper
½ tsp (2 mL) cinnamon
¼ tsp (1 mL) fresh ground nutmeg
¼ cup (65 mL) cream
4 tbsp (60 mL) butter

Method

Peel sweet potatoes and cut into quarters. Cut each quarter in half again. Place in a pot and cover with cold water. Add all but half a teaspoon of the salt and one tablespoon (15 milliliters) of the brown sugar. Bring to a boil, reduce heat, and simmer for about 15 minutes until very tender. Potatoes should mash easily when pressed with a fork. Drain potatoes and return to pan over very low heat. Return to burner until all moisture has evaporated (about two minutes). Remove from heat. Mash until very smooth. Combine the rest of the salt with the pepper, cinnamon, the remaining sugar, and nutmeg in a small bowl, then stir in the potatoes. Place cream and butter in a saucepan. Heat until butter melts. Stir into potatoes and serve.

Creamed Callaloo ❧

Makes four servings.

Ingredients

2 cups (500 mL) water
1 lb (500 g) fresh callaloo (washed, with stems removed)
2 tsp (10 mL) butter
2 tbsp (30 mL) all-purpose flour
2 cups (500 mL) coconut milk
dash of white pepper to taste
dash of fresh ground nutmeg to taste

Method

Blanch the callaloo for two minutes in hot water, drain well, and set aside. Melt butter in a small saucepan, stir in flour, and cook over medium-low heat for one minute, stirring constantly. Using a wire whisk, stir in coconut milk and bring to a boil. Whisk for one to two minutes or until mixture thickens. Stir in pepper and callaloo into sauce. After a few minutes, spoon into serving bowl and sprinkle lightly with nutmeg. Garnish as desired.

Jamaican Curried Mutton ❧

Makes six to eight servings.

Ingredients

2 lb (1 kg) shoulder of mutton (cut in small pieces)
2 tsp (10 mL) Jamaican curry powder (more if desired)
2 tbsp (30 mL) vegetable oil
2 sliced medium onions
2 chopped scotch bonnet peppers (seeds removed)
2 cups (500 mL) hot water
1 cup (250 mL) diced potatoes

Method

Season meat with salt, pepper, onion, and curry powder and allow to stand for an hour. Heat vegetable oil in a skillet, then add meat with seasoning. Cover and allow to cook in hot oil for about 20 minutes, stirring occasionally. Add water and potatoes, cover tightly, and cook on low heat until meat is tender and gravy is thickened. Add more water if necessary. Serve hot over cooked rice.

Guests from Chris Blackwell's The Caves on the cliffs of Negril often drop by this pub for a drink and a chat.

Pumpkin Rice ❧

Makes four servings.

Ingredients

1½ lb (750 g) rice
4 cups (1 L) broth
1 lb (500 g) pumpkin
4 tsp (20 mL) olive oil
1 tsp (5 mL) butter
1 small onion
salt and pepper to taste

Method

In a large saucepan place the cubed pumpkin in half the oil with half the butter and let it soften, then add all but one cup (250 mL) of the broth and a bit of the salt and pepper. Cook for about 10 minutes, bringing the mix to a simmer without actually reaching a rolling boil. In another saucepan sauté the chopped onion with the remaining oil and butter, then add the rice and stir for a couple of minutes. Add the pumpkin and a half cup (125 mL) of the hot broth, keeping it simmering while stirring constantly. Then add the last half cup of the broth as the rice dries out, stirring often to keep the mix from sticking and adding water if necessary. When the rice is done, add some more butter and serve hot.

Roasted Plantain and Pumpkin Soup &

Makes 10 servings.

Ingredients

2 ripe plantains (remove ends but keep skin intact)
4 tbsp (60 mL) butter
2 tbsp (30 mL) olive oil
2 diced shallots
6 diced scallions (leave bit of green ends)
2 diced garlic cloves
1 small diced piece of scotch bonnet pepper (or jalapeño pepper) with seeds removed
2 sprigs fresh thyme, or 2 tbsp (30 mL) dried thyme
2 tsp (10 mL) ground coriander
2 tsp (10 mL) ground cumin
2½ lb (1¼ kg) peeled, seeded, and coarsely chopped Caribbean pumpkin
8 cups (2 L) vegetable stock
salt and pepper to taste
garnish of roasted pumpkin seeds and chopped fresh cilantro or chives

Method

Roast ripe plantains in 400° F (200° C) oven on greased sheet until skins turn black and start to burst. Remove from oven, let cool, and peel skins away from fruit. In a tall soup pot heat butter and olive oil until hot. Add shallots, scallion, garlic, scotch bonnet pepper (if desired), thyme, coriander, and cumin. Sauté until shallots are soft. Add diced pumpkin to soup pot, stir, and sauté until pumpkin starts to brown slightly. Add vegetable stock and simmer until pumpkin is soft. Taste for seasoning and add salt and pepper as needed. Let cool slightly. Cut plantain into coarse portions and add to soup. Put everything through a blender until thick and smooth. (Be very careful to hold lid of blender down if the soup is still hot.) If soup is too thick, add a bit of hot vegetable stock to thin. Reheat soup when ready to serve. Ladle into serving bowls and garnish top with roasted pumpkin seeds and chopped fresh cilantro or chives. A spoonful of sour cream is a great garnish, as well.

Note: Regular pumpkin can be substituted for Caribbean pumpkin.

Heineken might be a Dutch beer, but in Jamaica its popularity is second only to the island's very own Red Stripe.

John P. and Adelaide Marquand (the author's wife) promote the United China Relief Writers' Committee. Marquand donated royalties from his Mr. Moto detective series to the campaign, for which he worked as chairman.

John P. Marquand
Adrift with Mr. Moto in Beijing

When I arrive in Beijing, the city once known in English as Peiping or Peking, every-thing is cloaked in white haze, the barely breathable air a dry-ice poison of pollution and construction dust. I need sleep, but I'm eager to get my first look at the Chinese capital that inspired the work of American writer John Phillips Marquand, among others.

"Is so sorry-la," a slender-hipped young woman with mysterious eyes, singsong tones, and glossy poker-black hair says, apologizing for nearly knocking my eye out with an umbrella. Her hand touches her mandarin collar as she twirls her parasol confidently. *Is so sorry…* I recognize her words and imagine that even though her eyes give the impression she appears thoroughly modern, she's entirely untouched by the outside world. Oddly I clutch *Mr. Moto Is So Sorry*, the Marquand spy thriller partially set in mid-1930s Beijing. I must have misheard her, I think, as I drink in the city's seething scene.

China's population is a staggering 1.3 billion; Beijing's 13.8 million. The crowd on the street is thick, yet I feel alone, a state acutely alien to me since I'm usually accompanied by a husband of almost 20 years who carries my cameras, allows me to try out my ideas on him, and keeps loneliness at bay while I'm globetrotting. This time I'm traveling solo, vaguely hoping my husband will get his life in order. He's been floundering, attempting to raise money for penny stocks. Frankly, though I didn't resent helping him through a rough patch some time ago, his futile road of broken dreams has lasted five years, and "loans" from me now tally too much to justify. His constant state of debt has become a black hole. Worse, his blatant unhappiness at his financial state has drowned his once-free spirit. Fervently part of me still hopes he can get himself and our relationship back on track, even though I know I've risked what's left of a formerly good marriage by refusing to lend him more cash and by going off on my own. Still, I do miss his companionship and I don't agree with Rudyard Kipling's adage: "He travels better who travels alone."

Disoriented by the din from the vehicle traffic beside the continual push of pedestrians that throng Wangfujing, Beijing's commercial street, I drift aimlessly. Cars, mostly Siroccos, China's and Ford's joint-venture automobile, screech and honk, their progress as bipolar as the crush of sidewalk strollers. At the beginning of my journey I had no idea just how much frustration would lie ahead in this megalopolis, one of the 10 biggest in the world, where English speakers are as scarce as the signs of Beijing's heritage.

I've marked a page in *Mr. Moto Is So Sorry* and stop on the busy sidewalk to read it again, thumbing through the slim spy novel to find it. My action is perilous, like that of a fish struggling against the direction of its school. I stand my ground and read: "He did not know the dramatic intricacies of Peiping, where walls and gates divided the whole area into quarters like armed camps and where the houses themselves and parts of houses stood behind more walls, making Peiping the most private, remote, and mysterious city in the world." And this, a passage that intrigues me even more: "Out in this country, the way things are today, anything can happen, anything does happen. If a pink elephant walked in here now, I wouldn't turn a hair. I would only say it's China. Opium smuggling, gun running, bribery, warlords, bandits, spies—they're all outside the window there. The sky's the limit these days."

For more than a century Western fiction authors have used China, the "Yellow Peril," as a source of villains, one of the more infamous being Sax Rohmer's Fu Manchu. With the end of the Cold War, though, America has found other bad guys in the Russian mafia, home-grown white supremacists, and Osama bin Laden and the Islamic fundamentalist terrorists of Al-Qaeda, leaving sinister, stereotypical Orientals to out-of-print pulp novels and long-ago black-and-white films.

In *Thank You, Mr. Moto*, Marquand, through his American protagonist, describes an expatriate's time in Beijing. It's the colonial life of pink gin, Noël Coward–style smoking jackets, and coolies waiting in the wings to do one's bidding. I crave the exotic, something to take my mind off my domestic plight, and envy those decadent days when Beijing was a romantic's outpost rife with guilty pleasures. In my mind's eye I envision a stooped Chinese, spindly mustache twitching as he speaks Confucian wisdom that will clarify my life. I picture a sensual photograph of taxi girls in cheongsams posing for men in white linen suits. I conjure

In the
New China
tourism, both
by Chinese them-
selves and foreign-
ers, has increased
dramatically from
John P. Marquand's
days in the 1930s.
Sites such as this
bell at X'ian are
on many people's
list of things
to see.

the sight and sound of brocade-clad mandarin daughters playing lutes beside a lotus-lilied court-yard in the Forbidden City. A pedicab ride away, sinuous back alleys wend their way to villages under bright white stars in lush countryside. My nostrils twitch at the imaginary scent of paddy fields left to decay. Marquand decided on his first China trip that he had something of the Orient within him: the Chinese love of solitude, mystery, order, and especially *feng shui*, or balance. My personal desire is to steady my state of mind by steeping it in the images from Marquand's mid-1930s China.

Around a corner, away from the fray, I come upon a perpendicular street with a bicycle lane. There, basket bicycles and rickshaws slide by, the serene, wheeling rhythm a calming counterpoint to the incessant automobile traffic. In that serendipitous split second I feel the past: the oncoming vehicles stop, the bicycles turn, and the only sounds are the groans of old pedals, the *ding-ding-ding* of bells. The bicycles and handful of rickshaws are pollution-free and quiet. The swish of the few human-powered vehicles in the special lane is my only indica-tion that this modern metropolis is still the Peiping Marquand knew.

The rickshaws are dilapidated, their frames and drivers as thin and delicate as the limbs of daddy longleg spiders. Their special lane is a legacy from the era before Mao Zedong's death. Perhaps acting as a harbinger of the end of Mao's reign, the massive Tangshan earthquake struck in July 1976, claiming over a quarter of a million lives. In September of that year Chairman Mao finally succumbed to old age and was embalmed by China's scientists, his frail form put on display in a glass case in a mausoleum beside Tiananmen Square. Despite refrig-eration, Mao's corpse has deteriorated. Even one of his ears has fallen off, perhaps a further signal that China has moved on.

I remember thinking: *Tomorrow, if I can pry my jet-lagged self from my elegant haven of a room on the Horizon Club floor at the Kerry Centre Shangri-La, I'll chase down a souvenir of China's political father. I'll purchase Chairman Mao's Red Book and a curiosity wristwatch decorated with his deceptively avuncular, round-faced likeness.*

It was almost seven decades ago and before China embraced communism when Marquand, the restless New Englander, first set eyes on Beijing. The year was 1934, just months before he divorced his first wife of 13 years. As I, too, have done in my own fragile situation, Marquand traveled to flee a troubled home life and an estranged spouse. Sent to China by *The Saturday Evening Post* with the purpose of broadening his experience and the magazine's readership, he escaped the ensuing disappointment of a failing relationship by losing himself in a strikingly different locale while searching for subject matter.

On first impression I find that Beijing's charm eludes me. Not only am I unable to locate

This Chinese woodblock depicting a traditional courtroom trial gives us an idea of what the legal procedure was like in the time of Judge Dee.

Marquand's exotic images, but I'm having a problem relating to *my* subject matter. Truthfully, other than Marquand's penned portrait of old China, much of the writer's Mr. Moto series disappoints me. With that discomforting thought I realize I haven't been paying attention to my tourist map and am now lost in a mob of shoppers.

Halting, I survey my surroundings: girls in red sunglasses; young women and couples, always linked arm in arm or holding hands; an old man, yawning like a toothless tiger, dragging a child through the swarm. I reflect that the sexless, military-style blue-and-green garb of 20 years ago has been supplanted by capitalist chi-chi: Benetton, jeans west, Paul & Shark, Ports, Burberry, even Moschino and Ungaro, the fabrics likely woven near X'ian on the Silk Road where Robert Van Gulik's translation of the *Celebrated Cases of Judge Dee (Dee Goong An): An Authentic Eighteenth-Century Chinese Detective Novel* takes place. This fascinating account of one of feudalism's finest chronicles three renowned cases of a historical Tang dynasty district magistrate, showing the dual role in the seventh century of judge and detective responsible for peacekeeping and discovering, capturing, and punishing criminals. Van Gulik's cross-cultural collaboration with a Chinese tradition of crime and punishment was translated on the run in China's interior. After the Japanese invaded China in the 1930s, the diplomat and scholar fled Beijing. His subject captured his imagination, and in the late 1950s and 1960s while serving the Netherlands in Asian diplomatic missions, the Dutchman brought his fair-minded and quick-witted jurist and Old China to the world in dozens of new and still-beloved mysteries. His Perry Mason–style modus operandi takes place in the courtroom.

X'ian, too, along with an already soulless early 1980s Beijing with its restrictive political system, is Florida mystery writer Carl Hiaasen's setting in collaboration with the late Bill Montalbano for *A Death in China.* Hiaasen's fantastical wildness is missing from the novel, though his premise of Emperor Qin Shi Huangdi's quest for immortality is beguiling. Emperor Qin, the Son of Heaven, died in 210 B.C. In accordance with custom he had his ministers, family members, slaves, and horses buried with him. It was he who ordered construction of the Great Wall. The discovery of his tomb, which covers nearly 22 square miles, and his slightly larger-than-life terra-cotta army, some of whom sport mustaches and who wear their hair in elaborate topknots, leaves no doubt that at the very least the emperor desired a bodyguard in the afterlife. There are some 8,000 clay warriors, a lucky discovery in 1974 by peasants digging a well. The amazing all-male pottery soldiers wear flowing knee-length robes, breeches, and turned-round lapels, though their positions, body armor, uniforms, and faces are different. Emperor Qin left no record of the existence of his clay army and it remains an enigma. The protagonist of Hiaasen's novel, Tom Stratton, sets the scene by journeying to Beijing and then X'ian in an attempt to lay the past to rest and get on with life.

Stratton's mission reminds me that I must get on with my day and visit the Forbidden City before its intricate gates are closed. I had my destination written down in the stick-figure squiggles of Chinese by the hotel concierge, and I show this card to two young women, simultaneously asking directions to the Forbidden City. I'm met with blank stares. Not even a "Sorry-la."

I press on. The fashionable gear that parades by has likely been cut and sewn in a factory near Shanghai. These women may be wearing haute couture "Made in China" knockoffs, but at least my earlier encounter with the "so sorry-la" stroller's *chinois* elegance is right out of a Mr. Moto paperback. Marquand's six-book series, conceived in 1935 and initially abandoned in 1942 (a final novel, *Right You Are, Mr. Moto,* appeared in 1957) when World War II forced him to scrap the figure as a hero, became the basis for the popular motion pictures starring the bug-eyed, soft-spoken Peter Lorre as the gold-toothed, slyly mild-mannered Japanese secret agent. In *Mr. Moto Is So Sorry,* the title character exemplifies for readers the complexities of Asian culture. Moto has no problem accepting a political murder but apologies to an American friend as he is "so sorry" that the would-be killer, a Japanese military officer, was rude to his intended victim.

By now Beijing is oppressively hot and I'm footsore. An unreasonable late-autumn sun has penetrated the smog. I stop a man attired in a business suit. With a polite "Excuse me, sir," I dangle my Chinese message before his eyes and point to my destination circled on the tourist map. Then I ask in English, "Please, which way is the Forbidden City?" He walks on as if I'm invisible. Could it be that so few Chinese outside my hotel with its 24-hour butler service, business-oriented club lounge with hors d'oeuvres, bar service, classical music, library, and charming staff speak or understand even a smidgen of English? I vaguely remember that most tourists see China on a guided tour.

I don't really care that I'm lost. Marquand's life was varied and adventurous and I'm following his lead. The author was an artillery commander in World War I, a war correspondent, an advertising copywriter, a Far East buff, a top-secret intelligence consultant on biological warfare during World War II, and a judge for 15 years with Book-of-the-Month Club.

Reflecting on Marquand's career, I note that his Mr. Moto series was immensely popular with middle-class America, but literary types sniggered, both because of the genre and because the books were penned serially for magazines (all with *The Saturday Evening Post* except for *Last Laugh, Mr. Moto*, which was done for *Collier's*). Historically correct, though, the action of *Mr. Moto Is So Sorry* occurs when northern China was in turmoil, with only feuding warlords standing between the invading Japanese Imperial Army and Beijing.

Mr. Moto took his first bow in *The Saturday Evening Post*'s serialized "No Hero" (retitled in book form as *Your Turn, Mr. Moto*), along with the subsequent novels' typical central figure, a thirtyish American with a shady past and low self-esteem. The Yank meets a corrupt foreigner, usually British, in an exotic locale and is thrust by this sinister figure into harm's way. The American is often at the end of his rope and, as was the case with Marquand, has an unsettled personal life. The formula includes a liberated and beautiful woman whom the jaded American distrusts, as the twice-divorced Marquand would, but later falls head over heels for, ultimately rediscovering his worth. Meanwhile, the indefatigable Mr. Moto comes to the rescue.

Mr. Moto Is So Sorry is set in the same period as *Thank You, Mr. Moto*, and both books have nearly identical characters. Still, Marquand's lyrical words resonate. "It was a city of the imagination, a city of the spirit falling into a dreamlike ruin; falling into memories as fantastic as the figures on a Chinese scroll; always changing but never changed," he writes in *Mr. Moto Is So Sorry*, and in my mind I hear the clatter of metal rickshaw wheels thin against the stone, the slap of tired feet as bony coolies pull wealthy foreigners or Russian agents through Beijing's gas-lit streets.

Now I wish I'd learned a few traveler's phrases in Mandarin, having given up asking directions to the Forbidden Palace. Bored by the repetition of storefronts and streets, I find myself back

The bicycle was *the* mode of transportation during Mao Zedong's regime.

on bustling Wangfujing where shopping is everything. The store windows and their wares wink seductively. The airline staff on my long flight from Canada chattered incessantly about the incredible deals, so I surrender and search out the location of a shopping tip one of the flight attendants gave me. For once I don't get lost. A short street marked Goldfish Lane near the opulent Palace Hotel reveals the Austrian ladies' shop Wolford. I allow myself to be enticed by European bodysuits and stockings, sold by but not made by Chinese.

Back on the busy sidewalk, I detect a guttural sound beside me and turn. A man in Adidas sneakers and garden-green polyester trousers clears his throat, then spits, enacting an ancient Chinese custom. Later, during the outbreak of severe acute respiratory syndrome (SARS), the government tries to curb its citizens' habit.

Marquand wasn't just well-known as a mystery writer. He's considered the mid-20th century's most successful novelist of manners, netting a Pulitzer prize for his satirical novel, *The Late John Apley*. Marquand continually strived for critical acclaim and was paid millions of dollars during the 1950s, the last decade of his life. A Harvard graduate, he enjoyed the fruits of his success but at the end of his life found himself "risen from the ranks" to discover in "the upper echelons an emptiness that made the game hardly worth the candle."

The game hardly worth the candle. For the next few days I jostle with the crowds in the vehicle-packed streets but see no mystery in this curious Communist hive of commercial capitalism. The scenes—even the *hutongs*, the narrow Chinese lanes of Marquand's experience—evade me, and when I discover them around Shichahai, they're strewn with garbage and sullen, glassy-eyed hawkers of cheap household goods. Ungainly tour buses jam the entrance. China's culture was once protected from foreign aggression by the Great Wall and from foreign influence by the 1968 Cultural Revolution. In fact, until 1984 Special Economic Zones virtually iron-curtained China from the West.

I vow not to waste any more time on shopping, newly determined to seek out the Forbidden City. This time I ask a hotel staffer to write my destination in Chinese and then inform a cabdriver verbally. I sit in the taxi's back seat on white toweling. We pass through the diplomatic district, and I see that the American embassy is barricaded from public access. Chinese soldiers in worsted green uniforms stand red-faced in the heat. The driver and I have our own barrier—language. Bored by the traffic and enforced silence, I gaze idly at the rearview mirror. My brain is working overtime, and I imagine that the driver's bulbous eyes belong to Peter Lorre. Mr. Moto is my chauffeur!

Finally we arrive at the Forbidden City. While there I enjoy actor Roger Moore's audio guide in English. His British-accented words entertain, and though he's merely a voice on a tape, I feel connected to my world once again. Moore, or James Bond, as I begin to see him as, is the first native English speaker I've heard since my flight from Canada. The grounds of what is officially known as the Imperial Palace Museum sing with the splash of fountains. Moore tells me there are no less than 9,999 rooms. The outside of the buildings are red, green, and gold gilt decorated with drawings of playful kittens, flowers, and swans. The ceramic rooflines swoop up at the edges charmingly and are embellished with cocks and mythic creatures. The stone floors are cool even in the midday swelter. Delicate willows, leafy bamboo, and dark firs shade the narrow paths. A group of schoolchildren are on an outing, and they wave little red flags and sing a patriotic song, eyes shining. I cross a small bridge, and Moore informs me suavely that the Fish Bridge was built during the reign of Emperor Qianlong. Two ancient philosophers conceived of the idea while they conversed over the fish swimming in the pond. The bridge was purposefully erected close to the surface of the water to make fish watching and the ensuing talk that goes with such enjoyable pastimes conducive. Inscribed in a stone archway nearby are poems written by the emperor. The stagnant water beneath the bridge is spored with mold, and underneath fat orange carp drowse.

The curvy paths are tight with visiting Chinese. Matrons sporting canvas sun hats and practical walking shoes snap photos of their husbands who pose unsmiling beside phosphorous-green waterways. Other couples sit knee to knee on benches, sharing afternoon snacks purchased in a kiosk at a crook in the paths. With lightning speed and skill they devour instant noodles with disposable chopsticks. When the noodles are gone, they slurp soup directly from Styrofoam bowls. A masked woman sweeps, raising a cloud of dust with a worn corn-silk broom. A flock of sparrows scatter, changing course.

I need to use the toilet and follow the signs to the public WC. When I enter the building, the stench of urine overwhelms me. I find a cubicle and squat over a hole in the ceramic floor, taking an odd traveler's pleasure in the fact that it's an Asian loo.

Before James Bond can finish his illuminating tour, loudspeakers scratch and screech with an announcement I can't understand. Noticing that the Chinese matrons and schoolchildren have disappeared, I realize the Forbidden City is closing and exit past the undulating glass-tiled rooflines of the pagodas at the east gate. The structures are a shimmer of watery hues in the late-afternoon sunlight. In the parking lot a flurry of bothersome salesmen push plastic butterflies and sun-bleached postcards at me. Still, I'm satisfied with my visit. The Forbidden City couldn't have changed much since Marquand's time, and I've been regaled by a familiar voice in the language I understand. Although it's a museum and thus for show, for a few hours I had the China I crave.

The next morning I rise early to visit Tiananmen Square. I walk the vast concrete desert of Mao's creation and unsuccessfully attempt to cross the maxi-laned highway that rings it. Seeing no break in the traffic, I retreat like a dog with its tail between its legs, gawking at the various landmarks: Qianmen (Front Gate), Tiananmen (Gate of Heavenly Peace), the History Museum and Museum of the Revolution, the Mao Mausoleum, the Monument to the People's Heroes. While I eye the nonstop morning traffic a military helicopter swoops noisily overhead. Thanks to the relentless rush hour, I miss the sunrise flag-raising ceremony performed by a troop of People's Liberation Army soldiers drilled to march at exactly 108 paces per minute. Unable to cross the road, I fail to spot the entrance to an underground city built 30 years before the revolution in case of a third world war.

Over the next week I take endless cab rides to see more sites. The pollution is punishing. I begin to feel as if I'm a patron in a silent movie theater. Because of my inability to speak Mandarin, there can be no verbal communication with the people I pass. I become a mute voyeur to Beijing's many moods. I stand at the edge of Taoranting Park by the lovely sewage canal and admire early risers practicing their crack-of-dawn tai chi exercises, their slow-motion gestures suiting that sleepy time of morning. I ramble through the Heavenly Temple, the New Summer Palace, the Old Summer Palace, the Drum Tower, and the Bell Tower and have the tickets to prove it. I bargain in Silk Alley and at the Hongqiao Market for pearls, linens, and Chinese clothes. Commerce is universal, and it feeds my need for a connection with other human beings. I brave the fetid concrete darkness of Yu Ding Qiao, the bird and animal market, where I gape at parrots and peacocks, dogs and cats, writhing snakes and chattering monkeys for sale. When I return from that heartless place, Beijing seems to me to symbolize pure predatory capitalism. I even wonder if anyone really cares about liberty and democracy as did the demonstrators who were cut down by army tanks in Tiananmen Square in 1989. Ideology appears to have been forsaken for the allure of quick profits.

By now my lovely hotel room could be mistaken for a department store. Italian lingerie, Austrian stockings, and Chinese silk scarves and pajamas are heaped in my suitcase, drape chairs, and spill out of every closet and drawer. I try to refrain from shopping but each of my outings takes a full day. The distances in Beijing are huge, the traffic a tenacious, eternal snarl, and whatever cabbie I get seems to find the longest way to get anywhere. Perhaps it's because the farther the drivers go, the more cash they make. Or maybe I'm paranoid and the drivers are lost, too. Often, a taxi lets me off at the wrong destination and then I have to hail a new cab and show my destination card again.

The strip on the back of my credit card with my signature is obliterated by too much use,

One wonders what Zhou Enlai and Mao Zedong would have thought of the New China and its zeal for Communist Capitalism. Shopping has become a national pastime.

my limit thoroughly spent by the enticements of the Japanese department stores and the draw of famous-name fashions sold cheaper than at home. Arms exhausted from dragging packages back to the hotel, my Chinese money supply for cab fare finished, I can no longer close my suitcase. I've given up hoping that anyone I encounter will speak more than a few words of English. Instead I talk to myself, and know I'm totally alone.

Time crawls like a jail sentence. I'm bored by Beijing, and Marquand's China simply doesn't exist except in the ticketed tourist sites. Despondent about my difficult marital situation in Canada, I've given up on Marquand's vision of Beijing as a means of emotional release. Instead, perhaps brainlessly, I've used shopping as a panacea. I ask for a cash advance on my credit card, something I never do, to purchase more silk scarves at the market. When I return to the hotel and look carefully at them, I spy tiny labels marked 100 percent polyamide. The scarves aren't what they seem to be, like a lot of China. I make another silent pact to stop shopping.

I can't even manage eating Chinese. In Hiaasen's *A Death in China* I came across the phrase "death by duck." Apparently the richness of Peking duck can trigger a heart attack, but there's no possibility of death by duck for me. The local menus are impossible to decipher, there are no pictures of the various offerings to point to, and I'm turned back from the kitchen door. With dishes written down in Chinese by the bemused and cheerful concierge, I try to get the food I crave—chicken, prawns, dumplings, even fried rice—but that backfires, too. I'm served tripe and chicken feet.

Construction dust from Beijing's Olympic building boom eclipses the sky. Each morning is a whiteout. Evenings, alone with a drink in my hand, I watch multihued sunsets reflected in the chrome-and-glass buildings next door. In my mirror to nature's version of *The Picture of Dorian Gray*, the sun is a plunging ball cloaked in a plume of silver. A hotel staff member who grew up in Beijing tells me she's never seen a star. I'm disheartened and desperate to speak in full sentences to someone, to be understood on more than a tourist's level. I've failed miserably. Marquand's bid for solitude has escaped me and his China has eluded me. I doubt it exists, though sometimes I daydream I'm in his "city of the imagination, a city of the spirit falling into a dreamlike ruin; falling into memories as fantastic as the figures on a Chinese scroll." And then my husband invades my reverie, making me less lonely for a split second until he admits his transgressions. I telephone him, but he doesn't answer.

I take to wandering my neighborhood, hardly speaking anymore. It's a pointless exercise in frustration. I spy a sex shop, head down neon-lit concrete stairs, and go in through a small plain door. A clean-cut lad in glasses and a stained lab coat offers me X-rated Japanese-language DVDs for a few American dollars each. Commerce is the only language I understand. I decline and study the merchandise kept under glass. The fluorescent lights and clinical atmosphere belie the dust balls that cuddle with the condoms and rubber vibrator sleeves. I wonder if I've stumbled into the Twilight Zone. For no known reason, other than that I'm in Beijing, I purchase the oddest items: a feather tickler made of horsehair, and tiny latex condoms studded with pink plastic knobs. They're coated in dust. When I return to the hotel, I toss them into the garbage.

Attempting to prevent further credit-card debt, I stay in the hotel. It's the height of National China Week, and the already busy streets are impossibly thronged, making walking a hazard and turning touring into queuing. I'm amazed there can be even more people. Worse, the trains and planes are full, the hotels are overbooked, and I've missed my chance to leave Beijing for the countryside and what I now believe must be the real China.

The next day I find myself in the sex-shop alley again, lured by a sign in English that says: HEALING MASSAGE. THIS PROFESSIONAL ESTABLISHMENT RUN BY THE BLIND MAN. I peek through the doorway and figure the place looks reputable. The price for a massage is a quarter of what my hotel health club charges. I withdraw more funds against my American Express card on the pretext that a massage will soothe my nerves.

When I fork over a ridiculously small amount of Chinese money to a woman at the entrance, she gives me a ticket and leads me into a softly lit room containing two massage beds draped in dreary floral polyester. Motioning toward one bed, the woman hands me a

China has one of the fastest-growing economies in the world, and this baby will likely reap the benefits of increasing prosperity as he gets older.

sheet, then closes the door behind her. I disrobe, cover myself with the sheet, and lie on the table. When the door swings open, I hear a gasp and open my eyes. The masseuse gestures wildly for me to put on my clothes. The door slams shut. When she returns, she puts the sheet over my street clothes and begins to knead, slap, and prod me. She finishes by snapping my toes and fingers through the cloth. As I leave, I apologize again, repeating the words I heard on my first day in Beijing: "Sorry-la." I see by the woman's expression that she doesn't understand my pidgin English.

Back in the hotel, my already inflamed sinuses even more aggravated by the relentless city pollution, I read voraciously, hardly leaving the confines of my lovely room. Maybe this is the expat life, I muse unhappily. There's a hotel butler and my every wish is his command. But life feels empty, and I know I'm marking time as I immerse myself in *The Late John Marquand*, Stephen Birmingham's biography of the writer. I almost smile when I read that in response to fan mail Marquand composed a form letter that began: "Writing is a lonely occupation..." On another occasion he said that "a writer should never marry," yet his biographer notes that the creator of Mr. Moto never enjoyed the enforced bachelorhood between his two marriages and spent a lot of his time visiting friends.

I wish I were home with my unhappy husband—anywhere, in fact, but under Beijing's deadly alabaster sky. I continue to read, then stare at Marquand's photo, wondering how he managed, why he wasn't lonely. Suddenly my reading glasses break in half. Tape is useless, and I can't imagine the interminable plane ride home without them. I call the concierge, who informs me there's a whole floor dedicated to reading glasses at Sogo, Beijing's Japanese department store. At Sogo I take the escalator to the fifth floor where locked cases make the merchandise untouchable. There are lots of glasses: Christian Dior, Armani, Silhouette, and more. Every color. Every style.

I begin a pantomime with a newspaper and my broken glasses in hand. The young salesman seems bored as he stands silently behind the Armani case. I fish out my note. He reads it and points to another case. I follow his direction. The other case is guarded by a young woman. I repeat my request, mimicking reading, showing my broken spectacles, and proffering the concierge's explanatory note. The woman doesn't open the case. She just gazes vacantly at me. I stare back and continue my sad theatricals. Finally I get it. There are no lenses in the frames. I need a prescription. The escalator whisks me downstairs. Vaguely I remember an optometrist and glasses boutique in a shopping center a mere block away.

The sign reads EYES ON AMERICA. I enter, approach a saleswoman, and do my now-familiar pantomime. When she doesn't respond, I lose my temper. "All I want is a pair of fucking reading glasses!" I shout. The clerk doesn't even blink. I repeat my incredible rudeness but only get the same lack of reaction. Desperate, I take the girl by the arm and lead her to a telephone next to the cash register. I dial my hotel's concierge, and when he answers, I'm close to tears when I ask him to speak for me. The clerk chatters to him, and I'm duly taken care of. Seconds later an optometrist appears. I'm tested and fitted for reading glasses. They're Armani and cost a mint, but they're mine.

On my last day in Beijing I strike up an instant friendship with a woman who works in my hotel. Mei Ling is Malaysian and speaks perfect English. She suggests we have dinner at a Thai restaurant called the Pink Loft. We amble down a narrow street lit by neon Chinese characters, sometimes holding hands as women or even men friends do in the Far East. The restaurant is on Sanlitun, the Chinese capital's hip/sleazy bar street, and when we get there we dine on the establishment's balcony, which is strewn with fuchsia and purple silk pillows.

Mei Ling orders chicken wrapped in pandan leaves with sautéed lotus-blossom greens for both of us after the waiter brings her a Gibley's gin and tonic and me a Stollie and soda. I'm happy for her company. Although it's my final day in Beijing and our first outing, Mei Ling and I are connected by language and by heart. We share secrets, and she assures me with Asian élan and wisdom that "The risks we take are calculated. So that's okay." Later she says, "We are on the right track."

After dinner and more drinks, we take a stroll, continuing our conversation. I tell her my innermost thoughts about my husband and admit that I'm afraid of being alone. She tells me, "When one door closes, another opens." When we come to a curb, I hesitate, reluctant to wade into the beep and blare of the traffic. But Mei Ling takes my hand and says, "Do not hesitate. Just do it. Trust me. They will stop for us." We step off the curb, and the cars halt as we thread our way safely through. Smiling at each other, we agree that crossing a street is a little like life. One must trust and take chances. Sometimes the past has to be left behind in order to forge ahead. My frustrations in Beijing have been erased and I've achieved a certain balance or *feng shui*. Like John P. Marquand so long before me, I've discovered what I came for.

Recipes

Kerry Centre Shangri-La (Beijing)

Crispy Shrimp with Wasabi
Beef Roll
Crispy Apple Chicken
Steamed Crab Meat and Bean Curd
Stir-Fried Noodle Country-Style
Kir Royal
Parson's Special

Pudong Shangri-La (Shanghai)

After 8
Yin-Yang White Chocolate Mousse Cake
Crispy Sugar Cookies

Grand Hyatt Shanghai

Capella

The
Lhasa apso,
as illustrated in
this poster from
the market in X'ian,
was the traditional
dog of the royal
Chinese court.

216

Crispy Shrimp with Wasabi ❧

Makes two to three servings.

Ingredients

1 lb (500 g) cleaned king prawns
1½ cups (375 mL) mayonnaise
1 cup (250 mL) condensed milk
6 tbsp (90 mL) wasabi or to taste
1 beaten egg
1 cup (250 mL) flour
1 tsp (5 mL) salt
1 tsp (5 mL) Chinese wine
1 tbsp (15 mL) vegetable oil (for batter)
4 cups (1 L) vegetable oil (for deep-frying)
1 cup (250 mL) water

Method

Mix thoroughly mayonnaise, condensed milk, and wasabi (use according to how spicy you want it) to make sauce. Season the king prawns with salt and Chinese wine, dip them in egg wash and flour, then deep-fry until crispy and golden brown. Remove the prawns, top with mayonnaise sauce, and serve with steamed rice.

Beef Roll ❧

Makes three to four servings.

Ingredients

1 lb (500 g) beef sirloin
2 tsp (10 mL) ginger
½ lb (250 g) mango
3½ oz (100 g) celery
2 tsp (10 mL) dried mushrooms
3½ oz (100 g) Cantonese sausage
½ lb (250 g) broccoli
1½ tsp (7 mL) oyster sauce
1 tsp (5 mL) fine sugar
½ tsp (2 mL) salt
½ tsp (2 mL) chicken powder
2 tsp (10 mL) flour
1½ tbsp (23 mL) chicken stock
1 tbsp (15 mL) vegetable oil (or as necessary)

Method

Slice beef sirloin thin, then chop celery, mushroom, sausage, ginger, and mango into small pieces. Roll the beef with the above ingredients. Steam the broccoli in double boiler and set aside. Pan-fry the beef roll until golden brown. Heat wok with oil and add chicken stock and powder, flour, salt, oyster sauce, and sugar. Put beef roll into the wok for a few minutes but don't overcook. Arrange the beef roll on a plate with broccoli and serve. If desired, accompany with steamed rice.

Crispy Apple Chicken ↝

Makes three to four servings.

Main Ingredients

1 lb (500 g) boneless chicken breasts
¾ lb (375 g) apples
1 tsp (5 mL) salt
1 tsp (5 mL) fine sugar
4 cups (1 L) vegetable oil
3½ oz (100 g) red and green chilies (or to taste)

Lemon Dressing Ingredients

6 tbsp (90 mL) white rice vinegar
¾ cup (185 mL) lime juice
1½ cups (375 mL) water
¾ lb (400 g) sugar (or to taste)
½ tsp (2 mL) salt
1 tsp (5 mL) custard powder

Rice Flour Batter Ingredients

1½ cup (375 mL) rice flour
1 cup (250 mL) cold water
½ tsp (2 mL) salt or to taste
pinch of pepper

Method

Slice the chicken into pieces and marinate with salt, sugar, and chili peppers for 10 minutes. Set aside. Clean apple and cut into thin strips. Mix rice flour batter ingredients thoroughly. Combine lemon dressing ingredients and apple well. Deep-fry the chicken with batter until golden brown. Heat up the lemon dressing, pour onto chicken, and serve.

Note: Regular flour can be substituted for rice flour.

Steamed Crab Meat and Bean Curd ❧

Makes four servings.

Ingredients

1 lb (500 g) soft bean curd
½ lb (250 g) prawns
½ lb (250 g) crab meat
¾ lb (375 g) carrots
7 tbsp (105 mL) flour
2 tsp (10 mL) salt
1 tsp (5 mL) fine sugar
1 tsp (5 mL) chicken powder
1 cup (250 mL) superior stock
cornstarch for thickening

Method

Cut carrots in triangle shapes. Dice crab meat and prawns. Steam the carrots and crab meat until cooked. Blend bean curd with chopped prawns, salt, chicken powder, sugar, and flour thoroughly, forming a paste. Put cooked carrots in a pan and place the bean curd paste in the middle. Steam for 10 minutes. Add superior stock and crab meat and thicken with cornstarch. Pour the sauce onto the bean curd paste and serve.

Note: Soft bean curd is also referred to as silken tofu.

Stir-Fried Noodle Country-Style ❧

Makes four servings.

Ingredients

½ lb (250 g) prawns
½ lb (250 g) pork butt
¾ lb (375 g) bean sprouts
½ lb (250 g) green peppers
½ lb (250 g) red peppers
¼ lb (125 g) onions
¼ lb (125 g) yellow chives
1 lb (500 g) long-life noodles
1½ tsp (7 mL) salt
2 tsp (10 mL) caster sugar
7 tbsp (105 mL) oyster sauce
4 cups (1 L) vegetable oil

Method

Cut green and red peppers, onions, and yellow chives julienne. Blanch the prawns, then deep-fry the noodles golden brown in oil and put them into boiling water until cooked. Strain the noodles and set aside. Heat up a wok containing oil and stir-fry prawns, red and green peppers, and onions. After a few minutes, stir in noodles, bean sprouts, oyster sauce, salt, and sugar. Then add yellow chives and serve.

Note: In China long noodles celebrate long life. The longer the noodles you eat, the longer your life will be. Chinese eat long-life noodles on their birthdays. Great care is taken not to cut the noodles.

Rats don't have much cachet in the West, but in China they're lucky symbols. Perhaps the Chinese feel naming a cigarette after the creature wards off cancer.

Kir Royal ❧

Ingredients

½ fluid oz (15 mL) crème de cassis
champagne

Put crème de cassis in a champagne flute, fill rest of glass with chilled champagne, mix thoroughly, and garnish with a red maraschino cherry and a lemon twist.

Parson's Special ❧

Ingredients

5 fluid oz (150 mL) orange juice
1 fluid oz (30 mL) lemon juice
½ fluid oz (15 mL) simple syrup
½ fluid oz (15 mL) grenadine
1 egg yolk
12 fluid oz (355 mL) lemon-lime soft drink

Method

Shake in a martini shaker with ice, pour into martini glasses, and garnish with orange wedges.

After Eight

Ingredients

1 tsp (5 mL) amaretto
4 tsp (20 mL) Kahlúa
4 tsp (20 mL) Cointreau
4 tsp (20 mL) fresh cream
2 tsp (10 mL) green crème de menthe

Method

Pour amaretto, Kahlúa, and Cointreau over ice, then stir and strain into a martini glass. Mix in cream and crème de menthe. Garnish with grated dark chocolate flakes.

Communism may still hold sway in today's China, but shopping is the order of the day and night.

Yin-Yang White Chocolate Mousse Cake ↩

Main Ingredients

1 egg (separated into yolk and white)
½ tsp (2 mL) gelatin
1 tbsp (15 mL) white rum
¼ lb (125 g) white chocolate
⅔ cup (165 mL) cream
¼ piece orange zest and juice
¼ piece lemon zest and juice

Method

Melt white chocolate. Whisk egg yolk and white with juice of lemon and orange in a double boiler while raising temperature to obtain a thick, foamy mix. Soften gelatin with cold water. Boil about two teaspoons (10 milliliters) of the cream and add gelatin, melting it. Pour the gelatin/cream over the foamy egg mix. Fold the egg mix into the melted white chocolate and add rum. Whisk the rest of the cream until whipped. When the chocolate mixture is at room temperature, fold the whipped cream into it slowly. Pour into a pastry ring mold and allow it to set.

Crispy Sugar Cookies ✑

Ingredients

¼ cup (65 mL) butter
¼ cup (65 mL) icing sugar
¼ cup (65 mL) brown sugar
3½ tbsp (53 mL) orange juice
3 tbsp (45 mL) cake flour
1½ tbsp (23 mL) sesame seeds

Method

Mix all the ingredients in a bowl, form into a disk, and allow to set in the refrigerator. Warm up oven to 350° to 400° F (180° to 200° C). When ready, remove cookie disk from refrigerator, place on a baking sheet, and cut into whatever shapes desired. Bake for 10 minutes or until golden brown. Top Yin-Yang Chocolate Mousse Cake on previous page with orange and grapefruit slices. Then place the mousse and the Crispy Sugar Cookies on a plate and serve with lemon sorbet and red fruit coulis.

Capella ✑

Ingredients

1½ fluid oz (45 mL) vodka
½ fluid oz (15 mL) limoncino
½ fluid oz (15 mL) lemon juice
1½ fluid oz (45 mL) cranberry juice

Method

Shake well, then pour into a margarita glass.

Note: Cloud 9, the "Highest Bar in the World," is located on the top floor of the Grand Hyatt Shanghai, level 87 of Jin Mao Tower, and was selected as one of "The World's Great Gathering Places" by *Newsweek* (November 15, 1999).

Graham Greene had three self-admitted Havana hot buttons: the availability of sex, the bar El Floridita, and the free-flowing cocaine supplied to gamblers by American gangster boss Meyer Lansky.

Courtesy Hotel Sevilla/Havana

Graham Greene
Love, Intrigue, and the Tango in Havana

A jinetera, Cuban slang for *jockey*, hisses at a cigar-sucking tourist whose lips are wet from the moist tip of his smoke. "You buy cigar?" the illegal salesman whispers, sidling closer. "Cohiba. Romeo and Juliet. Montecristo Churchill No. 2? Cheap." The *jinetera* and the tourist move off together and, as I watch, they're "swallowed up among the pimps and lottery sellers of the Havana noon." Thus wrote British author Graham Greene in *Our Man in Havana*, his 1958 satire of international skullduggery.

It's almost a half century later, and Fidel Castro's revolution has swept away the lottery sellers, but the prostitutes posture and strut again, with Habana Vieja's seedy opulence serving as their stagy backdrop. They're young, very black women with impossibly high, rounded derrieres, and coffee-colored mulattoes whose lesser curves are maximized in spandex. They pose against the sunlit yellow-and-pink pillars of the colonnades, stand beside the sparkling, wave-lashed Malecón, and loiter impatiently in the tamarind-petaled suburbs of nearby Vedado and Miramar. The women are as erotic as Cuba, still recognizable as the Pearl of the Antilles. No matter what era of history, this is indisputable. I believe if Graham Greene, novelist, escapist, spy, fervent Roman Catholic, and womanizer, who died in 1991 at age 87, had set his pale blue eyes on Havana's whores he would have found this city as irresistible now as he did when he traveled there to take his pleasure.

Greene reminisced about his visits to Havana in the early 1950s in his candid memoir *Ways of Escape*: "I came there for the sake of the Floridita restaurant (famous for daiquiris and

Most adults in Cuba, such as this one, are literate; in fact, the literacy rate of the country is 98 percent, slightly higher than that of the United States, Fidel Castro's longtime nemesis.

Morro crabs), for the brothel life, the roulette in every hotel, the fruit machines spilling out jackpots of silver dollars, the Shanghai Theater where for one dollar and twenty-five cents one could see a nude cabaret of extreme obscenity with the bluest of blue films in the intervals."

I must admit I, too, am drawn to Havana for the sake of El Floridita's Papa Doble, the double daiquiri created here for Ernest Hemingway, and for the louche atmosphere that's an easily acquired Havana taste. Like Greene, I'm thrilled by the endless hot evenings at sidewalk bars where hobnobbing with the *jineteras* and beggars is de rigueur. Havana seems to me a lost place, and its decades of hope and sadness parade by in fits and starts—like the 1950s cars, the cracks in their rusting hulks hidden by coats of shiny house paint, like the beautiful old beggar woman who taught me to tango.

It's a humid Havana night, and I'm squashed between two cigar-puffing couples on the makeshift sidewalk tables of El Castillo de Farnés, a restaurant on the corner of Avenida de Bélgica and Obrapia. I quaff a majority of *mojitos* at this drinking den that claims to have hosted Fidel, his brother, Raúl, and Che Guevara in 1959. A photo, proof of their visit, hangs on the wall inside the air-conditioned eatery. My Cuban cocktails go down smooth and quick. Sweet, like sucking on a piece of freshly cut plantation sugarcane. Fragrant, like breathing in a mint garden.

A street teen takes the snuggle of space between the restaurant window and my wooden chair. He strikes up a conversation, quick as a lit match. It's about the ruin the U.S. trade embargo has brought. The establishment's bouncer, Juan, eyes him, and the kid moves on. I admire the bouncer's comportment. His simian features belie our century, but his hard work and sensitive manner suit both the patrons' and Cuba's emotions. I watch as Juan, a descendent of the African sugarcane slaves who once made Cuba the world's richest colony, swipes tables clean. He takes a one-armed beggar by the shoulders, leading him away from a stony-faced tourist, gently but firmly conducting the arguing amputee back onto the narrow sidewalk that rocks with pedestrian traffic.

The action has begun. My attention is caught by a child, a boy, who appears at the open mouth of a sewer directly below a parking space on the sidewalk in front. His face is destroyed by burns. The boy darts in, and Juan sorts him from under a table's feet. An imp, the child grins lopsidedly and returns to his lair, head sticking up from his sewer hideout. The boy reminds me of a leprechaun, with eons of experience behind him. Mischievously and perversely the boy lights a match, then holds the flame to the gas tank of a parked Honda motorbike. A youthful prankster, he's as full of himself as any precocious First World child. When the Honda's owner appears, the street urchin winks at the crowd, then disappears underground.

A dancer practices Santeria, the Afro-Cuban faith that uses human interpreters to conduct rites of divination, sacrifice, exorcism, and initiation.

The street has become a three-ring circus, a schizophrenic stage. Six feet over on the restaurant's makeshift patio, a magician entertains tables for one American dollar per trick and, as when the maestro Fidel Castro took power, snow-white doves flutter on his shoulders.

I sway with the *mojitos* and the music. The night feels fluid. Street people loiter, and there are so many that even Juan can't control them. They're young and old, maimed and whole, black, brown, and white, and at intervals they break into wild dance, but not to their music, *son* and salsa, but to the rhythmic next-door island beat of Jamaica. I recognize Shaggy and, later, Bob Marley's rousing call of *"Rastafarrr!"* The music is infectious. The raucous night, the sour-sweet smell of sweat and perfume, and the sound stones me. The street life of Habana Vieja claims me.

A beggar woman approaches, then hovers near, moving like a snake released from a basket. She is ancient, yet her shoulders and hips are as twitchy as a sixteen-year-old's. She speaks a *santeros* in my ear. She's practicing Santeria, the Afro-Cuban faith that uses human interpreters to conduct rites of divination, sacrifice, exorcism, and initiation. The woman worships Ochún, a goddess of love, and she explains that this is why she is still vital and such a sensual dancer. She talks to me about love, and while she speaks she is never still. Her hips, shoulders, and arms undulate like Medusa's hair. I rise and dance with her. She teaches me to tango, cheek to cheek, to the wail of *"Rastafarrr"* until the marigold-and-mauve dawn rises through the particles of construction dust that herald the rebirth of the exquisite nearby slum, the seaside Malecón. Only a few of Havana's many architectural masterpieces, the Malecón's ornate residences were constructed for wealthy Spanish sugar barons in the first half of the 19th century. These once-elegant villas were still havens for the elite in the wild time when Greene began his erotic affair with Havana.

It was just after World War II. Tourists had returned to Havana in droves, seeking sun and sin. The lesbian acts at the Blue Moon and the Shanghai Theater's live sex shows were all the rage, not only for the highly sexed British writer but for the typical American visitor attracted by vice and needing no passport to take the short ferry ride from Key West. *Los exhibiciónes* attracted women, too, who cheered a black Cuban dubbed Superman, whose erect penis measured 12 inches as he made love to a black girl onstage.

Greene's other self-admitted Havana hot button, besides the sex and El Floridita, was the free-flowing cocaine supplied to gamblers by American gangster boss Meyer Lansky. Cuba has always been a dicey destination, and it was used as a base for Prohibition rum-running to the Florida Keys, Hemingway's theme in his 1937 novel *To Have and Have Not*. With Greenesque irony, Cuba's Mafia connection was forged in 1938 when Lansky, the Jewish godfather, was invited by Fulgencio Batista, Cuba's self-promoted chief of the army and charismatic strong-man, to clean up Havana's casinos. Havana's government-run establishments had earned a reputation as being fixed. Lansky seized the opportunity handed to him, brought in his own croupiers and pit bosses, and rewarded Batista with kickbacks. Spurred by his financial success, Batista, affectionately known to his cronies as the "pretty mulatto," ran for president. In 1944, though, four years later, President Franklin Roosevelt sent a message through Lansky, asking Batista to resign in favor of free elections. Batista's candidate lost and, for a while, the strongman became a man of leisure in Daytona Beach, living close to Lansky's Florida head-quarters and schmoozing with American sugar barons and politicians. Reportedly the Cuban brought with him $20 million in pin money. Thus began a lucrative alliance between Batista and American interests that only terminated with the returned president's overthrow by Castro on January 1, 1959.

During Greene's initial visits, he admitted "never stay[ing] long enough to be aware of the sad political background of arbitrary imprisonment and torture." I feel Greene must have been in pure escapist mode not to notice the abject poverty, just one of the sad realities of Batista's U.S.-backed police state. Today the poverty is attributed to the American embargo. To its many unfortunate souls, Havana is the City of Broken Dreams. Greene's self-admitted naivete seems unusual for a writer who, in his 1966 novel *The Comedians*, sharpened his pencil on the Third World politics of Haiti's Tontons Macoute and their voodoo dictator Papa Doc Duvalier.

By the 1950s, Greene was a man famous for his independent political views and was no admirer of the Americans. His widely publicized attacks on U.S. foreign policy in Vietnam are chronicled in the 1955 novel *The Quiet American*, a book that uncannily foreshadows America's disastrous role in that country's civil war. Master spy Kim Philby maintained that *The Quiet American* was his friend Greene's best work.

A little more than a decade before his debauched sojourns in Havana, the novelist was dragooned into the murky backwaters of Britain's Secret Intelligence Service (SIS). He joined the SIS under pressure to give more of his time to the war effort. Greene resigned his position in the organization in 1944 but served informally until the early 1980s, collecting information under the guise of author in return for expenses. In private he joked that the SIS was "the best travel agency in the world." Greene's cover as a novelist of growing international stature and writer on assignment was unlikely to raise enemy eyebrows, even during a crisis. His tasks included interviewing dissidents, acting as a conduit for messages, reporting on security measures, and recruiting local contacts.

Cuba offers universal health care to its citizens, but the quality of life remains poor.

During his service in World War II, Greene was known to MI6 as officer 59200, the same code number he gave to his hapless protagonist James Wormald's gullible immediate superior in *Our Man in Havana*. But unlike Wormald, the middle-aged vacuum-cleaner representative and reluctant spy, Greene was a man with a naturally deceptive nature. Spying for the firm was certainly better than enduring the boredom of the Pioneer Corps where he might have ended up digging latrines with other middle-aged men. The novelist was happy to keep his family at a distance in Oxford, both for their safety and to allow him freedom for his some-times perverse ways. Greene, the ultimate escape artist, had a wife, children, and mistresses as well as a continuous parade of prostitutes whom he sometimes requested to fire up a fetish—burn his flesh with cigarettes.

When renowned filmmaker Alexander Korda made *The Fallen Idol* from Greene's screen-play in 1947–48, the British director and Greene hit it off. Through Korda, Greene entered a clandestine clique that included the moviemaker's associate William Stephenson, better known as the Man Called Intrepid. In 1948 Greene journeyed to Vienna and Prague under the guise of a scouting trip for Korda's production of *The Third Man* (made from Greene's screenplay). In reality his trip was arranged by an agent for the SIS.

The tragicomedy of *Our Man in Havana* is a direct take on Greene's own experience in spying. His tongue-in-cheek attitude had its roots in World War II when he was posted to the colonial capital of Freetown, Sierra Leone, for the bureau responsible for counterespionage. His position as station chief consisted of 14 farcical months of self-admitted bungling. On the outward journey from Liverpool in a cargo ship, he and his fellow passengers were assigned to watch for submarines and were made to man machine guns. When Greene discovered the ship was carrying a cargo of dynamite and depth charges, and that one good hit would blow them to bits, he got drunk and stayed that way for the entire voyage.

Greene's mandate in West Africa was to watch foreign ships in the harbor for signs of enemy espionage activity and report by cable to headquarters using code. His cover had him pretending to be a colonial policeman. His personal insight into how a spy's life could be sab-otaged by a comedy of errors began when he locked his codebooks in a large safe delivered to him for that purpose, and then was unable to open it. He finally destroyed the safe to get at his codebooks, then reported that the safe had been damaged on the journey out. He requested a new safe, but it never arrived. Instead, it found its way to the bottom of the Atlantic when a German submarine attacked the ship carrying it. Greene spent his afternoons cooling his mouth with tropical drinks at local establishments just as his characters do, and true to his early spying experiences, he portrayed secret agents as bumbling amateurs.

On his return to England and directly under Philby, the future defector to the Soviet Union, Greene was placed in Section V, keeping track of operations at SIS stations in Tangier, Gibraltar, Lisbon, and Madrid. Greene's job was to supervise counterintelligence operations for neutral Portugal, a hotbed of enemy agents. The writer tracked a card-index file that contained all the names and information of the known German agents in Portugal. The operation was spearheaded from a secret location outside London, a pleasant country house in the Hertfordshire town of St. Albans. There Greene stumbled across a German agent code-named Garbo, whose outrageous make-believe would shape the fantastical plot of the novel Greene would eventually set in Cuba.

The real-life Garbo, born Juan Pujol García, offered his services to German intelligence operating in Madrid and was given the task of developing a spy ring in England. The Spaniard had no desire to winter in Britain, so he purchased a Michelin Blue Guide to England, a quality map, and a few military reference books. Then, making his way to Lisbon, he began to feed the Nazis detailed reports on Britain's defenses, all richly concocted by his imagination. Garbo maintained his information was sourced from agents he'd recruited in England. There was Fred, a waiter in Soho; a sweet-faced secretary in the government ministry; and a Venezuelan man in Glasgow. And more would come.

In *Our Man in Havana*, Wormald uses Garbo's real-life antics, imaginatively spying purely for what Greene called "a paying game." Taking his cue from Garbo, Greene has Wormald fabricate secret information based on a map of Cuba, a few books, and a copy of *Time*, then selling his creations for a monthly wage. The amateur spy needs the income to keep his beloved daughter, Milly, in saddle, riding pants, and horse. Milly's admirer, handsome Captain Segura, was modeled after the Red Vulture, Batista's evil henchman Major Esteban Ventura, who specialized in torture and mutilation and carried a cigarette case fashioned from human skin. Wormald's made-up moles could have been Garbo's: Teresa, an exotic dancer, collects pillow talk; a whiskey pilot provides air-reconnaissance information; an engineer spies on military installations. Just to heighten the sense of unreality, illustrations of Wormald's latest vacuum cleaner, the Atomic, are spun as secret weapon components.

Like Wormald's duped British masters, the German Command regarded the Portuguese spy as their prime source and his information invaluable. They became totally dependent on his tales of convoy movements and troop exercises. Garbo penned vivid accounts of London nightlife, including drunken orgies. Of course, the Germans especially appreciated his accounts of the weak morals of the English.

In the winter of 1942 Garbo approached the SIS in Lisbon and arranged a second employer.

He agreed to travel to England and, with the help of British intelligence, concocted events to benefit the English war effort. He had 27 fictional agents, one of whom died of cancer and had to be replaced. To keep up the act, Garbo was arrested for suspicious conduct and released 48 hours later for lack of evidence. Hitler was so grateful to Garbo that he awarded him the Iron Cross Class 11. As the Normandy invasion approached, Garbo sent convincing reports that there was no planned invasion; it was just a rumor meant to confuse the Germans. Greene had a highly honed sense of black humor, and from his comfy country office in Section V, he gleefully followed Garbo's merry dance.

Greene's first draft of what would become his "entertainment" *Our Man in Havana* was begun in the 1940s as a screenplay. He placed the story in 1938 and set it in Tallinn, the capital of Estonia. When he gave it to the Brazilian filmmaker Alberto Cavalcanti, thinking the director could clear it through the censors, he was told that a film that spoofed the secret service would never be issued a certificate. Greene put the work away and soon after, in the early 1950s, started his purely pleasurable sojourns to Batista's Havana. While there it dawned on him that "here in this extraordinary city, where every vice was permissible and every trade possible, lay the true background for my comedy." Greene also concluded that situating the piece in 1938, before the war, was the wrong period. "The shadows in 1938 of the war to come had been too dark for comedy; the reader could feel no sympathy for a man who was cheating his country in Hitler's day.... But in fantastic Havana, among the absurdities of the Cold War (for who can accept

Dictator Fulgencio Batista didn't give up power without a fight. For years Fidel Castro, shown here, waged revolution from the Sierra Madre until his eventual victory at the beginning of 1959.

the survival of Western capitalism as a great cause?), there was a situation allowably comic…"

When Greene visited Cuba again in 1957, this time to collect background color for *Our Man in Havana*, the country was squirming under Batista's cruel hand. By then Castro's power play included nocturnal bombings that kept tourists and their money away. Greene stated: "Strangely enough, as I planned my fantastic comedy, I learned for the first time some of the realities of Batista's Cuba…. Now, while the story was emerging, I set about curing a little of my ignorance. I made Cuban friends, I took a car and traveled with a driver around the country. He was a superstitious man and my education began on the first day when he ran over and killed a chicken. It was then he initiated me into the symbols of the lottery—we had killed a chicken, we must buy such and such a number. This was the substitute for hope in hopeless Cuba."

Greene eventually flew to Santiago de Cuba, the country's second-largest city, in the lush and mountainous Oriente Province. It was Batista's military headquarters against the unstoppable firebrand Fidel, who was waging a guerrilla war from his hideout in the nearby mountains. There the novelist became caught up in a spying experience as absurd as any in *Our Man in Havana*. Greene describes the episode in *Ways of Escape*. It began at a late-night party with middle-class Havanans during what Greene called "the heroic period." Greene was told stories of brutal beatings by Batista's henchmen, and the Castro supporters asked if Greene would smuggle in sweaters and socks to Santiago, destined for the fighters in the mountains. A foreigner was equally suspect but had reason to possess winter clothes. The province was riddled with military roadblocks, and the airport had a customs check.

A young woman made the arrangements. A courier for Fidel, she was anxious that Greene meet Fidel's genuine representatives. She warned the novelist that Santiago was rife with Batista's spies, especially in the hotel where Greene would be staying. She told him a curfew was in force, there were arbitrary arrests, and it wasn't uncommon for early risers to discover bodies hanging like rag dolls from lampposts. The woman said the hanged ones were lucky—a notorious nearby Santiago building rocked with the screams of victims being tortured and mutilated. The female courier would arrange to travel on the same plane as Greene. She would remain nameless for their safety, and Greene mustn't let on that he recognized her. The woman would contact him at his Santiago hotel for the handover of clothes.

The next morning a *Time* correspondent called on Greene, who was still in Havana. His mission was to accompany the novelist to Santiago and try to get something for his column. Greene felt he couldn't decline. Later, in his writing, Greene described the stench of Santiago: "The smell of the police station lay over the city. I was back in what my critics imagine to be

Automobiles are among the most colorful sights in today's Havana; sometimes they're downright macabre.

Greeneland." As the novelist breakfasted in his hotel room and awaited the female courier's telephone call, there was a knock on his door. It was the *Time* correspondent accompanied by a fellow who claimed to be Castro's public-relations man in Santiago. The instant Greene laid eyes on the middle-aged, mustachioed man "Mr. X," he was positive he was in Batista's camp. He was certain the man was a spy and that he himself was suspect. When the telephone rang, he asked his visitors to leave. The female courier gave Greene an address on Calle San Francisco. Greene never heard from the woman again, but while he walked in the heat, Mr. X. and the *Time* correspondent pulled up and reassured the novelist they were all on the same side. They drove to the rebel leader Armando Hart's house where Greene saw Hart having his hair dyed by a barber.

In the morning, *Our Man in Havana* clutched in my *mojito*-shaken hand, I follow Greene's journalistic trail to Santiago de Cuba where I plan to interview the novelist's mysterious female courier, Nidia Zaralia, no longer a girl, but an accomplished elderly woman. Earlier I checked into Greene's hotel, the revamped Casa Grande, and was harassed by street touts wanting dollars to guard my rental car. So far I've seen busloads of tourists, but no obvious spies, though I know street people are often paid political informers for Fidel. When I enter Nidia's modest bungalow, she's sitting in a comfy flocked chair and is happy to reminisce through an interpreter. "I met Greene in 1957 through my good friend Amelia Bolívar, who was studying African culture," she tells me.

Silently I remember Greene's statement in *Ways of Escape* that his partying Castro supporters were middle-class Cubans.

Nidia removes her thick-lensed glasses and says, "I lived in a rooming house in front of the Writers' Center. I was visiting with my friend, and a Mercedes pulled up. At first we thought it was another friend's cousin, a millionaire in sugarcane, but then a tall man who looked like an American tourist in his fifties came out. I remember his blue eyes."

I recall the unusual pale hue of Greene's eyes and his reputation for being a man with a splinter of ice in his heart.

Nidia continues. "When he said he was Graham Greene, I was surprised. I'd read his book about the Mexican revolution, *The Power and the Glory*. We went for a ride with him to have a conversation and told him about the revolution—at that time it was centered in Santiago de Cuba. After, we went to a restaurant, El Chico, where he agreed to bring a suitcase of warm socks and sweaters on the plane to Santiago. Greene's interest was to interview Fidel. We would arrange it through Armando Hart, my boss in the movement."

Nidia points to a photo of Hart, who went on to become Cuba's minister of education, then minister of culture. I ask her about Greene's attitude.

Nidia smiles. "Greene worried it would be dangerous and wanted someone with him." She says that after her telephone call to Greene at the Casa Grande she waited in a car near a street named Pio Rosado. She remembers the event with a clarity that comes with time for thought. "It was hot, and when I saw him walking, I took him to a different house. Not Hart's."

When I tell her that Greene maintained in his autobiography that he saw Hart having his hair dyed, Nidia is adamant. "No, we were at the count's house. Hart said, 'No meeting with me. Greene can wait and meet Fidel.' I was surprised. The journalist who'd accompanied Greene was already at Count Douaneys. I think he was a spy for the FBI. I watched by the window, and Greene, the journalist, and the count who owned the house talked. I put the suitcase in a closet, and later a North American took it to Fidel. Greene called me before he left Cuba. He'd waited a week, but the timing to meet Fidel wasn't right. Batista's army was shooting revolutionaries. Greene said he couldn't wait any longer. He had to go to Africa to interview Mau Maus. The [London] *Times* got the interview with Fidel the day Greene left."

Before I leave, Nidia poses for my camera in front of her study wall lined with 50 photos of the revolution. Her presence in each picture resurrects the brilliant past: the images of guerrilla fighters, including El Jefe Máximo, embody the dedication and spirit that is still the revolution for many. Born in 1922, Nidia was more than the slip of a girl Greene perceived her to be. She would have been a handsome woman of 37. Greene's missed opportunity for an interview with Fidel must have been galling.

Like Greene, I return to Havana to wait. I've asked for an interview with Fidel and am told maybe, maybe not. I wait a week, calling every day, and hear the refrain "There are 600 people on the list who are in front of you." Frequently I'm questioned about why I'm on a tourist's and not a journalist's visa.

I'm stymied in my efforts to visit Guantánamo for the same reason. The U.S. naval base on Cuban soil has been turned into a camp for Al-Qaeda and Taliban prisoners. I give up on a press visit to Guantánamo but am relieved and agree with a Greenesque comment by Wormald's friend, Dr. Hassalbacher: "You should dream more, Mr. Wormald. Reality in our century is not something to be faced." Recently I've seen newspaper photographs of Guantánamo prisoners kneeling with hoods over their heads.

My time is up, but I've been in Havana's searing light so long that in my mind's eye I hardly need to wander. I know that on every street corner a beautiful black woman, a mulatto, or a blonde in flamingo pink Lycra struts her stuff. I can feel the sun's burning eye dart through the wooden louvers of the pillared Spanish villas that grace the sea-battered Malecón.

I make a last pilgrimage to El Floridita, the incandescent, red-velvet, air-conditioned bar that hasn't changed an iota since Greene frequented it. I perch on a leather barstool, and a

Originally, rich sugar barons inhabited Havana's seaside Malecón, but in later years the neighborhood's ornate residences fell into disrepair and the area became a slum. Today a massive restoration job has brought many of the Malecón's edifices back to their former glory.

middle-aged man in flowered shorts and tropical shirt moves in beside me, chilling his mouth with a daiquiri. He says he's a first-time American tourist who knows nothing about Cuba, Castro, the people, and especially the politics. He has no opinions but is very interested in everything I say about Cuba.

After draining numerous icy drinks, he slips and tips me off. He states with a tone of derision that Castro is fearful of a U.S. takeover and for that reason the dictator can't sleep nights and either opens up a backroom casino or turns up at the Canadian embassy, looking for a game of chance, usually cards. At that moment I know the tourist is probably a CIA agent, and a Greene quote flies into my brain. Greene writes in *Our Man in Havana* that playing the lottery and believing in blind luck is "the substitute for hope in hopeless Cuba." Not necessarily for Castro, but for the people's sake, I hope not. Hurriedly I leave El Floridita and the middle-aged American spy, who continues to freeze his soul with countless daiquiris.

Back in a safe Canada, I'm left with my shady experiences, my hope for Cuba's people, and my lessons from the beggar woman in love and the tango. I know full well that for a short while I inhabited what can only be described as Greeneland, a place where spies lurk in bars and intrigue lies just around the next corner.

Whether they're Cohibas, Romeo and Juliets, or Montecristo Churchill No. 2s, cigars are as ubiquitous as sunshine in Havana.

Recipes

Bodeguita del Medio

Picadillo (Chopped Meat)
Cuba Libre
Boniatillo (Sweet Potato Custard)
Casserole Chicken
Sangria

El Floridita

Mulata
Graham Special

Hotel Ambos Mundos

Mojito
Daiquiri

Street art in Cuba often has a political flavor such as this depiction of a rally in support of Fidel Castro, El Jefe Máximo.

246

Picadillo (Chopped Meat) ↻

Makes four to six servings.

Ingredients

2 lb (1 kg) chopped beef
1 small garlic bulb
1 onion
1 green pepper
½ cup (125 mL) tomato paste
½ cup (125 mL) lime juice or vinegar
½ cup (125 mL) olive oil
salt to taste

Method

Chop the meat and marinade with salt and vinegar or lime juice. Fry the garlic, green pepper, and onion well diced in the oil, then add the chopped meat and fry it slowly. Later add the tomato paste to taste.

Cuba Libre ❧

Ingredients

1 cola soft drink
1½ fluid oz (45 mL) Cuban white or amber rum
1 lime slice
ice

Method

Pour the rum into a tall glass, then fill it with cola and ice. Stir and garnish with the lime slice.

Boniatillo (Sweet Potato Custard) ❧

Makes six to eight servings.

Ingredients

2 lb (1 kg) sweet potatoes
4 cups (1 L) sugar
1 tbsp (15 mL) anise
2 cups (500 mL) milk
6 tbsp (90 mL) butter

Method

Boil the cubed sweet potatoes in water for about 20 minutes until tender. Drain and allow to cool, then puree. Melt the butter slowly in another pot with the pureed sweet potato, then add the milk, sugar, and anise and continue stirring until thick.

Casserole Chicken ෴

Makes four to six servings, depending on the size of the chicken.

Ingredients

1 whole medium-size chicken
1 garlic bulb
1 poblano chili
1 tbsp (15 mL) oregano
½ cup (125 mL) lime juice
½ cup (125 mL) tomato sauce
1 cup (250 mL) diced ham
½ cup (125 mL) cooking wine
salt to taste

Method

Marinade the chicken with garlic, oregano, and salt. Roast the chicken in the oven. Prepare a consommé with the giblets, then add chopped poblano pepper and garlic, tomato sauce, cooking wine, and salt. When consommé is ready, strain the liquid and cook slowly in the oven. Add diced ham. Remove the consommé from the heat after five minutes and pour over the roast chicken in the oven, then continue cooking it for five minutes.

Sangria ☙

Ingredients

1 tsp (5 mL) sugar
1 fluid oz (30 mL) lime juice
4 fluid oz (120 mL) soda water
4 fluid oz (120 mL) red wine

Method

In a large glass dissolve the sugar and add the lime juice. Then put in the soda water and red wine. Stir and add ice cubes.

There may be a great deal of antipathy between Cuba and the United States, but people in Havana did show some support for Americans after September 11, 2001, as this poster demonstrates.

Mulata ❧

Ingredients

1 fluid oz (30 mL) lemon juice
1 fluid oz (30 mL) crème de cacao
2 fluid oz (60 mL) dark Cuban rum
crushed ice

Method

Frappé ingredients thoroughly.

Graham Special ❧

Ingredients

½ fluid oz (15 mL) Italian vermouth
½ fluid oz (15 mL) white Cuban rum
juice of half a lime
½ tsp (2 mL) sugar
cracked ice

Method

Shake well, strain, and serve garnished with a pineapple slice and two cherries.

Mojito

Ingredients

1 tbsp (15 mL) sugar
1 fluid oz (30 mL) of lemon juice
1½ fluid oz (45 mL) white Cuban rum
sparkling water
3 ice cubes
2 sprigs of mint (with stem)
dots of angostura

Method

Put sugar and lemon together and stir them until sugar is dissolved. Smash mint with a muddler and add sparkling water, ice cubes, rum, and angostura. Garnish with a sprig of mint.

Note: A muddler is an unusual cocktail accessory used for crushing the mint for a *mojito*. It resembles a small baseball bat.

Daiquiri

Ingredients

1 tbsp (15 mL) of sugar
1 fluid oz (30 mL) of lemon juice
1½ fluid oz (45 mL) white Cuban rum
ice cubes
dots of maraschino liqueur

Method

Place sugar and lemon in a blender, blend them, add ice, and blend them again. While blending add the dots of maraschino liqueur.

In his younger days André Malraux (seen here in 1942) was something of an adventuring political activist, sort of a French Ernest Hemingway with a wide streak of the kind of socio-political savvy that informed American novelist John Dos Passos's best work.

Courtesy of Louis Chevasson Collection

André Malraux
The Awesome Allure of Cambodia's Angkor Wat

When he died of a heart attack in 1998 in a shack near Cambodia's border with Thailand, dictator Pol Pot robbed millions of Cambodians of what they desired— justice. During his brief but brutal tenure, the enigmatic mass murderer dimmed all but one light in his country and that was small comfort: he was no temple robber. Pol Pot's Khmer Rouge revered Cambodia's ancient temples during their genocidal rule.

In 1923 two young French adventurers, André Malraux (1901–1976) and his wife, Clara, led a looting expedition to Cambodia's remote Banteay Srei temple in the Angkor area. Malraux would go on to achieve fame with a series of novels, including his third, *The Royal Way*, which romanticizes the escapade in Cambodia. Malraux's temple robbing is certainly objectionable, but it doesn't hold a candle to Pol Pot's monstrous actions. The Communist despot was responsible for killing more than two million of his countrymen. Still, stealing a poor colony's antiquities is morally indefensible, but then Malraux had more than a few flaws. In subsequent novels such as *Man's Fate* (his best fiction; it's based on his travels in late 1920s China) and *Man's Hope* (which draws on his experiences in the Spanish Civil War) and especially in his later memoirs, he constructed an exaggerated aura of heroism for himself both in Spain where he flew with a French squadron fighting on the Republican side, and in Occupied France where he trumpeted his exploits as a resistance leader during World War II.

When André Malraux and his wife were plundering the temple Banteay Srei in the early 1920s, jungle still consumed a good deal of the Angkor complexes. Today the jungle still encroaches.

Ironically the sometime liar and onetime thief of a Third World country's treasures would serve as France's culture minister, be feted by Charles de Gaulle, and would ultimately be buried in the Panthéon, the French republic's secular shrine.

Malraux and his wife posed in Cambodia as well-heeled philanthropists. When their ruse strained their budget, they headed into the jungle in search of the obscure early Hindu temple Banteay Srei, aiming to seek their fortune amid phallic towers carved with huge faces. They traveled on horses so small their heels dragged on the ground. The villagers they stopped had never heard of the temple. Their guide, Xa, persisted until they found an elder who recalled the site and for a fee agreed to take them there. Later, referring to Angkor Wat itself, Malraux graphically described his first sight of the Cambodian jungle and the treasures it holds: "In each opening, beyond the leaves, he tried to glimpse the towers of Angkor Wat above the skyline of trees bent and twisted by the lake winds; in vain, the leaves, reddened in the twilight, closed in on the paludal universe."

The couple had arranged to be picked up by Henri Marchal, a *conservateur* who had diligently striven to unearth Cambodian temples for a decade. Hidden by the jungle's lush greenery were the broad moats, the flagstone causeways, and the magnificent arches of the Angkor Thom complex. At Marchal's house Malraux and Clara sipped chilled Cinzano from French crystal. Later they were driven in Marchal's Ford Roadster past rice paddies and tall forests, past Angkor Wat's momentous ruins, and on to Bayon where they marveled at the 200 god-king faces and cobra-headed *nagas* that topped the pineapple-shaped towers.

Under the supervision of the *conservateur* they assembled the carts, bullocks, horses, and guide for their expedition. The affluent airs they put on in their guise as philanthropists took their last pennies, and they were forced to put forward the date of the excursion.

Their way was marked by spiders the size of dinner plates suspended in silken webs. The never-ending shrill of cicadas was punctuated by the squawk of strange birds that swooped in the jade canopy above. The grating of their saws as they performed their robbery caused heavy-winged birds and scrambling monkeys to flee, and the carved stones had a sunset hue even in the afternoon light. The metal teeth of their hacksaws sounded louder than the grating call of parrots, and the blades' edges snapped, probably because the ancient Khmer builders used no mortar in piling the intricately chiseled blocks stone upon stone.

After three days of toil, Malraux and his confederates removed corner stones representing two smiling *devatas* (protective goddesses). Malraux and his wife planned to sell the bas-reliefs to the highest American bidder. Finally, back in Siem Reap with their weighty booty, they acquired a truck to transfer the camphor Chinese coffins that now held the priceless objects. Their destination was a steamer that would take them across Tonle Sap lake, down Tonle Sap river to Phnom Penh, along the Mekong River, and eventually to Saigon. Malraux, no fool, for all his youth, was careful not to arouse the suspicion of the French authorities. If caught, he planned to use the excuse that his action wasn't theft since the Khmer statuary wasn't in a museum or protected. It was on open display.

As the steamer cut through the water on its long voyage, Malraux and his wife slept fitfully, dreaming of jungle insects and the lilting smiles of the goddesses they'd ransacked. Upon landing in Phnom Penh they were put under house arrest in a hotel. Days turned to months, and though there was lax surveillance and the couple dressed for dinner in haute couture, they were snubbed by the expatriate society that shared the dance floor.

Meanwhile the French authorities discovered that Malraux's archaeological credits were bogus and, worse, that the temple sacker was a calculating art thief who had already arranged contact with dealers in Asiatic statuary. Clara, realizing the seriousness of their situation, decided to fake a suicide attempt to draw attention to their plight. The scheme failed but affected their faithful guide, Xa, who made Clara hide presents of rare Khmer statuary, including an *aspara* (dancing goddess). The booty was tucked and wrapped in her shimmering lamé dresses, packed in their trunks, and would be delivered triumphantly to France. Still under hotel arrest, Clara tried another tactic and went on a hunger strike. This time she had a measure of success and was released,

Although many of the temples at Angkor were originally dedicated to the Hindu pantheon, Buddhism prevails and the religion's monks are a common sight among the ruins.

but her husband was sentenced to three years in prison for vandalism. Ten months after Malraux's conviction a new lawyer hired by Clara appealed and the writer was eventually released.

André Malraux's story is so impossibly romantic and compelling that when I travel to Cambodia I know I have to experience his obsession firsthand. It takes me a long time to get to Cambodia, but after I arrive time seems to stand still. Actually it tumbles backward as I journey through rippling paddies of emerald tilled by plodding, placid water buffalo, and witness Khmer women, heads sheltered in purple and red squares of hand-loomed cloth, bending low under the relentless sun. Their hands work like pendulums as they slice the tiny pearl-hued rice stocks or splash their wooden pails of muddy water on iridescent life-giving fields.

Called Kampuchea for a time, this Indochinese country of 13 million largely gentle and tolerant Buddhists has repeatedly been torn asunder. For almost a century (1863 to 1953) Cambodia was under French suzerainty, and the nation still evokes the sophisticated aura the French imbued along with the gracious hostelries they left behind.

The Hôtel Le Royal in Phnom Penh and the Grand Hôtel D'Angkor were favorite stops for Somerset Maugham, Charles de Gaulle, and Jacqueline Kennedy, among many others. Later Prince Norodom Ranariddh (son of King Norodom Sihanouk, the country's head of state off and on from the 1940s until the present) stayed virtually around the clock behind Le Royal's thick walls in 1997 prior to his violent removal as prime minister by rival Hun Sen (a former Pol Pot Khmer Rouge and onetime foreign minister and prime minister during the Vietnamese occupation of Cambodia). It is Le Royal where I lay my head when I'm not wandering. This lovely redone relic of French colonialism gives no clues to the death and desecration of the recent past; in fact, its sleepy elegance makes one almost forget that Phnom Penh's hinterland is strewn with human bones and is booby-trapped by an estimated 2.6 million landmines.

Cambodia experienced a brief period of independence from France under Sihanouk, years in which it became increasingly embroiled in the bloody conflict being fought next door between North Vietnam and South Vietnam (and its U.S. ally). Then, in 1975, with the final collapse of Lon Nol's U.S.-backed, anti-Communist government, Cambodia entered its most tragic era ever. The seemingly demented Pol Pot and his Khmer Rouge henchmen came to power and marched the country straight into hell.

Known to his comrades as Brother Number One, Pol Pot (real name Saloth Sar) set about changing the very fabric of Cambodia, literally ripping it asunder. He and his Maoist cronies designated 1975 Year Zero and drove millions of people out of the cities. All capitalist trappings and anything deemed foreign were stamped out in a crazed attempt to catapult the nation back into total agrarianism. Private property, money, religions, traditional music, dance, art, literature, and even traditional marriage were banned. International telephone links were cut and foreigners fled. Physicians, teachers, and all Cambodian who had worked in the employ of foreigners were tortured and killed. Even hospital patients, the elderly, and children were forced on the death march to the countryside known as "the killing fields." Untold thousands perished from starvation and disease. In December 1979, however, the Vietnamese invaded and quickly ousted Pol Pot, but the war with the Khmer Rouge rebels continued to rage throughout the 1980s and early 1990s.

Now I write from the perspective of a new century, but Cambodia still struggles to wake from its nightmares. Although Pol Pot died in 1998 and the Khmer Rouge guerrillas, trademark red and white scarves noosing their necks, seem finally vanquished, Cambodia continues to live on the edge, its relative calm ever fragile. Sihanouk is once again king, but real power remains in the hands of Prime Minister Hun Sen. Despite all the turmoil and terrible events, however, the temples of Angkor abide as shining examples of Cambodia's rich history and culture.

When I finally get my first eyeful of the sublime grandeur that is Angkor, I'm greeted by a chorus of ragged children, round eyes prematurely old. "Madame, madame, only one dollar!" they chant with dogged persistence borne of need, surrounding me in a twister of dust, bare feet, and scrawny legs. One pushes into my hand postcards of Angkor Wat and the dusty town of Siem Reap, just four miles from the ruins. Another waves Buddha amulets that sparkle in the sunlight. "Madame, madame, you help me," they cajole, their faces sad and beautiful. Jostling and shoving, the urchins are wild things with a desperate air. Their playground is the fabled ruins of one of the world's greatest architectural achievements, a UNESCO World Heritage Site that was recently proclaimed by *National Geographic Traveler* as one of the "world's top 50 must-see places."

Behind the tussle of dusty children, the beggars, the bicycles, the elephants, and the stands selling drinks and hairy brown coconuts filled with clear milk, Angkor Wat rises. I walk through light and shadows thrown from the monumental structures down a 12th-century road decorated with splendid stone balustrades carved with five-headed *nagas*, cosmic water serpents, heads raised to the heavens.

"Madame, madame, madame!" the children continue to sing across a 100-yard-wide moat choked with refuse and water lilies. The children's voices, sweet and strident, pursue me on an invisible breeze scented with the fragrance of the pristine white blooms of a frangipani tree and the heavy odor of rotting fruit. Their voices grow silent when soldiers, dressed in green with rifles at their sides, come into view. The hard-faced young men try to bully me for a tip or a bribe. I pretend I don't understand their pidgin English and continue down a mercifully shady

Regimes
and despots
come and go,
but the Buddha
face of the south
entrance to Angkor
Thom endures.

and safer stone path that leads up steep stairs to an indoor and outdoor myriad of cavernous temples and five lotus-shaped towers. Every single inch of the structure is swathed in sandstone carvings. On the walls and galleries are 1,500 *apsaras*, sensual, bare-breasted celestial dancers so real they shimmy and sway before my eyes. Each is in a different pose or costume. Like joyous and voluptuous angels, they seem to fly at me across the frescoes.

Angkor Wat is fashioned from dreams, specifically the erotic ones of King Suryavarman II to honor himself, the Hindu god Vishnu, and the bounty brought by the waters of the nearby lake Tonle Sap. The mammoth *wat*, or temple, of Angkor is the center jewel of scores of religious shrines that soar and crumble across 76 square miles of northwestern Cambodia. I stand amid an artistic and religious allegory depicting the epic tales of Hindu myths. The intricately carved temples, towers, dancers, and serpents are such a confusion of shapes and movements that my mind and senses are overwhelmed. I am simultaneously startled, mystified, frightened, and thrilled.

In a dark corner a barefoot monk draped in a saffron robe lights an incense stick with a broken wooden match, the thin spear of rising smoke as thin and elusive as he. It's his meager offering to his lord Buddha. The altars of this majestic site have changed from Hindu to Buddhist to animist over the six centuries that have passed in these hallowed halls. The monks are male and female, but it's difficult to tell the sexes apart, since they all appear to be emaciated skeletons with shaven heads. Like the children who follow me, the monks have saucer eyes that have seen too much, and bodies that are ravaged and prematurely old—courtesy of the

A view of the inner complex of Angkor Wat: the outer walls of the architectural wonder are two miles long, its central tower as tall as Notre-Dame in Paris—and more stunning.

Copyright © by Tyson Brooks

Khmer Rouge's years of terror and the continuing poverty that pervades this troubled land.

The outer walls of Angkor Wat are two miles long. The central tower is as tall as Notre-Dame in Paris, and more stunning. The place is the size of Manhattan. The ruins of Angkor are as mysterious to me as Tonle Sap, the Great Lake of Cambodia, and the river of the same name that connects it to the mighty Mekong. When the Mekong floods, the river Tonle Sap reverses its flow and the floodwaters fill the Great Lake. Tonle Sap doubles in size during the rainy season—drowning great forests, ensuring water for rice paddies, and providing the greatest harvest of freshwater fish in the world. This natural phenomenon occurs between June and October each year. Historians say the glories of the great temples were built to honor the gods that fill the largest freshwater lake in Southeast Asia. Tonle Sap's source is the spring meltwaters of the far-off snowcapped Himalayas.

It's impossible to comprehend Angkor Wat in a few days—hopeless to see it all within the limits of the human eye. And there are more marvels: at the Bayon temple site inscrutable near-identical stone faces, eyes closed and with slight smiles, are aligned toward the cardinal points of the compass; at Ta Prom tree roots like gigantic brown boa constrictors strangle, cling, and climb ornate walls. Everywhere faces and figures loom from Hinduism—Kala, a jawless monster commanded by Shiva to devour its own body; and Garuda, the half-man, half-bird transporter of the god Vishnu. Wherever you look unspeakable demons and sensual naked sandstone shapes silently observe all who pass.

To set one's eyes on the fabled ruins of Angkor Wat and Thom and on Cambodia's gentle people is to have heaven and hell etched in the mind forever. Whenever I think of Cambodia I recall the twister of tagalong children hawking their small wares, I see the smile of an amputee beggar as wide, beautiful, and miraculous as the nurturing Tonle Sap, but I also glimpse the piles of skulls heaped in temples and bearing mute witness to past horrors. Cambodia endures, though, and I dream of mauve and while lotus blossoms spinning down a river that slides behind Khmer shanties set high and safe on wooden stilts. I sniff the scent of incense lit by saffron-clad monks in dank temples. I bask in the radiance of a people who, though crippled with poverty, refuse to succumb. And I conjure up the staggering accomplishment that is Angkor, a willing accomplice to an obsession that has gripped kings and despots, a writer named Malraux, politicians of all stripes, tourists and travelers, all of whom have partaken in the affecting dream called Cambodia.

Despite all of the tragedy and terror Cambodia has experienced during the past three decades, children in a village on Tonle Sap still hope for a better future.

Recipes

Restaurant Le Grand (Raffles Grand Hôtel D'Angkor)

Green Papaya Salad
Pumpkin Soup
Sour Fish Soup with Pineapple
Stir-Fried Beef with Black Pepper
Braised Fish in Palm Sugar and Ginger
Cambodian Fried Rice
Pumpkin Custard
Deep-Fried Rice Flakes with Banana
Rice Dumpling with Palm Sugar

This Cambodian food basket has all the ingredients for an excellent Khmer meal.

A Cambodian woman sells produce at a village market. Life has finally begun to return to something approaching normalcy for war-beleaguered Cambodia.

266

Green Papaya Salad ✐

Makes eight servings.

Ingredients

1 small red chili
3 garlic cloves
3 shallots
1 tsp (5 mL) shrimp paste
2 tbsp (30 mL) palm sugar
3 tbsp (45 mL) fish sauce
5 tbsp (75 mL) lime juice
1¼ lb (600 g) grated green papaya
3½ oz (100 g) tomatoes (cut in wedges)
2½ oz (75 g) dried shrimp
1½ tsp (7 mL) basil leaves
3 tbsp (45 mL) chopped, roasted peanuts

Method

To prepare the salad dressing, use a stone mortar to combine the chili, garlic, shallots, and shrimp paste. Pound until soft, then add the palm sugar, lime juice, and fish sauce. Check the seasoning and adjust if necessary. For the salad, mix the grated papaya, tomato wedges, dried shrimp, basil, and peanuts, then add the dressing and serve immediately.

Pumpkin Soup ❧

Makes 10 servings.

Ingredients

3 tbsp (45 mL) vegetable oil
12 oz (350 g) chopped lemongrass
1 lb (500 g) sliced onions
6 lb (3 kg) pumpkin (cut into pieces)
1¾ oz (50 g) cumin powder
2 cinnamon sticks
8 cups (2 L) chicken stock
4 tbsp (60 mL) sugar
salt to taste
3½ fluid oz (100 mL) coconut milk

Method

Heat the oil and sauté the onions and lemongrass until fragrant, then add the pumpkin, cumin powder, sugar, salt, cinnamon sticks, and chicken stock. Allow the pumpkin to cook until soft in texture. Pass the soup through the blender (discarding the cinnamon sticks and lemongrass) and strain. Reheat the soup and check the seasoning. Serve the soup in individual cups, garnished with coconut milk.

Sour Fish Soup with Pineapple 🙠

Makes 10 servings.

Ingredients

8 cups (2 L) fish stock
½ cup (125 mL) fish sauce
½ cup (125 mL) tamarind juice
3 tbsp (45 mL) sugar
chili pepper to taste
14 oz (400 g) sliced fish fillet
7 oz (200 g) tomato (cut in wedges)
10½ oz (300 g) cubed pineapple
4 tsp (20 mL) sliced galangal
4 tsp (20 mL) julienned marjoram leaf
2 tsp (10 mL) deep-fried garlic

Method

Bring the fish stock to a boil. Add fish sauce, tamarind juice, sugar, and chilies and slightly reduce heat. Then add the remaining ingredients into the soup and keep at a gentle boil for five to seven minutes. Adjust the seasoning to taste. Serve the soup in individual cups, garnished with julienne of marjoram leaf and deep-fried garlic.

Stir-Fried Beef with Black Pepper ❧

Makes 10 servings.

Main Ingredient

4 lb (2 kg) cubed beef fillet

Marinade Ingredients

2 tbsp (30 mL) sugar
2 tbsp (30 mL) black pepper
2 tbsp (30 mL) chopped garlic
3 tbsp (45 mL) oyster sauce
2 tbsp (30 mL) soy sauce
2 tbsp (30 mL) salt

Seasoning Ingredients

2 tbsp (30 mL) Chinese wine
1 tbsp (15 mL) chopped garlic
3½ fluid oz (100 mL) chicken stock
1 tbsp (15 mL) dark soy sauce
2 tbsp (30 mL) oyster sauce
2 tbsp (30 mL) crushed black peppercorns

Dip Ingredients

3 tbsp (45 mL) lime juice
1 tbsp (15 mL) black pepper
salt to taste

Method

In a bowl marinate the beef with specified ingredients for at least half an hour. Heat a little oil in a wok until very hot and briskly fry the beef; the beef should just be seared but remain rare inside. In a new wok sauté the garlic with a little oil, add the beef and Chinese wine, and stir-fry. Pour in the chicken stock and other seasoning ingredients. Allow sauce to reduce until it thickens. Serve with dip.

Braised Fish in Palm Sugar and Ginger ❧

Makes 10 servings.

Ingredients

2 lb (1 kg) serpent fish cut into steaks
5 oz (150 g) palm sugar
1 tbsp (15 mL) black pepper powder
2 tbsp (30 mL) chopped garlic
3 tbsp (45 mL) sliced ginger
3 tbsp (45 mL) soy sauce
2 tbsp (30 mL) dark soy sauce
½ tbsp (8 mL) fish sauce
8 cups (2 L) fish stock
4 tbsp (60 mL) vegetable oil
1½ oz (40 g) julienned spring onions
1½ oz (40 g julienned green mango

Method

For the sauce, place a pot on high heat, then add the oil and quickly sauté the garlic. Next caramelize the palm sugar and add the pepper, ginger, fish and soy sauces, and fish stock. To cook the fish, place the steaks in the hot sauce and allow braising over low heat for two hours. Serve in a casserole dish with julienne of green mango and spring onions.

Cambodian Fried Rice ❧

Makes 10 servings.

Ingredients

10½ oz (300 g) diced pork sausage
3½ oz (100 g) diced prawns
1¾ oz (50 g) chopped garlic cloves
5 beaten eggs
1¾ oz (50 g) diced long beans and carrots
3 lb (1.5 kg) steamed rice
1½ oz (40 g) chopped spring onions
2 tbsp (30 mL) Chinese wine
2 tbsp (30 mL) oyster sauce
3 tbsp (45 mL) soy sauce
1 tsp (5 mL) salt
1 tsp (5 mL) black pepper
½ cup (125 mL) vegetable oil

Method

In a wok heat the oil to deep-fry the sausage, then put aside. Sauté the garlic and prawns with a little vegetable oil over medium-high heat, then add the eggs and vegetables and continue to stir-fry until eggs are set. Put aside. Using the same wok sauté some garlic and add the rice, stir-fry for a few minutes, add prawns, eggs, vegetables, sausage, and remaining ingredients. Keep stir-frying. Adjust the seasoning to taste and continue frying the rice until it's well cooked and gets a "wok smell." Serve the fried rice on a platter and decorate with lettuce leaves and sliced cucumbers and tomatoes.

Pumpkin Custard ❧

Makes 40 slices.

Ingredients

1 whole small pumpkin (about 2 lb/1 kg)
20 egg yolks
½ lb (250 g) sugar
1⅔ cups (400 mL) coconut milk
1 tsp (5 mL) salt

Method

Form a sufficient big hole on the top of the pumpkin to remove the seeds from the inside. To prepare the custard mixture, mix egg yolks, sugar, coconut milk, and salt in a bowl, then whisk well together until homogenous. Pour into the pumpkin through the hole. To cook the pumpkin, place it in a steamer and steam until cooked.

Even in André Malraux's day the mystique and allure of Angkor Wat attracted tourists, despite the difficulty of getting there.

Deep-Fried Rice Flakes with Banana ❧

Makes 25 servings.

Ingredients

2 lb (1 kg) rice flakes
10½ oz (300 g) sugar
2 cups (500 mL) coconut milk
2 cups (500 mL) coconut juice
½ coconut (grated)

Batter Ingredients

14 oz (400 g) rice flour
2 cups (500 mL) coconut milk
5 oz (150 g) sugar
1 tsp (5 mL) baking powder
1 tsp (5 mL) salt
1 tsp (5 mL) black sesame seeds

Stuffing Ingredients

1½ lb (750 g) peeled bananas

Method

Combine the rice flakes, sugar, coconut milk, juice, and grated coconut. Put aside for four hours or until the rice flakes soften. Prepare the batter by combining all ingredients and whisking the mixture until smooth. Cut the bananas for the stuffing into small cubes. Form the rice flakes into walnut-size balls and stuff with bananas. Dip the rice flake balls in the frying batter and deep-fry over high heat until golden brown. Serve as a dessert or snack.

Rice Dumpling with Palm Sugar ❧

Makes 10 servings.

Main Ingredients

3 lb (1½ kg) glutinous rice flour
3½ oz (100 g) rice flour
3 cups (750 mL) coconut milk

Stuffing Ingredients

1 lb (500 g) palm sugar (hard)

Method

Cut the palm sugar into dices and put aside. Mix the flour and coconut milk. To make the dumplings, form the flour-coconut mixture into small balls and stuff each one with the sugar. Cook in boiling water; the dumplings will float to the surface when cooked. To serve, quickly rub them with the shaved coconut and serve while warm.

Note: Asian cooking is adaptable. If you can't find all the ingredients, substitute others. However, don't substitute strong flavors for delicate ones. If in doubt, leave it out. Check Ingredients Glossary for further tips about unfamiliar ingredients.

Ingredients Glossary

Allspice: The name originated from the popular notion that the pimento berry contains the characteristic flavor and aroma of cloves, nutmeg, cinnamon, and pepper, all combined in one spice.

Callaloo: The edible spinachlike leaves of the dasheen plant. Substitute spinach if unavailable.

Chinese Wine: A bitter, strong, distilled beverage that can be made from a base of rice, wheat, or sorghum. Sherry can be substituted.

Coconut Juice: The natural juice from inside the coconut, coconut milk is made from soaking grated coconut flesh in hot water.

Coulis: This ingredient is made by crushing fruit and adding a little sugar.

Curaçao: Made from the dried peel of oranges on the Caribbean island of Curaçao. The liqueur can be colored orange (known as Orange Curaçao, or just Curaçao), blue (Blue Curaçao), green (Green Curaçao), or left clear (White Curaçao). All variants have the same orange flavor with small differences in bitterness. Blue and Green Curaçao are often used to provide color in mixed drinks.

Deglaze: To dissolve caramelized juices in the bottom of a pan with liquid.

Fava Bean: Also known as broad bean. The cultivation of this bean is so ancient there is no known wild form.

Fish Sauce: Based on the liquid from salted fermented fish, this sauce is extremely strong-smelling and is used as soy sauce would be. Fish sauce can be found at Asian grocers.

Galangal: A root in the same family as common ginger. It has a hot, gingery flavor and can usually be found dried in Asian food specialty shops.

Galliano: A yellow herbal liqueur named after an Italian war hero.

Hoisin Sauce: Made from fermented soybeans, garlic, and various other spices, this sauce is a reddish-brown and has a sweet, slightly spicy flavor.

Lemongrass: Often used in Oriental cooking, this herb can be found at most Asian or Mexican grocers. Choose stalks that aren't dry or brittle.

Limoncino: A sweet lemon liqueur.

Maraschino Liqueur: Made from cherries and processed much like brandy. Cane sugar is added and the alcohol is aged. It resembles a sweet cherry-infused liqueur. One of the most popular Italian brands is Luxardo.

Mojito: Everyone in Havana seems to make a *mojito* differently. Hotel Ambos Mundos insists on white rum while other establishments such as La Zaragozana say amber is just fine. Dark rum will make a Mulata *mojito* (see recipe section in "Graham Greene: Love, Intrigue, and the Tango in Havana"). Angostura bitters are a unique touch to Ambos Mundo's *mojito*.

Palm Sugar: A dark, coarse, unrefined sugar made from the sap of various palm trees. There is no Western counterpart. However, a reasonably similar flavor can be had from equal parts of maple syrup and brown sugar.

Pickapeppa Sauce: Created at Shooter's Hill, Jamaica, in 1921, this sauce is still made there today. Prepared with cane vinegar and aged in oak barrels, Pickapeppa has a sweet but mellow flavor that makes it very versatile.

Plantain: A banana-like fruit readily available at Asian and Caribbean grocery stores.

Poblano Chili: About the size of a sweet bell pepper but tapering at the end, the poblano can range from mild to hot.

Rose-Flower Water: Distilled from rose flowers, rose-flower water is widely used in the Middle East as a flavoring.

Rum: The quintessential Caribbean drink is produced by distilling molasses, a byproduct of the sugar industry. There are three types of rum. White rum is usually not aged in oak casks. Golden or amber rum is aged between six months to two years in oak barrels. Dark rum is aged for two to four years and is better as a sipping drink rather than a cocktail mixer.

Saffron: Available from most specialty-food stores, this spice is one of the most expensive in the world. Saffron is handpicked from the dried stigma filaments of the saffron flower. It takes 75,000 flowers to produce one pound (500 grams) of saffron.

Salt Pork: A salt-cured layer of fat that's cut from the sides and belly of a pig. The closest similar ingredient is bacon, which is leaner and smoked. You can substitute bacon by blanching it in boiling water for a minute to get rid of the smoked taste, then fry until crisp.

Sangria: A versatile drink with a long pedigree in Spain. It's definitely worth experimenting with fruit or fruit juices. Some people even add rum.

Scotch Bonnet Pepper: Considered by many to be the world's hottest pepper. Use sparingly.

Serpent Fish: A long, thin, compressed fish with red lines running around its body. Substitute steaks from any white fish (sole, whitefish, et cetera).

Simple Syrup: Many mixed drinks in the Caribbean and elsewhere call for a syrup made by boiling two parts water to one part sugar. Let the result cool, then add to the drink as called for by the recipe.

Sour Oranges: Also known as Seville oranges, this fruit is native to Southeast Asia. For 500 years they were the only orange type in Europe. Seville oranges were the first oranges introduced to Florida by the Spaniards.

Superior Stock: A complex stock consisting of chicken and pork, with onions, garlic, and ginger added for flavor. In restaurants it is sometimes served as a soup free of charge. Superior stock is readily available in Chinese food specialty shops.

Tamarind Juice: Made by boiling tamarind pods and extracting the juice. A far easier method is to buy tamarind paste (essentially concentrated tamarind juice) at an Asian grocer and dilute it in water (five teaspoons/25 milliliters in a half cup/125 milliliters of water). Tamarind adds a sweet and sour taste and brownish color to food.

Turmeric: A member of the ginger family, this Indian spice is best known for adding color to curries.

Vermicelli: Also called bean threads, these are thin noodles with a white/translucent hue when cooked.

Wasabi: A Japanese-style mustard or horseradish.

Restaurant and Hotel Information

Vietnam

L'HÔTEL MAJESTIC
1 Dong Khoi Street, District 1
Ho Chi Minh City, Vietnam
Tel.: (848) 829-5517 or (848) 822-8750
Fax: (848) 829-5510
E-mail: *hotelmajestic@hem.vnn.vn*
Web site: *majestic-saigon.com*

Graham Greene's favorite Saigon hotel: "It would ever be seven o'clock and cocktail-time on the roof of the Majestic, with a wind from Saigon River" (*The Quiet American*). Opened in 1925, this French colonial queen has been carefully renovated with modern creature comforts. Somerset Maugham and, more recently, French film star Catherine Deneuve and France's president, have booked the Majestic Suite when in Saigon. This vast and elegant suite is the height of colonial decadence, though all of the river-view rooms facing Dong Khoi have incredible street life. A stay here in a room with a view is worth the whole trip and every *dong* you'll spend.

HOTEL SOFITEL METROPOLE
14 Ngo Quyen Street
Hanoi, Vietnam
Tel.: (844) 826 6919
Fax: (844) 826-6920
E-mail: *sofmet@netnam.org.vn*

Renovated in 1992, this French colonial darling of Indochina has a fascinating history and has grown even more elegant through the years. It rates along with Sri Lanka's Galle Face as one of the seven most famous hotels east of the Suez Canal. Built in 1901, it was Vietnam's first five-star hotel and is still its best. It has played host to a stellar set. In 1923 Somerset Maugham checked in to finish his novel *The Gentlemen in the Parlour*. In 1936 Charlie Chaplin and Paulette Goddard honeymooned here. In 1945 U.S. parachute commandos arrived to disarm Japanese troops and entered the hotel wearing jackets bearing the American flag. At the very end of World War II the hotel served as the temporary home of Japanese POWs, mainly French subjects. In 1951 Graham Greene worked on *The Quiet American* here. During the Vietnam War, it was the Hanoi base for diplomats and press. In 1960 Ho Chi Minh visited, and in 1972 Jane Fonda stayed for two weeks while she made her infamous broadcasts to U.S. troops.

CONTINENTAL HOTEL
132–134 Dong Khoi Street, District 1
Ho Chi Minh City, Vietnam
Tel.: (848) 829-9201 or (848) 829-9255
Fax: (848) 824-1772 or (848) 829-0936
Web site: *www.continental-saigon.com*

Graham Greene writes: "The dice rattled on the tables where the French were playing *Quatre Cent Vingt-et-un* and the girls in the white silk trousers bicycled home down the rue Catinat." Built in 1880, this famous hostelry underwent a major renovation in the late 1980s. Greene and his protagonist in *The Quiet American* sipped cassis at the now-defunct Continental Shelf verandah bar, as did spies and correspondents through the wars. The hotel is the setting for the 1957 film version of *The Quiet American*. This landmark hotel is a must-stop.

Cuba

La Terraza de Cojímar
161 Calle Real
Cojímar, Cuba
Tel.: (537) 55-9486

Ernest Hemingway's spirit haunts this place. The walls are decorated with fishing photos of Papa and his cronies in and around Cojímar.

La Zaragozana
352 Calle Montserrat
Havana, Cuba
Tel.: (537) 867-1040

Established in 1830, this Habana Vieja restaurant is said to be the first eatery in Havana. Typically Spanish in design with stucco walls, terrazzo floors, and dark wooden chairs and tables, it resembles an old-fashioned Spanish bodega.

El Paseo
Parque Central Hotel, Parque Central
Neptuna y Prado
Havana, Cuba
Tel.: (537) 860-6627
Fax: (537) 860-6630

Innovative cuisine in a central location in Habana Vieja.

Hotel Ambos Mundos
153 Calle Obispo
Havana, Cuba
Tel.: (537) 860-9530
Fax: (537) 860-9532

The restaurant in Hotel Ambos Mundos has an excellent location on Calle Obispo, Ernest Hemingway's favorite street in the heart of Habana Vieja. The hotel itself has plenty of charm and convenience. Ask for a room with a view of Havana's harbor. Be warned that if you take the room beside Hemingway's old 511, there may be many comings and goings. Rooms are comfortable enough, but you may want to ask the maid to remove the plastic mattress pad.

BODEGUITA DEL MEDIO
207 Calle Empedrado
Havana, Cuba
Tel.: (537) 867-1374

Along with Ernest Hemingway's purported scrawl on the wall of this rustic Habana Vieja bar and restaurant, you'll find the autographs of Salvador Allende, Fidel Castro, Harry Belafonte, and Nat King Cole. To get into the Hemingway mood, order a *mojito*.

EL FLORIDITA
557 Calle Obispo
Havana, Cuba

There is no bar in Havana's Habana Vieja more firmly identified with Ernest Hemingway than El Floridita, home of the Papa Doble.

Jamaica

IDLE AWHILE RESORT
Norman Manley Boulevard
Negril, Jamaica
Toll Free: 1-877-243-5352
Tel.: (876) 957-3303
Fax: (876) 957-9567
E-mail: *info@idleawhile.com*
Web site: *www.idleawhile.com*

This sophisticated and intimate beachfront boutique hotel, designed by the talented Jane Issa, is an ideal retreat from the bustle of crowded lobbies and beaches. Idle Awhile caters to families, singles, and couples. The beachside restaurant has an excellent Rasta cook. Ask for the Ital Special.

COUPLES RESORT
Negril, Jamaica
Toll Free: 1-800-330-8272
Web site: *www.couplesjamaica.com*

This all-inclusive resort for couples, designed by Jane Issa, offers bohemian decor and luxury and is situated on 18 acres facing the crescent-shaped Bloody Bay on Negril's famed white-sand beach. Couples is rated "best in Jamaica" by *Condé Nast Traveler* readers' polls and by *Travel and Leisure*.

Round Hill Hotel and Villas
Montego Bay, Jamaica
Toll Free: 1-800-972-2159
Tel.: (876) 956-7050
E-mail: *info@roundhilljamaica.com*
Web site: *www.roundhilljamaica.com*

The location of this resort on a 100-acre peninsula was once part of Lord Monson's Round Hill Estate, a sugar plantation that was later changed over to coconuts and pimento (allspice), both of which are still produced today. Round Hill was opened as a resort in 1953. Its 29 acres were subdivided into lots, and prominent American and European society types were invited to build "cottages" and invest in the hotel. Shareholders have included Noël Coward, Adele Astaire, Oscar Hammerstein, Clive Brook, the Marchioness of Dufferin and Ava, and Viscount Rothermere. The resort subscribes to the old-money attitude of "why flaunt what you've always had?" So even in the finest villas there are brass lanterns instead of crystal chandeliers and checkerboard tiles rather than marble floors. Rumor has it that reggae legend Shaggy as well as Bob Marley's wife, Rita, have stayed at Round Hill recently. The movie *How Stella Got Her Groove Back* was filmed here.

Goldeneye Resort
Oracabessa, St. Mary, Jamaica
Tel.: (876) 975-3354
Fax: (876) 975-3620
E-mail: *goldeneye@cwjamaica.com*
Web site: *www.islandoutpost.com/goldeneye*

Goldeneye Resort is a 15-acre hideaway on a bluff between the sea and a lagoon. Ian Fleming wrote all of his James Bond novels here. Fleming's original house is surrounded by luxuriant gardens and forest-shaded villas overlooking the sea. A very exclusive retreat.

The Caves
Light House Road
Negril, Jamaica
Tel.: (876) 957-0270
Fax: (876) 957-4930
E-mail: *thecaves@cwjamaica.com*
Web site: *www.islandoutpost/caves*

The Caves was designed by Greer-Ann and Bertram Saulter. The hotel consists of 10 handcrafted cottages at the edge of the sea. The two seafront acres hide many secrets—sundecks and nooks, even grottos in the cliff itself. One of these grottos is intended for dining and is lit with candles and strewn with flowers. The Caves is a wonderful getaway on the Negril cliffs.

TENSING PEN HOTEL
Light House Road
Negril, Jamaica
Tel.: (876) 957-0387
Fax: (876) 957-0161
E-mail: *tensingpen@cwjamaica.com*
Web site: *www.tensingpen.com*

Tensing Pen has evolved since the early 1970s into a unique collection of wood, thatch, and cut-stone cottages. Set in a cultivated jungle of tropical vegetation, each cottage features simple but elegant interiors crafted by local artisans from bamboo, mahogany, cedar, and other indigenous materials.

Mexico

MAMA MIA'S
Umarán Number 8, Centro
San Miguel de Allende
Guanajuato, Mexico 37700
Tel./Fax: (52-415) 152-20-63 or 152-36-79

Mama Mia's has moved from Puerto Vallarta to San Miguel de Allende. The food is mainly Italian, and the clientele consists of tourists and upscale locals. There is live music almost every night, and rumor has it that Willie and Lobo still occasionally play.

HOTEL QUINTA REAL
311 Calle Pélicanos
Marina Vallarta
Puerto Vallarta
Jalisco, Mexico 48354
Toll Free (in United States): 1-877-278-8018
Toll Free (in Canada): 1-866-818-8342
Toll Free (in Mexico): 1-800-508-7923
Tel.: (52-322) 221-22-77
E-mail: *qrvallarta@mexicoboutiquehotels.com*
Web site: *www.mexicoboutiquehotels.com/qrvallarta*

The Quinta Real is an ideal getaway for discerning travelers. The suites boast splash pools and local art, and the outdoor pool area is sublime with just the right amount of sunlight and the shade of numerous palm trees. The hotel's beach club is accessed by a short golf-cart drive.

Casa Las Brisas
Playa Careyero
Punta Mita, Nayarit, Mexico
Toll Free (in the United States): 1-877-278-8018
Toll Free (in Canada): 1-866-818-8342
Toll Free (in Mexico): 1-800-508-7923
Tel.: (52-322) 221-22 77
E-mail: *casalasbrisas@mexicoboutiquehotels.com*
Web site: *www.mexicoboutiquehotels.com/casalasbrisas*

In retreat from a high-energy life building chic hotels and restaurants in Canada and the United States, the affable Marc Lindskog switched gears to erect the more intimate six-room, villa-style Casa Las Brisas on one of the world's most beautiful and secluded beaches in a town near Puerto Vallarta.

Sri Lanka

Galle Face Hotel
2 Galle Road
Colombo, Sri Lanka
Tel.: (94) 1 541010
Fax: (94) 1 541072
Web site: *www.gallefacehotel.com*

Built in 1864 in a Victorian style, Galle Face Hotel soon became one of the most exquisite accommodations east of Suez. Facing the Indian Ocean, it is a charming throwback to British colonial life on the island. The hotel has been patronized by Indira Gandhi, Alfred Krupp, Noël Coward, and Sir Arthur C. Clarke, among others. Clarke wrote *3001: The Final Odyssey* here.

Earl's Regency Hotel
Thennekumbura
Kandy, Sri Lanka
Tel.: (94) 8 422122
Fax: (94) 8 422133
E-mail: *erhotel@sltnet.lk*
Web site: *www.aitkenspencehotels.com/earls_regency*

Perched high above the Mahaveli River, Earl's Regency Hotel is a good base for exploring Kandy and the venerated Temple of the Tooth (purportedly belonging to Buddha). There are 100 rooms, a spa, a championship golf course, and an excellent staff.

KANDALAMA HOTEL
Kandalama, Dambulla
Sri Lanka
Tel.: (94) 84100
Fax: (94) 84109
Web site: *www.aitkenspencehotels.com/kandalama*

Kandalama Hotel has Sir Arthur C. Clarke's "favorite view in all Sri Lanka." The author spent his 80th birthday in this hotel. Flanked by two UNESCO World Heritage Sites, the first-century B.C. Dambulla rock temple and the fifth-century Sigiriya rock fortress, Kandalama was built to fit into its natural environment. The hotel is surrounded by lakes, forests, and rocky outcrops and is home to a variety of wildlife.

Grand Cayman

BELLA CAPRI
P.O. Box 30008 SMB
West Bay Road
George Town, Grand Cayman
Tel.: (345) 945-4755
Fax: (345) 945-4968

Bella Capri is a traditional Italian restaurant and one of Dick Francis's favorite haunts.

PAPPAGALLO
P.O. Box 184 WB
Birch Tree Hill Road, West Bay, Grand Cayman
Tel.: (345) 949-1119
Fax: (345) 949-1114
Web site: *www.pappagallo.ky*

Pappagallo is situated on a 14-acre bird sanctuary overlooking a natural saltwater lagoon. The area surrounding the restaurant is so rich in natural wildlife that most of the book *Birds of the Cayman Islands* was researched and photographed here. Pappagallo's oldest employee is Humphrey Bogart, the African gray parrot that greets patrons at the doorway.

NEPTUNE RESTAURANT
P.O. Box 31990 FMB
Trafalgar Square, West Bay Road
George Town, Grand Cayman
Tel.: (345) 946-8709

A local seafood restaurant with a more relaxed atmosphere.

Morocco

LE CHABLIS
9 rue Ibn Zaidoun
Guéliz, Marrakech
Morocco
Tel.: (212-44) 43 94 26
Fax: (212-44) 43 89 81

Le Chablis is one of the best French restaurants in Marrakech. It's located in Guéliz, Marrakech's new city, where the banks, offices, and trendy cafés are found.

DAR JAMAI
100 yards from Hôtel Palais Jamai
Old City, Fez
Morocco
Tel.: (212-55) 63 43 31

In English Dar Jamai means "House of Jamai." This is the house where the staff of the royal palace would have stayed and eaten during the days when the sultan occupied what is now the Hôtel Palais Jamai. If you make it to Fez, you should stay where Paul and Jane Bowles did. Jane freaked out on *majoun* in one of this 19th-century hotel's suites and never touched the stuff again. The building was beautifully redone in 1999, but for the most authentic experience, ask for a suite in the old palace. The 115-room, 25-suite hotel and its beautiful gardens and pool area overlook Fez El Bali, the most fascinating medina in Morocco. You'll have no trouble hearing the calls of the muezzins at 4:00 a.m. here.

L'ANMBRA
47 route D'Immouzzer
Fez, Morocco
Tel.: (212-55) 64 16 87
Fax: (212-55) 73 36 33

A traditional Moroccan restaurant with excellent food and music. Seating is on traditional floor couches.

LE DOUIRA
Hôtel Le Royal Mansour
27 avenue de L'Armée Royale
Casablanca, Morocco 21000
Tel.: (212-22) 31 30 11 and 12
Fax: (212-22) 31 25 83

The hotel's restaurant serves Moroccan/French cuisine.

EL KORSAN RESTAURANT
Hôtel El Minzah
85 rue de la Liberté
Tangier, Morocco 90000
Tel.: (212-39) 93 58 85
Fax: (212-39) 93 45 46

Hôtel El Minzah, where El Korsan Restaurant is located, was built at the command of John Crichton-Stuart, fourth marquess of Bute, a British aristocrat with extensive interests in Tangier's International Zone.

People's Republic of China

KERRY CENTRE SHANGRI-LA
1 Guang Hua Road
Chaoyang District, Beijing
People's Republic of China
Tel.: (86-10) 6561 8833

Kerry Centre is an ultramodern luxury hotel in the Chaoyang District, Beijing's diplomatic, commercial, and financial center. The hotel has excellent service. Stay on the Horizon Club floor; it's worth its weight in Chinese money, with 24-hour butler service, a library and hors d'oeuvres, and cocktails. A perfect place to rest your head after a long, jet-lagged night.

PUDONG SHANGRI-LA
33 Fu Cheng Road
Pudong, Shanghai

People's Republic of China
Tel.: (86-21) 6882 8888
Fax: (86-21) 6882 6688

The award-winning Pudong Shangri-La is located in the Lujiazui Finance and Trade Zone of Shanghai. Prominently sited along the famous Huangpu River, the hotel has breathtaking views of Shanghai's legendary riverfront, the Bund, and the Oriental Pearl television tower.

GRAND HYATT SHANGHAI
Jin Mao Tower
88 Century Boulevard
Pudong, Shanghai 200121
People's Republic of China
Tel.: (86-21) 5049 1234
Fax: (86-21) 5049 1111
E-mail: *info@hyattshanghai.com*
Web site: *shanghai.grand.hyatt.com*

Be at the top of the world in the planet's highest hotel.

Cambodia

RAFFLES GRAND HÔTEL D'ANGKOR
1 Vithei Charles de Gaulle
Khum Svay Dang Kum
Siem Reap, Cambodia
Tel.: 855-63-963-888
Fax: 855-63-963-168
Web site: *www.raffles.com*

A classic colonial hotel that has become synonymous with the Angkor temples themselves. Many great writers such as Somerset Maugham have enjoyed this establishment's elegance. Truly one of the great hotels of the world.

Index

*V*ictoria Brooks is the creator and editor and a contributor to the *Literary Trips: Following in the Footsteps of Fame* series. She is also the author of the novel *Red Dream*. Recently she received the Excellence in Caribbean Travel Writing 2001 Award. Victoria counts among her honors her meetings with Sir Arthur C. Clarke in Sri Lanka, with deceased literary lion Paul Bowles in Tangier, and with horseman/mystery writer Dick Francis on Grand Cayman. These experiences are chronicled in *Literary Trips* and now in *Famous Faces, Famous Places & Famous Food*. Victoria is the editor of *www.GreatestEscapes.com*, the Internet magazine for travelers, and her evocative travel stories have been published in many international and national magazines, including *Reader's Digest*. She lives in Vancouver, Canada, when she isn't exploring the world.

Travel...and Reading About It
Life's Greatest Escapes!

Greatest Escapes Publishing is a multimedia company that produces online content as well as traditional books. We are passionately devoted to the very finest in travel writing, seeking to inspire the wanderlust of our readers rather than simply giving them a list of sights, restaurants, and hotels. Read the Greatest Escapes travel webzine (*www.greatestescapes.com*), a monthly compendium of award-winning travel stories from around the globe.

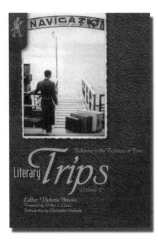

Literary Trips
Following in the Footsteps of Fame
edited by Victoria Brooks
ISBN: 0-9686137-0-5
$19.95 U.S.; $29.95 Canada

Literary Trips 2
Following in the Footsteps of Fame
edited by Victoria Brooks
ISBN: 0-9686137-1-3
$19.95 U.S.; $29.95 Canada

The *Literary Trips* series is packed with stories about famous writers and the locations around the world they're associated with, including Bruce Chatwin's Australia, Tennessee Williams's New Orleans, D. H. Lawrence's New Mexico, Robert Louis Stevenson's Hawaii, Maeve Binchy's Ireland, Rohinton Mistry's Bombay, Pablo Neruda's Chile, Agatha Christie's England, and much more. The remarkable Paul Bowles is the subject of an essay in the first book and also wrote the foreword—his last piece of writing prior to his death in November 1999. Sir Arthur C. Clarke, the subject of an essay in the second book, wrote the foreword to that volume.

"...irresistible..."—CHICAGO TRIBUNE

Literary Trips and *Literary Trips 2* are available online at *www.literarytrips.com*
(in whole or by the chapter), in bookstores across North America.
To order by phone, call 604-683-1668.

Greatest Escapes
PUBLISHING

"Steamy and sexy....
Stunning and unforgettable!"
—CHRISTOPHER ONDAATJE

Red Dream
an exotic novel
BY VICTORIA BROOKS

ISBN 0-9686137-2-1
$15.00 U.S.; $22.95 Canada

*P*art fact, part fiction, *Red Dream* is set against the bloody palette of Vietnam's history. Vietnam, when it was French Indochina. Vietnam, when it was a country divided.

The Characters

La Doctoress Jade Minh, an exquisitely beautiful woman with a hole for a soul and a secret. The faithful Van, Jade's distinguished scientist husband. The mysterious Chou, the South Vietnamese embassy's slippery legal eagle who lusts after Jade with creative perversion. The lovely Suzette, illegitimate and abandoned, who searches for herself and finds love with Kiet, a South Vietnamese government official drafted into his country's army.

And the War That Ruins Everything

Available in bookstores everywhere.
Signed copies are available online at *www.literarytrips.com* or by calling 604-683-1668.